The Kennedy–Johnson Tax Cut

The Kennedy–Johnson Tax Cut
A Revisionist History

Martin F. J. Prachowny

Queen's University at Kingston, Canada

Edward Elgar
Cheltenham, UK • Northampton, MA, USA

Published by
Edward Elgar Publishing Limited
Glensanda House
Montpellier Parade
Cheltenham
Glos GL50 1UA
UK

Edward Elgar Publishing, Inc.
136 West Street
Suite 202
Northampton
Massachusetts 01060
USA

A catalogue record for this book
is available from the British Library

Library of Congress Cataloguing in Publication Data

Prachowny, Martin F.J.
    The Kennedy–Johnson tax cut : a revisionist history / Martin
F.J. Prachowny
        Includes bibliographical references and index.
        1. Taxation—United States. 2. Income tax—United States.
    I. Title.
    HJ2381.P73   2000
    336.2'00973'09046—dc21   00–037621

ISBN 1 84064 417 6

Printed and bound in Great Britain by Biddles Ltd, *www.biddles.co.uk*

Contents

Charts, Figures and Tables

CHARTS

FIGURES

TABLE

Acknowledgments

Given the opportunity, I believe the three chairmen of the Council of Economic Advisers in the Kennedy–Johnson Administration would have cooperated with my attempt to write this historical account of stabilization policy in the 1960s, in which they played such a prominent role. Alas, Walter Heller, Gardner Ackley and Arthur Okun are no longer with us and they are unable to share their knowledge and understanding with me and the reader of this book. Nevertheless, they organized and donated their private papers to publicly accessible libraries without imposing onerous restrictions on their use. This made it possible for me to reconstruct much of the historical record of this period. For their foresight and generosity, I am grateful.

This is also the place to express my thanks to my colleagues, John Hartwick and Gregor Smith, who read the manuscript and made helpful comments.

My biggest debt is to my wife, Marguerite, who shared all the activities involved in this research project over the past three years. Her organizational skills during the archival searches and editorial interventions in the writing process are not easily detected, but they immeasurably improved the final product.

For shepherding this book through the publication process both quickly and smoothly, special thanks go to Alan Sturmer and Barbara Slater.

Bibliographical Note

A bibliography is usually at the end of a book, but this explanatory note is placed at the beginning to allow the reader to understand and verify the citations and references in the chapters that follow. While it is straightforward to make reference to published books and articles, archival material, on which many of the assertions and quotations in this book depend, is much more difficult to cite accurately. The aim here is to allow other researchers to find any specific document cited in the text by providing the name of the collection, the box number, the file title and the "name" and date of the document. This information would be cumbersome if placed directly in the text or put into footnotes; therefore, a short-hand convention is needed. There are three lists of archival material in the bibliography, each arranged chronologically and numbered. The lists refer to one of the libraries in which the archival material is found: the prefix K stands for the John F. Kennedy Library in Boston; B refers to the Bentley Historical Library at the University of Michigan in Ann Arbor; and J stands for the Lyndon B. Johnson Library in Austin, Texas. Some of the documents can be found in two or even all three of these locations, but I visited them in the order in which they are listed and they are placed in the list in which they were first seen. This system allows a simple bracketed reference such as (K1) to be put in the text and the details of that document are then found in the bibliography.

Documents produced while in the service of the United States government are in the public domain. To the extent that these collections contain private papers, Walter Heller and Arthur Okun donated the copyright to the United States. Permission to quote from the personal writings of Gardner Ackley has been granted by the Bentley Historical Library. I am grateful to the staff of all three libraries for their courteous help in meeting my requests for information.

Introduction

The most prominent landmarks on this historical journey are two pieces of legislation. *The Revenue Act of 1964* is popularly known as the Kennedy–Johnson tax cut, although neither of these two presidents did any of the heavy lifting required to bring to life this best-known event of postwar stabilization policy. Its sequel, *The Revenue and Expenditure Control Act of 1968*, on the other hand, is an orphan and is simply known as "The Surcharge" despite the realization that President Johnson sacrificed the last of his political capital to get this bill through Congress.

In any event, this book deals only tangentially with presidential involvement in macroeconomic management and much more with the decisions, advice and actions of the three Chairmen of the Council of Economic Advisers (CEA) during the 1960s: Walter Heller (29 January 1961 to 15 November 1964), Gardner Ackley (16 November 1964 to 15 February 1968) and Arthur Okun (15 February 1968 to 20 January 1969). They are the true authors of the "new economics" that attempted to manipulate total aggregate demand in the US economy to coincide with "potential" output which in turn was consistent with the ultimate goal of "full employment."

The role of the Council is critical in reconstructing this policy experiment. With the notable exception of McLure (1972), most of the profession has accepted the evaluation that fiscal policy in the early 1960s was a success and that the Council was the source of that success. Here is a sampling of previously expressed opinion:

> If asked to cite the clearest example of successful fiscal policy in the United States, most economists would point to the period 1961–1965, during which a succession of expansionary measures that culminated in the major tax reduction of 1964 brought the economy out of the doldrums of stagnation and back on the track of fast growth and high employment. The conditions for success were favorable. The economy was far below its potential, inflation had been wrung out of the economy by the conservative policies of

President Eisenhower, and the budget at the outset was clearly restrictive as measured by the full-employment surplus. In this environment President Kennedy was able to develop a consensus about the direction in which fiscal policy should move. Since there was ample slack in the economy, there was little danger of overshooting into inflation. (Dernburg, 1985, p. 442)

[L]ittle blame was seriously put on the shoulders of CEA. No doubt economists had to a large degree oversold such items as "fine tuning" in the flush of their 1963–64 success, and clearly "steering" was one thing and "fine tuning" another, but what effect, given the lack of information at their disposal, any degree of professional skill might have had is very questionable. (Norton, 1977, p. 213)

In considerable part because economists usually gave the right advice during the 1960's about how to use national fiscal and monetary policies to achieve these ends, and because much of their advice was sooner or later accepted, the 1960's, taken as a whole, undoubtedly represent the finest decade of America's economic history. (Ackley, B59, p. 14)

Probably the Oscar on the shelf of the CEA is the Kennedy–Johnson tax cut. More than any other major economic policy decision of the [past] 50 years, this was originated and promoted by the Council of Economic Advisers. The tax cut itself was an economic and political success, but it was also part of a package that generated some problems. First, it was visualized as fitting into a picture in which economic growth would be rapid — 4 percent per annum or more — and in which growing budget surpluses would be a drag on the growth of the economy unless constantly offset by the distribution of fiscal dividends. (Stein, 1996b, p. 19)

Americans' esteem for economists paralleled the rise in GNP, but only until it became obvious that the nation was on a severe inflationary binge. ... Not surprisingly, by the time they left the Executive Office Building, the new economists were being blamed for the fiscal errors of the 1960s, and the new economics had fallen somewhat into disrepute. ... Looking back over the period beginning with mid-1965 one can only conclude that discretionary fiscal policy failed miserably to live up to its advance billing. (McLure, 1972, pp. 59, 63)

As far as I can determine there has not been a thoroughly objective and detached evaluation of the Kennedy–Johnson tax cut. Most of the historical record has been provided by the participants: Heller (1967), Okun (1968), Schlesinger (1965), Sorensen (1965), the oral history involving interviews with past CEA chairmen by Hargrove and Morley (1984) and testimony by CEA chairmen before the Joint Economic Committee (JEC), especially in 1963–65. In the same category is an internal CEA study (J92) entitled "Fiscal Policy History," probably authored by a member of the staff, David J. Ott, in late 1968. It was intended to be part of the administrative history project (J95) required of all major units in the government, but Okun suggested that it be kept secret for a minimum of 20 years (J91) and even then he predicted (J94) that "the scholar who is out to trace the fiscal policy decisions of late 1965 – early 1966 will not get much help from this manuscript."

Independent and arm's-length studies such as those by Flash (1965), Norton (1977) and Stein (1988) cover a longer time span and a broader set of topics, but they do not contain a detailed economic analysis of fiscal policy in the 1960s. Two recent fiftieth-anniversary symposia in the *American Economic Review* (Feldstein, Solow, Stiglitz, 1997) and the *Journal of Economic Perspectives* (Schultze, Stein, 1996) are devoted more to personal reminiscences and re-affirmations of previously claimed achievements than anything substantive. Stein (1996a, Chapters 15–18) and McLure (1972) come closest to what is needed. The first of these is a balanced and nonpartisan study, rich in insight and sympathetic to the revolutionary nature of the CEA's plans for fiscal policy in the 1960s. Its strength is a detailed account of how decisions were reached, but what it lacks is more easily seen as a matter of the author's preferences. Nevertheless a more quantitative evaluation of the Kennedy–Johnson fiscal experiment is still needed, which Stein (p. 517) admits is "beyond my capacities as an econometrician." The second, an early and effective critique of the Kennedy–Johnson Council and their enthusiasm for aggressive fiscal policy, anticipates many of the conclusions to be reached here, but in 71 pages including a discussion of the Nixon period, this essay does not have sufficient elaboration and documentation to be considered the last word on the subject. To fill the remaining void, what follows is macroeconomic history written for those specialists who are looking for a detailed economic evaluation — both qualitative and quantitative — of this path-breaking experiment in activist stabilization policy.

This book can be considered to be revisionist history. It is more critical of the performance of the members of the Council of Economic Advisers in the Kennedy–Johnson administrations than has been the case in the past. This re-assessment is perhaps inevitable since Walter Heller set an overly confident and self-congratulatory tone in the Godkin Lectures that he gave at Harvard University in 1966, before the dust had settled on the fiscal-policy experiment. It is supremely ironical that Heller would have better served his long-term goal of more active fiscal policy had he taken a more skeptical approach when these lectures were published in his book, *New Dimensions of Political Economy*. Contrary to his claim (1967, p. 72) that this was a "textbook tax cut" and that "Careful appraisal of the tax cut's impact on GNP shows a remarkably close fit of results to expectations," it will become obvious that Heller's presentation of textbook macroeconomic theory was deliberately fuzzy and that it is virtually impossible to connect the numerical predictions made in 1963 with the outcomes in 1964–65. Moreover the success of the "new economics" cannot be claimed on the basis of the elimination of the output gap by 1965. The story continued without interruption into 1968, with the last three years characterized by escalating Vietnam war expenses, rising inflation and an inability to legislate a timely tax increase. As John Kenneth Galbraith warned President Kennedy in 1962 (B2), "Tax reduction is highly irreversible." This lack of symmetry in fiscal policy in the 1960s is an important element in the subsequent demise of countercyclical stabilization initiatives by the time we reach the 1980s.

By the same token, this is not an ideological vendetta against Keynesian macroeconomics based on latter-day neoclassical theory. I now consider myself to be a "practical" macroeconomist without any doctrinal allegiances, but I have vivid and fond recollections of Keynesian theory as taught to graduate students at the University of Michigan exactly contemporaneous to the Kennedy–Johnson tax cut. Macroeconomic models available at that time were more than adequate to deal with business cycles; it was the Council's interpretation and implementation of these models that was less than ideal. The demise of activist policies is often blamed on the current dominance of modern neoclassical macroeconomic theory because it can prove that such policies are ineffective for their intended purposes. In an economy that has strong equilibrating powers, predictable changes in tax rates will not have any lasting effects on the demand for goods and services and employment, except perhaps by stimulating more labor supply. Despite this widely accepted view, one of the conclusions to be reached here is that the tax cut was very effective as an instrument of demand management and that it eliminated the existing output gap of about $30 billion. My criticism of the tax cut stems not from an assertion that Keynesian macroeconomics was inappropriate for the situation, but from the evidence that it was misapplied. It is the transition from established macroeconomic theory to policy making where quality deteriorated.

In that context, a critical re-assessment of the Kennedy–Johnson tax cut does not involve abstract economic analysis; instead it represents a judgment of economics in action outside of the ivory tower and beyond the journal article. Performance relative to a set of ideas, rather than the ideas themselves, is the focus of attention here. As such, an evaluation of this legislation makes it virtually impossible to avoid criticism of specific individuals and of the institutions that they served. In similar circumstances Gordon (1961, p. vii) wrote, "when one believes a policy to be wrong, one should attack the policy itself, not the person in charge of it." However he and the other economists who sent a letter to the Canadian Minister of Finance "wanted to say without disguise or ambiguity of any kind, not only that the policy and operations of the Bank [of Canada] are wrong, but that as professional economists we have lost all faith in their ever being made right under the present management." While Gordon was satisfied when the governor of the Bank, James Coyne, was fired, my goal is to expose the unalterable political nature of the Council and its consequent economic ineptness.

Success or failure in the policy arena is an evaluation of the process of implementation; yet this is a subject to which most economists pay scant attention. Our work is done when we have proven a theorem or subjected a hypothesis to empirical testing, but the translation of theory into practice is often perceived as too bland or boring to occupy the minds of our most prominent colleagues. Moreover we are aware that political considerations are often at odds with economic efficiency, but we are unable to make critical judgments in an explicitly political environment. Because of our lack of understanding we set very low standards of performance. It is a strange set of priorities for our profession to pursue theoretical errors with relentless energy and enthusiasm while we abide with equanimity or indifference policy errors that have large real costs to sizable groups in the population.

In economic policy advising, it is too easy to define and to take credit for success and almost as easy to avoid responsibility for errors. The economics profession has largely accepted Walter Heller's assessment of the Council's stellar performance during the implementation of the tax cut, but I hope to convince the reader that such self-serving propaganda should not be taken at face value. There is no way to soften the blow. Heller, Ackley and Okun, the most able of academic economists of their era, when put into the political context of the Council of Economic Advisers, made egregious mistakes that have remained hidden from view. At the same time, I remain convinced that they and other members of the Council acted with good faith and honest intentions and I certainly do not wish to impugn their motives by suggesting some far-fetched conspiracy. Also I will try to avoid criticism that comes with the benefit of hindsight by deliberately taking a 1960s perspective to this project. Exceptions to this self-imposed rule are acknowledged at the place where they occur.

The methodology employed in this book represents a major departure from my previous endeavors. I am not an economic historian by training and experience, but I have tried to concentrate on the reconstruction of events and their context from primary sources. In addition to reading the standard economic literature, I also combed the CEA and Congressional documents of the day for relevant information. Because that left some critical gaps in my understanding, I resorted to a search of the private papers of the CEA chairmen during this period. Public statements by the Council, including the *Economic Report of the President* (*ERP*), are not trustworthy sources of unbiased economic analysis and prediction; private communications, not initially intended for public inspection, often reveal what we need to know to reconstruct the historical record.

Citations for and quotations from these sources play an important part in documenting the assertions that are made in this study. My own reading of other historical works has left me with the impression that too many of them are inadequately documented and my reaction to this perception is to rely on direct quotation rather than paraphrase, on primary rather than on secondary sources and on transparency rather than style. Documents that are vital to this study, but difficult to locate, are reprinted *verbatim* in the Appendix to this book. The bibliography contains not only the list of published material cited in the text but also archival material.

Moreover this work includes a great deal of quantitative material. In order to allow for independent replication of my empirical results, I have included most of the data used in this study and their sources as appendices to the chapter where they are relevant. Also step-by-step calculations of important variables are included in the text to show the reader the process by which they were derived. It may appear old fashioned to print data in this electronic age, but this method is still the only one that provides a reliably permanent record.

OUTLINE OF THE BOOK

A short outline of the book concludes this introduction. The principal aim of this study is to reconstruct the policy framework and apparatus that initiated the application of "modern" fiscal policy as it was envisaged by the Kennedy–Johnson Council of Economic Advisers. The first step, found in Chapter 2, is to identify the nature of the macroeconomic problem to be solved: namely the elimination of the output gap of approximately $30 billion. Although the US economy was not technically in a recession in the early 1960s, the CEA was convinced of continuing underperformance and introduced their goal as the achievement of potential GNP, that level of output that could be produced by a labor input consistent with 4 per cent unemployment. The second step involves reconstructing the macroeconomic model that the CEA deployed in making their predictions. In other words, what was their view of the link between a $10 billion tax cut and the need to raise the total demand for goods and services by $30 billion? The answer to this question is undertaken in Chapter 3. The next step, in Chapter 4, involves estimating a small version of the $IS-LM-AS$ model of the macroeconomy and predicting, after the fact, the effects of the tax cut on output, interest rates and inflation rates for the following twelve quarters. The differences between the model forecasts with and without the tax cut and its timing are taken as the predictions of the effects of the tax cut itself. In Chapter 5 the emphasis shifts to the appearance of a negative output gap and the need to reverse the previous stimulus to aggregate demand. The lack of symmetry in 1967–68 is the focus of this discussion.

To this point, the analysis concentrates on the macroeconomic effects of the tax cut, but there was an equally important debate raging at the time concerning the budgetary effects. This issue will be raised in Chapter 6. Subsequently, in Chapter 7, the discussion turns to the need to translate economic advice by the CEA into policy recommendations and ultimately into legislation. The political process by which such results are achieved involves voters and their representatives assessing their self-interest in the policy proposal. There is no guarantee that optimal policies from the viewpoint of the "representative agent" are those that satisfy a majority of voters. The problem of finding the characteristics of the "median voter" is compounded by the existence of participation costs that disfranchise many voters and by the unpredictable effects of lobby and pressure groups. The long drawn-out battle over the 1968 tax surcharge is taken as a vivid example of the difficulties in getting the public to accept a tax increase. From all the previous material Chapter 8 attempts to draw lessons for the conduct of fiscal policy as a stabilization instrument. The main conclusion is that taxes are too blunt and unreliable an instrument to use for this purpose and that the "new economics" was discredited not by recent advances in macroeconomic theory, but by poor execution. An Appendix reproduces important documents that are part of the historical record of this period.

1

What Went Wrong?

When USAir Flight 427, a Boeing 737 aircraft, crashed near Pittsburgh on 8 September 1994 killing all 132 people aboard, the National Transportation Safety Board (NTSB) began an intensive and exhaustive investigation into the causes of the crash. Although essentially unsuccessful in this instance, it remains an impressive fact that investigators left no clue unexamined in order to discover the technical or human failure that led to this tragedy. There has been no official accounting of the expenses involved in this crash investigation, but Jonathan Harr (1996) indicates that resources for the investigation were not a limiting factor. For example, a just-retired Boeing 737 was put through "really extreme tests ... almost bizarre tests" to see if the crash scenario could be replicated. The unspoken rationale for this relentless search is that it will make future crashes less likely. If a structural weakness or pilot error could be identified, corrections would be made to prevent the same factor from causing another mishap. In the aircraft industry it has become the normal operating procedure to learn from mistakes in order to prevent their re-occurrence. In the process, despite newly designed aircraft, deregulation of the airline industry and more crowded airspace, flying has become less accident-prone. When the cause of the crash of Flight 427 could not be ascertained, the investigators were bitterly disappointed, in large part because they could not contribute to this improvement in reliability and safety. As one of the Safety Board team members, Gregory Phillips, acknowledged, "There's a tremendous amount of pressure, within myself and from outside, to find out what happened. I want to be certain I've looked at everything possible. I want to make sure there's nothing we can do that hasn't been done." (p. 55).

This obsession with airline safety has a cost attached to it: deliberate system redundancies, mandated inspections, maintenance and repairs and last-minute delays caused by unexpected safety concerns. These features add to the price of an airline ticket and reduce the number of passengers that buy them, but the assurance of a safe flight fills seats that would otherwise be empty. At least approximately, the safety costs incurred by airlines are balanced by the extra revenue that comes from safety-conscious passengers. In that context, any perceived disregard for the cause of a crash would lose the airline more in passenger loads and revenues than it would gain in cost savings and so profits would decline. Despite the painful process involved, the airlines have a self-interest in crash investigations. This does not mean that the NTSB can avoid conflicting vested interests. According to Jonathan Harr (1996, (pp. 41–2):

> The appearance of an independent, objective inquiry into the cause of an accident is crucial to the Safety Board's credibility. Yet the Board does not have the manpower or the expertise to conduct a major investigation on its own. It relies on what it refers to as "the party system," calling upon experts from the interested parties to assist in the investigation, on the premise, for example, that no one knows the working innards of a General Electric jet engine better than the General Electric engineers who designed and built that engine. ... Given the money, the reputations, and the potential exposure to liability that are at stake in determining the cause of a crash, the conflicts of interest in such a system seem clear and incurable.

Nevertheless, despite this adversarial approach, the NTSB is still able to function as a fact-finder. Thomas Haueter, an investigator with NTSB, pointed out, "People would like to drive the investigation in their own interest. It's up to me to control that." (p. 42).

POLICY ANALYSIS AND POLICY ADVICE

There is an obvious parallel in the economics profession to the fruitless investigation of Flight 427: the Great Depression. Despite many efforts by the best minds in the business, there is still no agreement as to the cause, propagation, transmission or remedy of the Depression of the 1930s. Romer (1993, p. 24) sums up the situation as follows: "Documenting the timing and severity of the Great Depression in the United States and abroad is more straightforward than explaining what caused the national and international collapse. Not surprisingly an experience as devastating and complex as the Great Depression has many different causes." At the time of Flight 427, the National Transportation Safety Board had investigated 374 major commercial airline accidents and found the probable cause in all but four cases. In economics, by comparison, the failure to agree on an explanation of the macroeconomic events in the 1930s is much more typical of the outcome of historical analysis.

Economics is not well equipped to deal with *post-mortem* investigations, especially when it comes to major stabilization-policy mistakes. It is impossible for a macroeconomy to leave evidence of all important events and decisions that would allow for a historical reconstruction and also for an identification of probable cause. There are no economic equivalents of flight-data recorders — the so-called "black boxes" — that are so vital in aircrash investigations. Nevertheless it will be argued that quantified, predictive models of economic behavior allow policy analysts to perform counterfactual research. More specifically an econometric model can be used to forecast important economic variables, especially in preparation for some major policy change. Then at a later date after the policy was implemented, the actual outcomes could be compared to the predictions and the difference between them represents an indication of what went wrong. The technical barriers to such an exercise are not high; what is missing is the will-power to learn from past mistakes and to apply these lessons to future policies.

The prevailing theme of this book is that the economics discipline needs some institutional change that makes learning from mistakes a more vital element of scientific progress. The economics profession does not have an equivalent to the NTSB, a government body charged with the responsibility of investigating economic "crashes" and to find the probable cause. In fact, with the notable exception of the Great Depression, economists do not spend a lot of time thinking about past mistakes. Despite great strides made in our understanding of economic forces, the availability of up-to-date information on the performance of the economy, the human resources of a multitude of research institutions and a vast policy-making bureaucracy, the prospect of examining past mistakes in minute detail is almost entirely foreign to the professional economist.

This book is intended as a historical and analytical account of "modern" fiscal policy as practised in the United States in the decade of the 1960s, starting with the Kennedy–Johnson tax cut of 1964 and ending with the Johnson tax surcharge of 1968. These two events in a relatively short time-span are often treated as separate episodes: the first hailed as a major success and the latter dismissed as a minor disappointment. Eckstein (1970, p. 90) observed that in 1965,

> The economy had shown, at least for 18 happy months, that it could prosper without war with sensible, modern economic management; doubts about fiscal policy were wiped out, and for a year or two, economists rode high

indeed. Then came the Vietnam War and the end, for a period at least, of modern fiscal policy. ... [T]axes were not increased because the President could not get the American people to pay for the war. In the end, the war paralyzed the political process, producing the surrealistic debate over the tax surcharge from mid-1967 to mid-1968.

One of the main theses of this study is that the inability to design and implement fiscal policy symmetrically around the recently enunciated goal of "potential output" is an indictment of the whole process of fine-tuning aggregate demand through tax changes, not just the later period as Eckstein would have us believe.

The demise of activist stabilization policy in the 1970s and 1980s, that is often blamed on the revolutionary approach to macroeconomic theory by the noninterventionist school of thought, is much more easily assigned to the failed policies of the 1960s. Had the Council of Economic Advisers in the Kennedy and Johnson administrations presented a clearer model of the links between taxes and aggregate demand, had they better understood the balance point of potential output, and had they been as persuasive in their advice to raise taxes in 1966 as they had been to lower taxes in 1963, countercyclical fiscal policy would have survived the neoclassical counterattack. Moreover fiscal policy would have been used more effectively during the 1982 and 1990 recessions, primarily because the budgetary deficits and accumulated debt would have been more manageable except for the irresolute position taken by the Council in 1966–68.

The point is that former policy advisers face a psychological barrier to undertake an evaluation of their own policy mistakes. The chasm between policy analysis and policy advice is too large to bridge. Heller recognized the challenge of learning from one's mistakes. In the preface to the 1967 publication of the Godkin Lectures, he asks, "had the policy process delivered a stronger dose of taxes instead of an overdose of tight money[?] ... Could economic policy be nimble and selective enough to keep total demand moving up while restoring balance to the economy? ... Would the 'new economics' succeed in minimizing the problems and maximizing the opportunities?" Not surprisingly Heller flinched when confronted by this opportunity: "Grounds for optimism in answering these questions will be found in this book, especially in its development of the theme that modern economic intelligence and advice have been woven into the everyday fabric of White House decision-making — for good." Martin Feldstein (1997, p. 100), a CEA chairman of a much later era that also witnessed macroeconomic mismanagement, looks at this period in a different way: "the experience of the 1960's and 1970's led the economics profession to a thorough-going rejection of ... its faith in the usefulness of fiscal policy." My argument is that Feldstein's evaluation would certainly have been more favorable if Heller had made a more serious effort to find out what had gone wrong in the 1960s.

Although more modest in tone in the 1990s than thirty years earlier, the Council still takes credit for "success" in policy implementations. The most recent example singled out by Stiglitz (1997, p. 109) is the auctioning of radio frequencies which are "proving their worth." Shortly afterwards *The Washington Post* (12 July 1997) reported that winning bidders were unable to meet payments on their bids and *The Economist* (17 May 1997) suggested that bid rigging was responsible for a recent auction of frequencies suitable for wireless data transmission, garnering only $13.6 million instead of the expected $1.8 billion. In these auctions, bidders are prohibited from "co-operating, collaborating, discussing or disclosing the substance of their bids or bidding strategies." Given the involvement of the CEA in the design of the complicated "simultaneous multiple-round auction," it would have been especially useful for Stiglitz and the Council to investigate and report to the economics profession how this collusion could have taken place and, more importantly, what disincentives are needed and available to prevent a re-occurrence. But learning from mistakes is not an aspiration that is embraced by policy advisers. Solow (1997, p. 108) is aware that government policies do not always bring about the results that are predicted by advisers. He writes, "even well-intended regulations create incentives for avoidance behavior. This will both diminish the benefits to be expected and, perhaps, generate welfare losses outside the intended scope of the regulation." But Solow is much too optimistic about the ability of the Council to forecast privately-optimizing adaptive behavior and to "design effective regulations," as if the Council had some supreme powers unavailable to other agencies.

Stiglitz also claims that the Council is able to represent the national interest against a multitude of lobbies in public-policy debates. "The question is whether government is simply an arena for bargaining by special interests, or whether government can rise above that to represent the will of all." (p. 113). Noble as that may sound, policies that satisfy everyone are even more demanding than a Pareto improvement, that merely requires that some members of the community not be harmed. Moreover it is naive to think that special-interest lobbyists are unable to wrap their cause in the flag and convince a confused public that they are pleading for the national interest. The point is that economists are ill prepared to predict which special interests will win in a competitive environment. We have no models beyond the Stolper–Samuelson theorem and rent-seeking behavior to show how the welfare of specific groups is affected by policy decisions and we have no predictions beyond assorted voting models to indicate which special interests will thrive and which will fail to survive.

Scarcely a year later, Stiglitz (1998) acknowledges the critical role of special interests in government decisions. He asks rhetorically:

> Why is it so difficult to implement even Pareto improvements? ... [A]l-though a few potential changes were strictly Pareto improvements, there were many other changes that would hurt only a small narrowly defined group (for example, increasing the efficiency of the legal system might hurt lawyers). But if everyone except a narrowly defined special interest group could be shown to benefit, surely the change should be made. In prac-tice, however, "almost everyone" was rarely sufficient in government policy-making and often such near-Pareto improvements did not occur. (p. 4)

Stiglitz provides examples of both successes and failures from his ex-perience at the Council of Economic Advisers, but is hesitant to con-clude that the existence of special interests makes outcomes quite un-predictable. The Council justifies its existence by its ability to stop "bad projects." Stiglitz (1997, p. 112) identifies two: the supersonic air-liner and high-definition television, but there is no annual list of those bad projects that went ahead despite CEA disapproval. For example, there are too many trade disputes that are decided in favor of industry interests at the magnified expense of consumer welfare and the CEA must acknowledge its inability to eliminate tax privileges and shelters. Surely the CEA is an overall loser in this sort of cost–benefit analysis, but it would be useful information to know why some "bad projects" are politically successful.

Unfortunately the political arena in which policy advisers operate is much different from the world of academia where policy analysts toil. It would be an unthinkable act of defiance and disloyalty for the CEA to publicize the failures of the administration for which they work. Worse than that, the Council is unable to promote discussion of both costs and benefits of proposed initiatives; only the latter are allowed to be mentioned. As a consequence, policies always turn out to be worse than anticipated. During the tax-cut discussions in 1963, Walter Heller and Gardner Ackley in their testimony to the Joint Economic Committee did not mention the possibility that interest rates might rise and investment fall, or that inflationary pressures might worsen if the tax cut proved to be too strong, or that a tax increase might be necessary in the near future when private demand recovered. It was certainly not possible to state that 4 per cent of the labor force was likely to remain unemployed even if the best prediction for the tax cut came to pass. Policy advis-ers, even those who were previously policy analysts, become captives of the need for extravagant claims. Any suggestion that there might be costs as well as benefits to a proposed policy change will activate lobby groups for the potential losers: borrowers if interest rates rise, fixed-income earners who fear inflation and the union movement protecting the residually unemployed. Since potential losers usually have stronger lobbying positions than potential winners, as will become evident in Chapter 7, the CEA has ample reason to disguise the costs of a policy change and to concentrate only on the benefits. In the White House, to mention economic costs is to admit to political weakness and even internal CEA memoranda that perform cost–benefit studies, with the notable exception of (B50), are difficult to find.

It is sometimes easy to forget that economic policy decisions are made in a confrontational environment. Economists are accustomed to conflict over theories, facts and interpretations, but in the political sphere it is institutionalized and palpable conflict that has a bearing on policy debates and outcomes: Democrats *vs* Republicans, the President *vs* Congress, the Treasury *vs* the Federal Reserve and, of course, a multitude of special interests against each other. In such an adversarial context, each side has to score debating points against its opponents and this makes the admission of mistakes an impossibility. According to Kearns (1976, pp. 290–91) President Johnson once told her,

> If we went around beating our breasts and admitting difficulties with our programs, then the Congress would immediately slash all our funds for next year and then where would we be? Better to ... work from within to make things better and correct the problems ... I wish it had been different. I wish the public had seen the task of ending poverty the same way as they saw the task of getting to the moon, where they accepted mistakes and failures as part of the scientific process. I wish they had let us experiment with different programs, admitting that some were working better than others. It would have made everything easier. But I know that the moment we said out loud that this or that program was a failure, then the wolves who never wanted us to be successful in the first place would be down upon us at once, tearing away at every joint, killing our effort before we even had a chance.

Lyndon Johnson was neither the first nor the last president who felt beleaguered by his opponents and unable to share the anguish of failure with the public. To add to this paranoia, Johnson did not tolerate internal dissent either, which made honest disagreements an act of disloyalty. Johnson's opinion of the bureaucracy, reported by Kearns (p. 299), was that, "I barely knew or saw them, yet there they were disagreeing with my policy and leaking materials to the press. It was a real problem all right. A President is entitled to people who'll execute his views." Academics on the Council of Economic Advisers, accustomed to the cut and

thrust of open debate to hone their arguments, would be forced to adapt
to Johnson's obsessions and self-censor their advice. What is surprising
is that those who labored in fear of Johnson's wrath did not make public
their experiences, and the lessons to be learned from them, after their
public service ended.

The thought of resignation in the face of accusations of disloyalty and
declining persuasiveness was even more remote in the minds of Council
members. Okun was of the opinion (J96) that, "The man who resigned
with a blast because the President didn't take his advice would be a
heel, not a hero." Ackley was more specific in his views as to the conditions under which a resignation is warranted. In the oral-history project
(Hargrove and Morley, 1984, p. 230) he said, "suppose you're asked to
go out as a public advocate of a position that you think is just dead
wrong. ... I was ordered to write [a] letter [probably (J27)], and under
great pressure I did write it and then told them that if they ever asked
me to do that again I would resign."[1]

These self-imposed limitations reduce the Council's leverage to ensure that their advice is accepted by the President. The only sanction
available to the members of the Council is resignation, with a public
explanation of the reasons taken for this action. Such a threat would be
more credible from Council members than from anyone else of equal rank
in the administration, not only because their status was determined in
the economics profession and not as political aides in the White House,
but also since they were typically "on loan" from economics departments
at prestigious universities to which they could easily return in the wake
of a resignation based on principle.

EX-POST POLICY EVALUATION

Although economics cannot rely on a "black box" to reconstruct events,
Okun (1968; 1970) suggested what might be called a "scientific approach" to policy evaluation: to compare actual GNP with what would
have transpired in the absence of the tax cut, with the difference ascribed
to the policy change. In the process, he had to estimate an econometric
model of the US macroeconomy in order to remove the effects of the tax
reductions on consumption and investment expenditures. Okun did not

[1] Ackley seems to have had a high tolerance for indignities. In June 1966, he was
informed of the President's demand for a daily "resume of press contacts" including
negative reports (B28). Thereafter, Ackley submitted a memorandum every day
for many months indicating whether or not he had any contact with journalists.

pursue the question of "What went wrong?" because he was already convinced that the tax cut was a great success; nevertheless, his procedure has at least the appropriate ingredients for answering this question. At this stage, it is useful to specify the proposed design of *ex-post* policy evaluation.

The CEA must have had in mind a macroeconomic model that connected the desired outcome of higher income and lower unemployment to the required policy change in terms of lower tax rates on personal and corporate income.[2] Parameter estimates were also needed to quantify this model. Did the Council rely on such an econometric model of the US economy to make its predictions? In an earlier contribution (OECD, 1965, Chapter 7), Okun admitted, "The Government has not constructed an econometric model of national income and product, but econometric techniques have been used to investigate the various sectors." (p. 150). He is convinced of the benefits from such an exercise:

> [F]orecasting that rests entirely on *ad hoc* judgments cannot take full account of the lessons of history that can be summarized in quantified and formalized economic relationships. Quite apart from accuracy, formal methods have a number of advantages. For example, a complete model is a demonstrably objective predictor; it cannot be accused of coloring the forecast to further its preferred policies or to correspond to the state of its viscera. (This shield can help to supply internal as well as external protection. Many an economic forecaster may have some private moments of doubt as to whether he is maintaining his objectivity and his courage as he prepares his outlook.) Secondly, the more formalized the forecasting method, the more readily it lends itself to systematic post-mortems. The full model reveals its own past errors in stark nakedness. And systematic post-mortems are essential to guide research efforts in refining forecasting. (p. 150)

As desirable as this sounds in the abstract, government agencies will always be reluctant to publicize the basis of their forecasts and the CEA has not made available in any of its publications the type of econometric model that Okun advocated. As the OECD study remarks, "A government may not wish to expose itself to the risk of embarrassment if its forecast proves seriously wrong." (p. 24). Not surprisingly, Taylor (1993) provides only an unofficial CEA view of econometric policy evaluation.

Internal communications within the Council reveal a desultory attempt at *ex-post* evaluation of the 1964 tax cut. Lee Hanson and Burton Weisbrod wrote to Heller (K67), "Now that the tax bill has taken final form and its passage appears imminent, we should devote serious consideration to devising criteria for assessing the impact of this cut. . . .

---

[2] The details of the CEA predictions will be discussed in Chapter 3. Here we are concerned with the methodology of forecasting.

For example, assume that the consumption ratio proved to be, say, 0.5 rather than, say, 0.9 as we assumed it to be." They and Locke Anderson (K69) suggested using survey data for this purpose and a number of agencies were petitioned to support such an effort. However, even after "three weeks of meetings and consultations on the subject of studying reactions to the tax cut" (K70), no study was produced and the opportunity to view the tax cut as a laboratory experiment was lost. Instead the Council wrote a review of recent macroeconomic developments in September 1964 (J13) which concluded, "In the nature of the case, the evidence of a direct causal relationship between the Revenue Act of 1964 and this year's favorable economic developments is circumstantial rather than the hard, sure proof of the scientist's test tube."

Even if it is impossible to reconstruct the CEA's model of the tax cut, let

$$Y = \alpha X + \beta Z + \epsilon, \qquad (1.1)$$

be such a model, where Y is the endogenous variable and X and Z are exogenous variables, of which the latter is considered to be the policy instrument. In fact there may be a multi-equation simultaneous model such as IS–LM which must first be solved to obtain a reduced form in equation (1.1). If Y_0 is the current value, but Y_1 is optimal, then a change of $\beta(Z_1 - Z_0)$ is required to reach the desired result. This situation is shown in Figure 1.1, where A is the current position and B is the predicted outcome of the change from Z_0 to Z_1. The estimated slope of the regression line, which is obtained from past relationships between Y, X and Z, is β and the intercept is αX. The actual outcome happens to be C, which allows us to ask "What went wrong?" by concentrating on the vertical distance $Y_2 - Y_1$. This distance is shown to be positive, but it could just as easily be negative.

The relationship between Y and Z may not be contemporaneous as envisaged in equation (1.1); therefore a more general formulation may be written as:

$$Y = \alpha X + \beta_0 Z + \beta_1 Z_{-1} + \beta_2 Z_{-2} \ldots + \epsilon, \qquad (1.1')$$

which then creates a number of policy errors, $(Y_2 - Y_1), (Y_2 - Y_1)_{-1}, (Y_2 - Y_1)_{-2} \ldots$, after a one-time change in Z. Again these may be positive or negative.

A number of explanations for the existence and size of $Y_2 - Y_1$ in Figure 1.1 are possible:

1. There is always some prediction error, which is captured by ϵ in equation (1.1). In the process of estimation, the standard error of the regression, σ, is calculated. If the residuals are normally distributed,

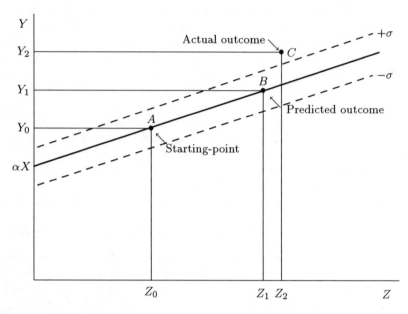

Figure 1.1   Identifying policy errors

ϵ will be between the two lines marked $+\sigma$ and $-\sigma$ two-thirds of the time. Thus if C were inside this region, we could conclude that the only thing that went wrong was unavoidable prediction error. Okun (1968; 1970), in his chart on p. 357, ascribes the entire change from Y_0 to Y_2 to the policy change; he does not allow for prediction error. In the case of equation (1.1′), a convenient summary measure of the multiple values of $Y_2 - Y_1$ is a root-mean-squared error.

2. But if C lies outside of a confidence interval based on multiples of σ, there must be some other explanation. One possibility is that the change in Z was accompanied by an increase in X that shifted the line upwards through C. In other words the experiment cannot rely on the assumption of *ceteris paribus*. For example, the CEA may have assumed that monetary policy would be neutral, but it turned out to be expansionary. According to Okun (OECD, 1965, p. 149), forecasting by the CEA "does [not] rest on any direct statement of intentions by the Board of Governors of the Federal Reserve System."

3. Alternatively the larger-than-expected value of Y_2 could be the result of the fact that Z increased more than was anticipated. This could happen if the cut in legislated tax rates in *The Revenue Act of 1964* had led to larger decreases in tax payments than expected. In other words it may not be possible to control the size of Z precisely. Okun

(OECD, 1965, p. 149) admits that, "The assumptions about Federal revenues take the form of predicting changes in the tax schedules from proposed and pending legislation. The dollar volume of revenues is crucially related to income levels and must be regarded as endogenously determined."

4. It is also possible that the relationship between Y and Z was misspecified and that the slope of the regression line should be higher or that a nonlinear relationship should be used.

5. Finally there may have been data revisions between the time of the prediction and the outcome to cause a discrepancy between the two, but this is essentially a minor problem because the size of the discrepancy is known.

The first four of these points can be captured by the following equation:

$$Y_2 - Y_1 = \epsilon + \alpha(X_1 - X_0) + \beta(Z_2 - Z_1) + (\beta^* - \beta)Z_0, \qquad (1.2)$$

where β^* is the slope of the line connecting A and C. By dividing both sides of equation (1.2) by $Y_2 - Y_1$, we obtain the proportion that each factor contributes to the total forecast error. *Ex-post* policy evaluation involves ranking these four possible explanations and trying to improve the design of policy implementation on the basis of the most important of these. For instance, it may be that changing tax rates leads to very unpredictable changes in disposable income, in which case, the government may want to use a different approach to fiscal policy. Or it may find that it needs to co-ordinate more closely with the Federal Reserve Board to estimate the combined effect of X and Z on Y.

This proposal for learning from one's mistakes puts a heavy burden on the Council of Economic Advisers. It must provide to the public a quantitative version of the economic model that it intends to use for predicting the effects of the policy change. Heller (1967, p. 69) was confident that the Council was able to perform this function:

> In part, this shift from a more passive to a more active policy has been made possible by steady advances in fact-gathering, forecasting techniques, and business practice. Our statistical net is now spread wider and brings in its catch faster. Forecasting has the benefit of not only more refined, computer-assisted methods but of improved surveys of consumer and investment intentions.

In commenting on the *ex-post* evaluation of *The Revenue Act of 1964*, Okun (1968; 1970, p. 356) promised that, "At the Council of Economic Advisers, we hope to improve the tools needed in this analysis and to remedy some of the limitations I have noted." Nevertheless it is hardly surprising when viewed in retrospect that the Council did not make forecasting an important element of its public duty. The last thing that members of the Council would want to do is to provide ammunition to their critics and to allow the profession to pinpoint what went wrong in any policy experiment. In this context, policy advisers want to provide in advance only the haziest of notions about the relationship between Y and Z and to make predictions that are also sufficiently vague to prevent verification. Then it is possible to take credit for success, but to avoid the blame for failure. To a policy analyst, the difference between C and B in Figure 1.1 is critical; to a policy adviser it is anathema. For the former, the size of $Y_2 - Y_1$ against some absolute standard is the basis for scientific progress, but to the latter it is self-incriminating evidence.

Not only would the *ex-ante* provision of a properly specified and estimated model expose the policy adviser to *ex-post* criticism, it would also marshal the forces of opposition by those groups who see themselves as potential losers when the policy change is made. For example, if the Council had relied on an *IS–LM* model to predict the effects of the tax cut, it would have become obvious that interest rates would have to rise if the *LM* curve had a positive slope. In the absence of expansionary monetary policy, some readily identifiable groups would have experienced a loss of welfare. Specifically, home owners with mortgages, consumers with auto loans and businesses with debt would have had to compare their extra interest costs against the increased disposable income they would have after the tax cut to determine whether they would receive a net benefit in this exercise. Such calculations are made easier by the availability of qualitative or quantitative predictions by the CEA; in a real sense, the Council would be helping its opponents, an act of altruism that would be unlikely to survive for long in a Darwinian world of partisan and confrontational politics.

POST MORTEMS WITH HINDSIGHT

The question "What went wrong?" sets the stage for the rest of the book. It is not only a historical journey through the corridors of power in Washington at the time of the 1964 tax cut, but more importantly, an analytical reconciliation between macroeconomic theory as it existed in the 1960s and the basis of the CEA's predictions concerning the tax cut and between these predictions and the actual outcomes. The analytical component derives from the need to apply the lessons from what has been called the most successful application of fiscal policy to the overall objective of stabilization of the macroeconomy in the face of unpredictable cyclical activity.

After the passage of so much time, it would be easy to mount a neoclassical attack on this quintessentially Keynesian policy experiment.

Criticism based on the distinction between predictable and unpredictable changes in fiscal policy would show the conflicting effects on nominal and real values in the macroeconomy, but it would not be fair to the proponents of the tax cut to blame them for not understanding the concept of "rational expectations" in 1963. Instead mainstream macroeconomic theory as it was taught in graduate courses at that time or found in Ackley (1961) and Dernburg and McDougall (1960) will be the basis for the evaluation of the Council's ability to formulate predictions for the tax cut. Moreover it would be feasible but unfair to use modern econometric techniques such as vector autoregressions to estimate equations such as (1.1) and then calculate policy errors, $Y_2 - Y_1$ in Figure 1.1. For the quantitative work in this book, I will rely on data and procedures that should have been available at that time, including two-stage least-squares and polynomial distributed lags. However I am aware that current desk-top computers and modern software programs have more power and versatility than the most potent mainframes of the 1960s, making what was once a Herculean task into an effortless procedure.

In the 1960s there were drawn-out stabilization-policy debates, including the subject matter of this book, but they were not overtly ideological in nature. As Friedman was misquoted at the time: "We are all Keynesians now." The intellectual climate has changed considerably since then and it is now almost impossible to write about macroeconomics without identifying with either the neoclassical or Keynesian schools of thought. It is not my aim to contribute to this pedandic debate. Although I am highly critical of the proponents of the tax cut for the low quality of their economic analysis and their lack of symmetrical support for a tax increase in 1966–67, this criticism is based solely on my assessment of the implementation of the tax cut and subsequent developments, all within an essentially Keynesian framework.

2

Estimating the Output Gap

A creation of *The Employment Act of 1946*, the Council of Economic Advisers did not have, in its first decade of existence, a strong guiding motive for its activities and advice. Leon Keyserling (1956, p. 70), a former chairman of the Council wrote, "The commitment of the Employment Act to full employment economics, rather than to countercyclical economics, has hardly been noted by most economists, and yet it represents a profoundly valuable and virile shift in mood and emphasis. Here is a unique opportunity for leadership by the CEA." This admonition was not taken to heart during the Eisenhower Administration, but after 1960 Walter Heller and the other Keynesian macroeconomists who were recruited by the Kennedy Administration resurrected this literal interpretation of *The Employment Act*. Heller was convinced that, "Standards of economic performance must be recast from time to time. Recasting them in more ambitious terms was an indispensable prelude to the shaping of economic policies for the 1960's which would be suitable to the tremendous output capabilities of the U.S. economy." (1967, p. 61)

To put these policies into the proper perspective required a target or goal to be reached by the policy maker or adviser. The choice made by the CEA for this purpose was potential output. This was taken to be the level of real GNP that would be produced if and when the unemployment rate was 4 per cent of the labor force. In common with contemporary Keynesian thinking, the goal was to be found in the goods market as a target for output, even though the immediate problem to be addressed was involuntary unemployment in the labor market. An alternative and more direct goal would have been a target unemployment rate and the government could have acted as an employer of last resort, as it had during the Great Depression.

Countercyclical fiscal policy that attempts only to forestall or alleviate a recession was thought to be inadequate, since the US economy was capable of producing more goods and services than would be demanded, even after a period of unusually strong private demand. During the late 1950s an uninspiring, low-level equilibrium had been accepted by the Eisenhower Administration as normal; their main concern was to avoid another major depression. With business cycles occurring all too frequently, this was not an idle preoccupation, but it was not ambitious enough for the economic advisers in the Kennedy White House.

In late 1962 and early 1963, as plans for the tax cut were formulated and debated, the US economy was experiencing relatively robust growth. In that context, the output gap based on the difference between actual and potential output served as a dramatic reminder of what additional aggregate demand through Keynesian stimulus was still needed. In the 1963 *Joint Economic Report* that recommended the tax cut to the full House and Senate, the problem was put in the following way: "What is the magnitude and speed of the expansion necessary if the economy is to reach full employment in the foreseeable future? ... In the fourth quarter of 1962, demand was some 7 to 8 percent below the full employment output potential." (p. 6). It would take another few years of unrelenting and unprecedented expansion of private demand to eliminate this gap. Not wishing to rely on luck, Kennedy and his advisers promoted the idea of a general tax cut to stimulate consumer and investment demand sufficiently to reach potential output within two years or less.

The Heller Council had created not only a bold policy proposal but also an informational innovation by producing charts that showed the size and duration of the output gap and giving a graphic representation of the "missing" demand for goods and services that could be produced in a full-employment macroeconomy. These appeared in each of the *Economic Reports of the President* authored by Heller and his colleagues. Chart 2.1 is a reproduction of the figure in the 1963 *Joint Economic Report*. This was the version of the output-gap chart most relevant for the tax-cut proposal in terms of timing its visual impact. It revealed that the US economy, despite its recent recovery from recession, had been producing considerably below its potential since 1955, a span of seven years of substandard performance blamed entirely on the Eisenhower Administration. It also had an optimistic conclusion by showing three projected paths back to potential output, each one depending on the speed with which the tax cut was implemented and assumptions about other policies. Not even path *A*, which involved an 8.3 per cent annual growth rate for eight quarters, was considered unrealistic. Paths *B* and *C* were, however, no less formidable; since potential GNP grew at 3.5 per cent, the gap itself would widen over time unless strong and resolute action was taken.

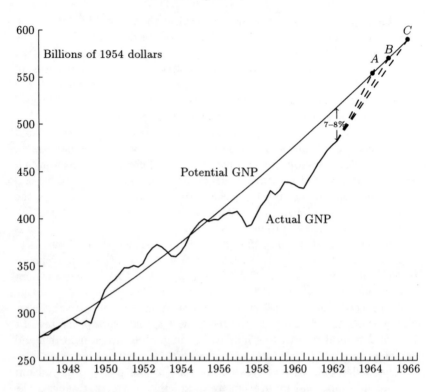

Source: Reproduction of Chart 1 in *Joint Economic Report* (1963, p. 7); based on
            data from US Department of Commerce (1966, Tables 1.2 and 8.1).

Chart 2.1   Actual and potential Gross National Product, 1947–66

It is the derivation of potential GNP and the output gap that is the
subject of analysis in this chapter. In the next chapter, the proposed
method of eliminating the output gap will be the focus of attention.
A statement of the recently discovered but now famous "Okun's Law"
provides us with three interrelated topics that will receive attention here.
Arthur Okun linked the output gap, $y_e - y$, to the unemployment gap,
$u - 4$, via the Okun coefficient, which he found to be 3.2, and obtained:

$$y_e - y = 3.2(u - 4). \tag{2.1}$$

First, we will review the method by which potential output, y_e, was estimated; second, the derivation of the Okun coefficient will be discussed;
and third, the assumption of 4 per cent unemployment as optimal will be
investigated. To conclude the discussion, the relation between inflation
and the output gap will be explored.

MEASURING POTENTIAL OUTPUT

Arthur Okun, more than anyone else, championed the cause of potential output as a macroeconomic target. From the beginning he was concerned with the costs to a nation's economy when it operated at a level of income other than at its potential. This was an early attempt to introduce the supply side of the economy alongside the Keynesian demand analysis. He declared (1962; 1970, p. 314), "Potential GNP is a supply concept, a measure of productive capacity. ... The full employment goal must be understood as striving for maximum production without inflationary pressures; or, more precisely, as aiming for a point of balance between more output and greater stability, with appropriate regard for the social valuation of these two objectives."

The Production-function Approach

In estimating potential GNP, Okun suggested (p. 314) that technology and the capital stock were "data" and not "variables," but that the labor input should be evaluated at 4 per cent unemployment. This suggests that potential output is derived from a simplified production function for the macroeconomy. The production function, written in natural logs, is as follows:

$$y = \alpha(k + c) + \beta(n + h) + \rho, \qquad (2.2)$$

where y is output, k is the capital stock and c is its utilization rate, n represents the number of workers and h is the number of hours that they work and ρ is an independent productivity factor; α and β are output elasticities of capital and labor, respectively. This is a Cobb–Douglas production function which, by the early 1960s, had been widely used for both industry-level and economy-wide estimation. To determine potential output, we first need a way of introducing unemployment into the production function and this is done by defining:

$$n = \ell - u, \qquad (2.3)$$

where ℓ is the natural log of labor supply and u is the rate of unemployment. On the basis of Okun's definition above, the output gap should then be written as

$$y_e - y = -\beta(u_e - u), \qquad (2.4)$$

with $u_e = 0.04$ or 4 per cent, a variable that is now called the natural rate of unemployment, but then was associated with "structural" unemployment.

The Okun Coefficient

Equation (2.4) would be wide of the mark as a way of connecting the two gaps in the macroeconomy. Okun argued that variations in u around 4 per cent unemployment would also influence other variables in the production function, namely ℓ, h and ρ. Because a reduction in u would also trigger an increase in these other variables, the Okun coefficient is much larger than β which would be in the vicinity of $0.6 - 0.7$ to reflect labor's share in total output. The 1962 *Economic Report of the President* (Table 2) provides some numerical estimates of the various contributions to the 1961 output gap of $40 billion or 7.7 per cent of actual output. In that year the unemployment rate was 6.7 per cent and a hypothetical reduction in unemployment to 4 per cent was assumed to account for $15 billion of that gap, so that each one percentage-point reduction in unemployment would raise output by $5.6 billion. Also operating at the economy's potential would increase the labor force and would generate another $4 billion in GNP; longer working hours would contribute another $5 billion; and greater productivity would create another $16 billion. From the numbers in Table 2 of the 1962 *Report*, the Okun coefficient can be calculated as $y_e - y$ divided by $u - u_e$ or $7.7/2.7 = 2.85$, although Okun originally reported a coefficient of 3.2.

The prevailing view continues to be that Okun's Law is a robust relationship. Solow and Tobin (1988, p. 9) are convinced that Okun's Law, "proved to be one of the most reliable and useful empirical regularities of economics." Gordon (1984, p. 539) asserts that, "This relationship has remained popular in macroeconomic analysis both because it has been sufficiently stable and reliable in the past two decades to deserve being labeled a law and also because it short-circuits the rather complex identity that links output and unemployment." Despite this overwhelming endorsement, both Adams and Coe (1990) and Prachowny (1993), applying a production-function approach to the estimation of the Okun coefficient, have found considerable instability in its value. However the data used for these studies begin well after the Kennedy–Johnson tax cut, making it paramount that equation (2.1) be investigated for the period 1955 to 1965.

In common with Okun's position, potential output is taken as the value of actual GNP in 1955:3, which is $396 billion in 1954 dollars. Then a growth rate of 0.035/4 per quarter is applied to this starting-point. These calculated values for y_e may not correspond exactly to Okun's, partly because of data revisions to GNP, but also because potential GNP at that time was only provided visually. Chart 2.2 plots values of $y_e - y$ and $u - 4$ for all quarters between 1955:3 and 1965:4. This information

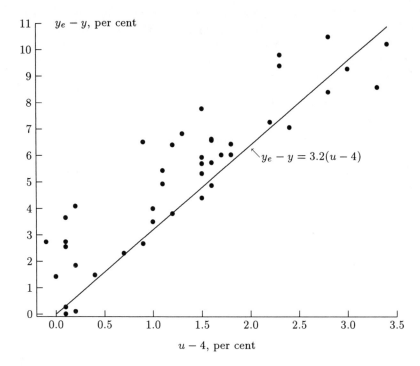

$$y_e - y = 3.2(u - 4)$$

Sources: u from Gordon (1993, Table A-2), y from US Department of Commerce (1966), y_e from quarterly growth rate of 0.875 per cent starting from $y = y_e$ in 1955:3.

Chart 2.2   Okun's Law, 1955:3 to 1965:4

is similar to that presented by the Council (1961; 1988, p. 27) for the 1950s. It shows that Okun's Law is not a very "tight" relationship. The ratio for $y_e - y$ to $u - 4$ varies from -27.26 in 1957:1 to 36.45 in the very next quarter. The mean value for all observations was 5.27 with a standard deviation of 9.12. The observations follow a clockwise loop pattern, with recessions tending to have larger coefficients than boom periods. The regression found the slope coefficient to be 2.636 with a standard error of 0.205 and a constant of 1.723, indicating that an Okun coefficient of 3.2 and a constant of zero leaves many more observations above the line than below it.

At the time that the tax cut was being planned, contemporaneous evidence on the size of the Okun coefficient should have given warning that it was far from stable, as weekly hours of work, capacity utilization and labor productivity varied independently of the unemployment rate.

As a result, a given unemployment rate could be associated with many different values of the output gap, depending mainly on its place in the business cycle. One is therefore tempted to suggest that the imprecision of this relationship should have been acknowledged and that a probabilistic evaluation of the Okun coefficient should have been accepted.

The Growth Rate of Potential Output

Estimating the output gap for any one period was not nearly as important to the CEA as estimating the growth rate of potential GNP. Heller (1967, pp. 61–2, emphasis in original) cast this imperative in the following terms:

> [N]othing was more urgent than to raise the sights of economic policy and to shift its focus from the ups and downs of the cycle to the continuous rise in the economy's potential. Policy emphasis had to be redirected from a *corrective* orientation geared to the dynamics of the cycle, to a *propulsive* orientation geared to the dynamics and the promise of growth. ... Estimating the trend rate of growth for this purpose was a comparatively unemotional — if technically intricate — matter of adding together the growth rates in labor inputs and productivity. When we initiated the "official" calculations in 1961, this growth in potential was running at a rate of $3\frac{1}{2}$ percent a year; it is now nearly 4 percent.

The reason why the growth rate of y_e became more important than a measurement of $y_e - y$ is that it allowed the CEA to plan for the future rather than reacting only to current and past problems.

The output gap, at any point in time, can be measured by having information about the unemployment rate and making an assumption that the Okun coefficient has remained constant since it was last estimated; however, unless one can predict unemployment for the next year or two, it is impossible to use this method for predictive purposes. In that case, if one knows the recent growth rate of potential GNP and is prepared to assume that it will continue, predictions become much easier, especially since y_e should not suffer from unpredictable cyclical variations. From this supply orientation, the growth rate of potential output, defined as the absolute change in y_e, is determined by

$$dy_e = \alpha dk^* + \beta(d\ell^* + dh^*) + d\rho^*, \tag{2.5}$$

with the starred values at their long-term sustainable rates of growth.

At the time that the Kennedy–Johnson tax cut was being proposed, the growth rate of y_e was announced as $3\frac{1}{2}$ per cent. Was this estimate derived, as Heller suggests, by predicting the growth rates of the factor inputs and productivity and then combined through the production function as in equation (2.5)? Okun (1962; 1970, p. 317) initially measured y_e for the period 1954–62 from the equivalent of equation (2.1). This is shown in his chart (p. 318) as the "wiggly" line for potential GNP. He then states, "One way of smoothing which eliminates all the ripples is to substitute a simple exponential curve that corresponds with the trend and level of the wiggly series. Such a line is obtained by a trend that goes through actual output in mid-1955 as a benchmark and moves upward at a $3\frac{1}{2}$ percent annual rate."

Also the 1962 *ERP* (p. 51) states, "The trend rate of growth of GNP, adjusted for changes in unemployment levels, has averaged about $3\frac{1}{2}$ percent in the post-Korean period. Thus, the path of potential GNP can be represented by a $3\frac{1}{2}$ percent trend from actual GNP in mid-1955. The 1961 value of the trend exceeds actual output by \$40 billion."

As a consequence, the path of y_e from 1955 to 1962 and onward was not forecast on the basis of "adding up" the growth of factors in equation (2.5) at their long-run sustainable values; instead, the growth rate of *actual* output, adjusted only for the unemployment rate, was used. Although ℓ, h and ρ are allowed to vary cyclically, no assumption was made about their noncyclical, long-term growth rates. In the process, the emphasis on potential output as a supply concept had lost its meaning; its growth rate had become an estimate of the path of actual output, raised once-and-for-all by a higher level of employment.

If we revert to equation (2.5) as the basis for estimating the growth rate of potential GNP, some predictions must be made for $dk^*, d\ell^*, dh^*$ and $d\rho^*$, as well as obtaining values for α and β. Chart 2.3 shows how index numbers for factors of production increased from a common base of 100 for the period 1955–62, the same timeframe as that used by Okun. The measure of k is the constant-cost, net stock of fixed reproducible tangible wealth minus consumer durables and residential housing, taken from Department of Commerce estimates published only in 1993; however, earlier estimates available to the CEA would not be much different since they rely mainly on the perpetual inventory method. Also the change in the real weekly wage in manufacturing is taken as the proxy for independent productivity changes, assuming that workers are paid the value of their marginal product. If we were to rely on an index for output per manhour, this would be $y - n - h$ and would automatically be calculated as a residual from the growth of output unaccounted for by factor changes. Hence, the smaller is the growth rate of capital and labor inputs, the larger is the growth of output per manhour and vice versa.

From this chart it is evident that y_e increases faster at $3\frac{1}{2}$ per cent than any of its underlying influences. Nevertheless the "adding-up" pro-

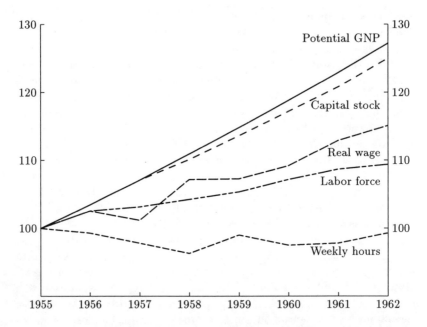

Sources: Economic Report of the President (1967, Tables B-20, B-26, B-28), US Department of Commerce, *Survey of Current Business* (September 1993, Table 22) and 3.5 per cent growth rate of potential GNP.

Chart 2.3   Indexes for potential GNP, capital, labor force, hours and real wage, 1955–62

cess may still make this CEA assumption look conservative. First, it is assumed that $\alpha = 0.33$ and $\beta = 0.67$ to give each factor its approximate share in output and to impose constant returns to scale. Second, these parameter values are combined with the following growth rates for 1955–62: $dk^* = 0.032, d\ell^* = 0.013, dh^* = 0$ and $d\rho^* = 0.020$. Third, substituting these values into equation (2.5) generates $dy_e = 0.039$, which is actually somewhat larger than the CEA estimate. If this growth rate were used in Chart 2.3, the index number for 1962 would have been 130.7 instead of 127.2 and the resulting output gap would also have been larger. Whatever the assumptions and calculations, this "adding-up" exercise would have been more in the spirit of the production-function approach to potential GNP originally suggested by Okun than that taken by the Council. One remains puzzled by their lack of interest in predicting long-term factor and productivity growth.

THE FOUR PER CENT ASSUMPTION

If equation (2.1) is the basis for measuring the output gap, a closer look at the assumption of 4 per cent unemployment as an optimal position is needed. Originally Okun (1962; 1970) suggested this number as a working proposition. He admitted, "It is interesting and perhaps surprising that there seems to be more agreement that a 4 percent unemployment rate is a reasonable target under existing labor market conditions than on any of the analytical steps needed to justify such a conclusion." (p. 314). Nevertheless Heller (1967) was convinced that the "estimates of the economy's potential and growth rate at 4-percent unemployment" were robust. He concluded that, "These guides have now [1967] passed the rugged test of five years' use as benchmarks for policies to match demand with capacity" (p. 62). Not only had the 4 per cent unemployment rate become an important target, a more ambitious goal was to lower this rate and in the process to raise the growth rate of y_e.

Counterbalancing the Council's optimistic position was a strongly held view at that time that current unemployment was mostly structural in nature; labor-market mismatches could be characterized as a number of square pegs that did not fit into an equal number of round holes. Any attempt to increase employment through higher demand for goods and services was doomed to failure as firms would not be able to find the required workers and would only drive up wages in the process. Heller, on the other hand, thought that this approach was much too pessimistic. He wrote (pp. 63–4, emphasis in original):

> Careful analyses of the statistical record within CEA convinced us that the structural-unemployment thesis was more fancy than fact, since the structural component of unemployment had *not* risen; that the 4-percent unemployment target was not only attainable but should be viewed as an interim target, later to be reset at a lower level (after manpower programs had increased labor skills and mobility); and that we had a sound method of translating the employment goal into a GNP target and thus defining the gap between actual and potential GNP.

Heller was ready to ridicule anyone less sanguine about possible improvements in the labor market than the Council: "Talk of 'structural unemployment' was loose in the land — indeed, very loose." (p. 63).

Structural Unemployment

The 1964 *Economic Report of the President* contains an appendix which is a shortened version of the testimony given by the three members of the CEA before the Subcommittee on Employment and Manpower of the Senate Committee on Labor and Public Welfare on 28 October 1963. This testimony was meant to convince Congress that the tax cut could stimulate aggregate demand sufficiently to reduce unemployment to 4 per cent. Acceptance of this proposal required a demolition of the argument that structural unemployment was in the vicinity of 5–6 per cent and that more demand for goods and services would merely generate inflation and not jobs. The Council summarized this view as follows (*ERP*, p. 169):

> The persistence of this high level of unemployment is sometimes cited as evidence of structural difficulties which will blunt the effect of the proposed $11 billion tax cut now being considered by the Senate Finance Committee and make it difficult to reach the interim full-employment goal of 4-percent unemployment, let alone our ultimate goal beyond the 4-percent level.

But the Council was convinced that the rising unemployment rate since 1957 was not the result of a deterioration in the mismatch problem, but a product of insufficient aggregate demand. However the only evidence cited (p. 170) is that business fixed investment had fallen from 10–11 per cent to 9 per cent of GNP without showing other sources of the demand for goods and services. They did not, at this point, try to persuade Congress that the growth of productive factors since 1955 far outstripped the demand for goods and services and that there was plenty of slack in the labor market. In other words they did not produce something like Chart 2.3 to buttress their argument.

The Council did not deny the existence of structural unemployment and pointed to unusually high unemployment rates among disadvantaged groups as "the essence of the problem." (p. 173). Although new skills training and general education were promoted as solutions to this problem, the Council also believed (pp. 175–6):

> [S]lackened demand since 1957 has intensified inter-group and inter-regional disparities in unemployment rates at the same time that it raised the total unemployment rate. Nonwhites, teenagers, unskilled and semi-skilled workers have suffered a greater-than-average increase in unemployment since 1957. But these same groups will also benefit disproportionately as demand expands and the over-all unemployment rate declines.

There follows a discussion of labor-market developments that leads to the following conclusion: "The evidence reviewed above does not yield persuasive indications that structural elements are today a significantly larger factor in unemployment than in 1957." (p. 178). However, much of this evidence is difficult, if not impossible, to assess without a proper analytical framework for the labor market. The emphasis on aggregate demand for goods and services and the neglect of the demand for labor throughout the heyday of Keynesian macroeconomics made such a framework seem superfluous. I have attempted to rectify this neglect by featuring an ideologically-neutral model of labor-market transactions; although this model was published in two books in 1994 and 1997, it does not rely on theoretical tools that were not available in 1963.

Setting forth this model at this stage will help us understand the Council's position on structural unemployment and the predicament of the labor market in 1962–63. Figure 2.1 summarizes the behavioral relationships in the labor market. The details and supporting arguments are in Prachowny (1997, Chapter 3). Labor supply is based on a reservation-wage model, since workers are mostly forced to accept or reject a fixed number of hours of work. This generates an unambiguously upward-sloping supply curve, L. Labor demand is a derived demand and firms want to equate the marginal product of each worker to the real wage; since there is typically declining marginal product, *ceteris paribus*, the demand curve slopes down. Despite this profit-maximizing decision rule, firms will usually have an unsatisfied demand for labor which consists of vacancies. These vacancies are optimally chosen as firms face both adjustment costs of hiring and firing workers and disequilibrium costs of being away from the optimal level of employment. As adjustment costs rise or disequilibrium costs fall, vacancies will increase. Actual employment will therefore be less than that demanded at every real wage rate and Figure 2.1 shows a labor-use curve, N, to the left of the labor-demand curve, N^d. The horizontal distance between them represents "unemployed jobs" or vacancies.

Equilibrium in the labor market is achieved at E, where supply equals demand. However, there is positive unemployment at this point as employment is found at E' and the number of vacancies equals the number who are unemployed. This points to the structural nature of equilibrium unemployment, which has also been labelled as the natural unemployment rate. Walter Heller and the Council thought that the distance between E' and E was about 4 per cent and that the labor market exhibited excess supply in 1962–63 with actual employment at a point such as A on the labor-use curve.

Neither the Council nor anyone else had direct estimates of the extent of structural unemployment, but Heller and his colleagues knew a proper measure of vacancies was critical for this purpose. They wrote (*ERP*, pp. 177–8):

> Since structural unemployment is a form of joblessness that persists over a protracted period even if unfilled jobs are available, an increase in structural unemployment would be clearly suggested if it were found that the number of job vacancies were rising along with the number of unemployed men. Unhappily we have no comprehensive and adequate series designed

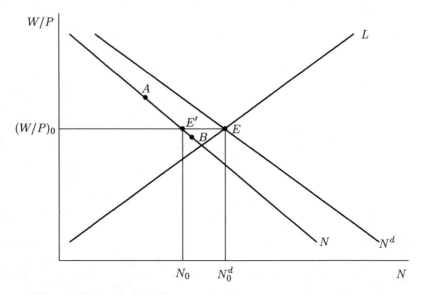

Figure 2.1   A diagram of the labor market

to measure job vacancies in the United States ... [Nevertheless] after adjustment for changes in the size of the labor force, the [National Industrial Conference Board] help-wanted index was substantially lower in 1960 and 1962 than in 1955–57, when the total unemployment rate was about 4 percent.

Accepting the existence of excess supply in the labor market, expanding aggregate demand through a tax cut would have to lower the real wage to increase employment. This could be achieved through higher inflation while nominal wage increases are held constant. In modern terminology this would require the tax increase to be an unpredictable positive shock in the goods market that is transferred to the labor market through higher goods prices and lower real wages, which in turn stimulate firms to hire more workers. In the process the unemployment rate falls in the movement from A to E' along the labor-use curve in Figure 2.1.

But the Council was more ambitious than merely striving for 4 per cent unemployment. Their prediction was that during the subsequent boom period, disadvantaged groups that had higher than average unemployment rates would do proportionately better. Once they received some training, they would reduce the bottlenecks that create mismatch or structural unemployment. They wrote (p. 174):

Bottlenecks in skilled labor, middle-level manpower, and professional personnel tend to become acute as unemployment approaches 4 percent. The result is to retard growth and generate wage-price pressures at particular points in the economy. As we widen or break these bottlenecks by intensified and flexible educational, training, and retraining efforts, our employment sights will steadily rise.

The tax cut, however, was paramount. They stated (p. 173, emphasis in original):

> Coal miners in Harlan County are structurally unemployed *now* and so are Negro and Puerto Rican youths in New York City. Yet, programs to reduce structural unemployment will run into severe limits *in the absence of an adequate growth of demand, i.e.,* in the absence of rapid expansion of total job opportunities. Such expansion is needed to assure that retrained and upgraded workers, for example *will* find jobs at the end of the training period and *will not* do so at the expense of job opportunities for other unemployed workers.

At this stage the Council could have linked the tax cut directly to the ultimate goal of reducing structural unemployment. In other words they could have argued that an aggregate-demand policy may have beneficial aggregate-supply effects. In terms of Figure 2.1, this involves shifting the N curve closer to the N^d curve by reducing the number of vacancies that firms tolerate in equilibrium. If the tax cut were large enough, it would create excess demand in the labor market, at a position such as B. Here the number of unemployed is less than the number of vacancies, but firms have the incentive to hire these extra workers and absorb the additional adjustment costs because the real wage has fallen sufficiently. This position cannot prevail, of course, and ultimately the real wage will rise again to $(W/P)_0$, but in the meantime, the on-the-job training received by workers who would otherwise be idle, will make the mismatch problem less of a bottleneck in the future and could permanently reduce vacancies. In the diagram, E' is now closer to E. In other words the argument in favor of "high-pressure" aggregate demand is that it keeps the labor force more flexible and skillful than merely trying to remain at "full employment" aggregate demand.

In a context of denying an immutable natural rate of unemployment, Tobin (1980, p. 61) made much the same suggestion:

> It is hard to resist or refute the suspicion that the operational NAIRU gravitates toward the average rate of unemployment actually experienced. Among the mechanisms which produce that result are ... loss of on-the-job training and employability by the unemployed ... and a slowdown in capital formation as business firms lower their estimates of needed capacity.

In Figure 2.1 a positive natural rate of unemployment arises from the general fact that there are some square pegs (the unemployed) which do not fit into an equal number of round holes (vacancies). If the economy experiences excess demand in the labor market at B, this would be analogous to forcing some of the square pegs into some of the round holes. The longer that pressure is applied the rounder the pegs and the squarer the holes become, with the end result that the number of mismatches has been permanently reduced.

Unfortunately developments in the labor market pointed in the opposite direction. Instead of a declining natural rate of unemployment, Gordon (1982) shows that the rate was rising throughout that time period. Estimating several versions of the Phillips curve and then imposing long-run equilibrium conditions, he concluded (p. 111) that the natural rate rose by 1.2 to 1.8 percentage points between 1956 and 1972, mostly for demographic reasons, such as the increased labor-force participation rates of women and young people. His estimates (p. 152) show the natural rate to be 4.9 per cent in 1947, rising slowly to 5.3 per cent in 1962 and to 5.6 per cent in 1970. Basically the structural-unemployment hypothesis on which Heller relied, suffered from too much emphasis on skill characteristics of the labor force and not enough on the costs of filling vacancies. Although training schemes that were favored by the CEA could make workers more mobile and easier to find by potential employers, identifying the needed skills is not a solution with a one-time cost, as voluntary quits create new vacancies in every subsequent period and the natural rate will fall only if firms face lower adjustment costs or higher disequilibrium costs or if the quit rate declines. Despite the passage of time and much effort, we still do not have a truly reliable time series for the natural rate in the 1960s, but if 5.3 per cent in 1962 is a better estimate than 4 per cent, then the output gap falls from 4.5 per cent to 0.64 per cent. In other words the need for a tax cut in 1963–64 is undermined by the possibility that the output gap was virtually nonexistent.

The Determination of Employment

The Council was confident that the tax cut would eliminate excess supply in the labor market. To assess this prediction we need to determine whether the labor market moved from point A in Figure 2.1 to E' or B after the tax cut. This requires an empirical version of the N curve in Figure 2.1 and is obtained by estimating the following equation:

$$n = \gamma_0 + \gamma_1 k - \gamma_2 w, \qquad (2.6)$$

where n is the number of people employed (LHEM in CITIBASE), k is the capital stock as previously defined and w is the real weekly wage in 1982 dollars (LEW77), all in natural logs. The regression was run with ordinary least-squares (OLS) and annual data for the period 1948–92. The estimates are as follows: $\gamma_0 = 8.395, \gamma_1 = 0.637$ and $\gamma_2 = 0.429$. All coefficients appear to be significantly different from zero, but there is serial correlation of the residuals. Using two-stage least-squares (TSLS) and autoregressive error correction for 1956–92 in Prachowny (1997, Chapter 1), the estimates are nevertheless virtually the same. Since the labor-use curve would shift upward over time as the capital stock accumulates, a static relationship between employment and the real wage can be obtained by noting that employment would remain constant if the real wage rose by $0.637/0.429 = 1.485$ per cent for every 1 per cent increase in the capital stock. If the real wage rose by more, employment would fall and vice versa. The regression line now written in its inverse form as

$$w - 1.485k = 19.563 - 2.330n$$

and individual observations for 1948–70 are shown in Chart 2.4.

It is immediately obvious that there is a very tight relationship between the adjusted real wage and employment. Also, throughout this time period, this version of the real wage fell and employment increased.[1] What this implies is that wage increases tended to be less than productivity improvements and firms had the incentive to keep adding to their labor input. We are not in a position to indicate the equilibrium real wage, since the reservation-wage model of labor supply is impossible to estimate in the absence of data on reservation wages. Hence one must resist the temptation to speculate whether excess demand or supply prevailed in any year.

The individual deviations from the regression line, small though they are, seem to have a cyclical pattern, with recession years below and to the left and boom years above and to the right of the line. During a recesssion one would expect that the real wage rises in response to a negative shock in the goods or money markets that puts downward pressure on inflation. In turn firms reduce the number of employees to raise the marginal product of the remaining workers to the higher wage rate. In other words there would be a move up along the labor-use curve. However, Okun argued that recessions lower the productivity of workers for a given capital stock. He wrote (1962; 1970, p. 321), "The record clearly shows that man-hour productivity is depressed by low levels of utilization. ... I have little direct evidence to offer on the mechanism by which low levels of utilization depress productivity. ... The positive relationship between output and labor productivity suggests that much

---

[1] Not shown are observations for 1971–92, for which this trend continued.

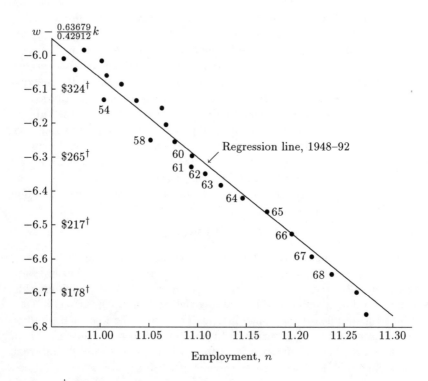

Note: † indicates weekly wage when $k = 8$.

Chart 2.4   Combinations of the real wage and employment, 1948–70

of labor input is a fixed cost for fairly substantial periods." While this postulated relationship is contrary to the overall evidence in Chart 2.4, the small deviations during a recession may be explained by this phenomenon. For example, in 1954 the regression line would have predicted a real wage that was 5.58 per cent higher than it was for the given level of employment ($n = 11.004$), which could be explained by a cyclical fall in productivity, given the value of $k = 7.801$ in that year. Again in 1958, another recession year, the real wage was 6.24 per cent lower than predicted by the regression line.

From that perspective 1962 and 1963, when the tax cut was being planned, are also recession years; in both years, the wage rate and productivity were depressed by about 3 per cent. A tax cut that stimulated demand for goods and services would have two beneficial effects on employment: (1) it would raise the productivity of all workers and firms would have an incentive to hire more workers at the going wage and

(2) the real wage would fall and this also would stimulate hiring. In other words eliminating the recession through expansionary policy is expected to move the employment point closer to the regression line and down the line as well, as actually happened in 1964–66. This prediction however, is based on evidence that was not available at the time, namely a regression based on time series to 1992.

THE OUTPUT GAP AND INFLATION

In 1963 potential GNP was a fragile and untested concept and measuring the output gap had many difficulties, but Walter Heller never hesitated in pushing for a tax cut. In the oral-history project (Hargrove and Morley, 1984, p. 199) he recounted, "Presidents Kennedy and Johnson accepted 4 percent unemployment as an explicit goal; they accepted 4 to $4^1/_2$ percent growth rates as a goal. They pitched their economics, on our advice, to the growing full employment potential of the economy instead of worrying about every wiggle in the economy and trying to flatten out the curves of the business cycles." There was no concern at the Council that such a program might have inflationary consequences if either the unemployment-rate or growth-rate target turned out to be too ambitious.

Although Okun, in his original paper, pointed to the inflationary dangers of having actual output above potential, subsequent discussion of the tax cut avoided the possibility of inflation. At the hearings held by the Joint Economic Committee to discuss the *Economic Report of the President* and the proposed tax cut in January 1963, Heller played down the inflationary pressures of a tax cut. He said, "when you have unutilized resources, unutilized manpower, unutilized industrial capacity, the force of expansionary fiscal and monetary policy expresses itself in higher output and more jobs rather than in higher prices." (*Hearings*, p. 29). Later, when asked by Senator Proxmire why President Kennedy thought that a planned budget deficit in 1962 would have been inflationary, but now in 1963 after continued expansion, this worry had eased, Heller responded (p. 36) by admitting that the forecasts for 1962 had been too optimistic. Of this episode Heller subsequently said, "The range of forecasts we were talking about ran from $565 to $570 billion and we put it at the upper end of the range." (Hargrove and Morley, 1984, p. 200). Actual GNP for 1962 turned out to be $560 billion. In other words a relatively small swing of $5 to $10 billion meant the difference between an inflationary tax cut and an output-augmenting tax cut and exposed the knife-edge properties of y_e.

In common with other Keynesian macroeconomists of that era, Heller had in mind an aggregate supply curve that was essentially horizontal until the economy produced at potential GNP and then it became vertical. However no explicit support for that hypothesis is produced in CEA publications or testimony. In retrospect the Council missed an opportunity to show that recent evidence pointed to very weak inflationary pressures as the economy moved closer to potential GNP. Chart 2.5 reproduces observations for the output gap for 1955:3 to 1965:4 from Chart 2.2 and relates them to changes in the inflation rate from the previous quarter.[2] This relationship would be consistent with what is now called an expectations-augmented *price* Phillips curve or an aggregate supply curve. Such a relationship may have been too much of a leap into the future at the time, since Phelps (1967) and Friedman (1968) did not introduce the importance of inflationary expectations until somewhat later.

Part of the Council's mandate was educational and persuasional activity. Heller said, "we had to sell modern fiscal policy to an unbelieving and highly suspicious public." (Hargrove and Morley, 1984, p. 200). However, the same effort did not go into persuading the public that the inflationary dangers of the tax cut were minimal. While charts showing the relationship between unemployment and the output gap proliferated in official publications, charts showing how the output gap and inflation were related were completely absent. Despite the widespread acceptance of the Phillips curve at that time, the Council was not prepared to take a step forward in inflation analysis by replacing the unemployment rate with its new-found concept of the output gap and replacing wage changes with inflation rates. Instead, to the extent possible, there was to be no acknowledged link between the tax cut and inflationary pressures.

The relationship between $\Delta\pi$ and $y_e - y$ for these 42 observations does not appear to be strong, but keeping in mind the scale of the vertical axis, the largest prediction error (in 1957:4) is only about $1/2$ per cent. The slope of this Phillips curve was quite small and moving the economy towards the elimination of the output gap through a tax cut would have had only minimal initial inflationary effects. Starting at $y_e - y = 7$ per cent where inflation was falling by 0.1 per cent per quarter and moving to $y = y_e$, would have generated only 0.31 per cent extra inflation in the first period. At full employment, the inflation rate would have increased by approximately $4 \times 0.314 = 1.25$ percentage points in the first year.

Presenting a Phillips-curve chart alongside an Okun's Law chart in

---

[2] The inflation rate is measured as the change in the GNP deflator from four quarters previously.

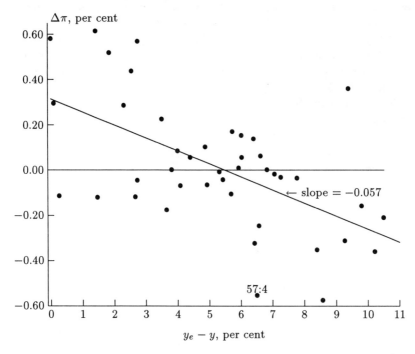

Source: π and y from US Department of Commerce (1966), y_e from quarterly growth rate of 0.875 per cent starting from $y = y_e$ in 1955:3.

Chart 2.5   Change in year-over-year inflation and the output gap, 1955:3 to 1965:4

Council publications would have made the tax-cut proposal stronger. It would have eased concerns that the tax cut would produce very little extra output but a lot of inflation. Given the short time horizon in political decision making, the additional \$30 billion in output against the inflation rate rising by less than $1/3$ per cent per quarter would be perceived as a very favorable trade-off and would have made such a presentation an extra weapon in the Council's arsenal.

Unfortunately Chart 2.5 opens a Pandora's box of unfavorable long-run consequences. It would not have taken long for someone to point out that as long as the economy remains at $y = y_e$, inflation will continue to rise by 1.25 percentage points per annum in every subsequent year and any long-term view would indicate that such a policy could not be sustained. Also evident from the regression line is the realization that the 4 per cent unemployment target was too ambitious. To obtain a constant inflation rate (i.e., $\Delta\pi = 0$), requires that the measured output gap should be $0.314/0.057 = 5.5$ per cent. In turn this requires that the target unemployment rate be raised by 1.7 per cent, if the Okun coefficient remains at 3.2. A natural rate of unemployment in the vicinity of 5.7 per cent is very close to Gordon's (1984) estimate of 5.0–5.6 per cent in 1958–65.

Since the estimated Phillips curve would have turned out to be a two-edged sword, the Council would have had good reason to deny its existence and to pretend that inflation came from misbehaving firms and could be controlled by "guideposts." In the oral-history project, Heller recounted (Hargrove and Morley, 1984, pp. 211–12):

> Bob McNamara always considered our wage-price guideposts as the most innovative thing that the Kennedy Administration — in particular, the Council — did. ... They had their genesis way back in 1961 when we began price and wage watching ... I brought Senator Gore to the White House one day to see Kennedy and plan a Senate rhetorical assault on the captains of industry in steel and other industries who would boost prices even in a slack economy. ... Then came the question of the steel industry perhaps raising prices in October 1961 because they were going to have their third installment of the previous wage bargain come in. That's when [Kennedy] wrote that letter, which I drafted with the help of Kermit [Gordon], saying in effect, "Look, if you behave on the price side, we'll help hold steel wages in check." ... It was Kermit Gordon, Bob Solow, and Jim Tobin — Bob Solow, in particular — who provided a lot of the intellectual moxie for those guideposts. ... And then, of course, came the steel crisis. We were convinced, rightly or wrongly, that what really broke the steel price increase was economics. By that I mean Kermit Gordon's persuasion that if you held out as much as 15 percent of steel capacity, then the price increases would collapse.

On the one hand the Council was predicting that prices would fall in the face of excess supply in the steel industry, but on the other hand it was not prepared to accept that same hypothesis for excess supply in the economy as a whole. Moreover Heller argued that unfettered market activity would lead to a welfare-improving outcome in the steel crisis, but he wanted to rely on political intervention through guidelines for every other industry to protect the national welfare. Even by 1984 when he was interviewed, Heller was reluctant to admit that the Council's thinking on inflation in the early 1960s was confused and contradictory.

My argument is that the Phillips curve would have shown a low short-run trade-off between the benefits of extra output and employment against the costs of higher inflation. Although economists are trained to think in terms of such trade-offs and to count both benefits and costs before they reach a conclusion, they are also trained to recommend a policy only if it achieves a Pareto improvement where some groups in the economy experience an increase in economic welfare but no identifiable group is made worse off. Economist-advisers, who have to count votes on behalf of their masters, try to avoid stating these trade-offs and costs for fear of creating an opposition. To the extent that such costs really exist, some groups in the economy will have to bear them, and in that environment, a Pareto-improving policy is impossible to devise. Economic advisers would then be reduced to the role of nay-sayers.

By predicting even a small rise in inflation in the wake of the tax cut, wage earners who were covered by long-term contracts would have found that real wage increases would have been smaller than they had expected; although their disposable income would have risen, they would have some uncertainty whether they would be better off or not. This could have led the union movement, which was still powerful at the time, to oppose the tax cut because it may have been perceived as favoring business at their expense. Their concerns would not have seemed unfounded: according to Chart 2.4, the productivity-adjusted real wage fell by 14.4 per cent between 1963 and 1966 as employment rose by 6.8 per cent. To forestall such important opposition, proponents of the tax cut would try to break the link entirely between higher aggregate demand for goods and services and inflation. Then there are no costs and no trade-off between benefits and costs and the tax cut is a Pareto improvement.

THE OUTPUT GAP AND FINE-TUNING

Once an output gap in the vicinity of $30 billion is accepted as fact, the need for corrective action is also clearly established. In a staff memorandum circulated at the Council (K28), under the heading "Economic prospects without tax reduction and reform," is written: "There are no forces now visible that would enable the economy to advance over the next several years at a faster average rate than it has since 1957. In any given year or quarter, of course, economic activity might be somewhat above or below this trend; but no long-term improvement would be expected." This is a clear indication that the Council advocated the tax cut, not as a measure to forestall a recession or to keep output growing at the present rate, but to make the major leap necessary to get back on the path of potential output.

With such an obvious objective and the means to achieve it, it is puzzling to realize that members of the Council frequently were bogged down with fine-tuning the economy. Heller, for instance, spent a great deal of time interpreting the latest trends in economic indicators for the President and putting the need for a tax cut into that context. In a long memorandum to the President entitled "The Slowdown in the Recovery and Its Implications for Policy" in March 1962 (K15, emphasis in original), he advised:

> Economic considerations would put a high premium on expansionary policy today. ... There is considerable danger that the private economy's pump has not been sufficiently primed to keep flowing, and the time to act is while there is upward momentum in the economy. ... If the situation got worse — and political realities permitted it — a quick, sure way of adding to purchasing power all over the country would be a temporary reduction of personal income taxes. ... [I]t's none too soon to start considering concrete sources of action in case it turns out that our forecasts *were* too optimistic — we aren't about to do a Saulnier [CEA Chairman during Eisenhower's second term], stick our heads in the sand, and lose elections.

Some months later, he was writing promotional or advertising copy for the administration in a memorandum entitled "Milestones in the 'Kennedy Expansion' " (K46), which he suggested be labelled as "The longest peacetime expansion since the Civil War, leaving aside the long climb out of the Great Depression of the Thirties."

If the economy was performing so well under Kennedy's stewardship, what was the purpose of the tax cut? As long as the Council took pride in the "Kennedy expansion," logical counterarguments to the critics were more awkward than necessary. Instead they should have minimized the significance of the continuing recovery and concentrated on the output gap. They should have asked boldly: "Does it matter if investment or some other category of demand improved slightly this quarter if we still need $30 billion to close the output gap?" Moreover emphasis on fine-tuning also made the inflationary threats of the tax cut more relevant and provided more ammunition to the opponents. By publicizing the length of the economic recovery it tipped the scales of probability in favor of inflation, whereas the large size of the output gap would have led to the opposite prediction.

Despite their early and unreserved acceptance of the importance of potential output as a goal for economic policy (e.g., K2), Heller and the other members of the Council could not always "raise their sights" to this level as Heller later claimed. They did "worry about every wiggle in the economy." The opportunity to take credit for the recovery that began in March 1961 was too strong to resist. As a result, fine-tuning the macroeconomy came to have a place equal to the elimination of the output gap in their list of objectives. Unfortunately this ambiguity in priorities weakened the urgency and relevance of the tax cut.

By the time the output gap disappeared sometime in 1965, so did any reference to its role in macroeconomic policy. The Council's inability, during 1966–67, to convince itself and others that a tax increase was needed stems from its reliance on fine-tuning arguments instead of the fact that actual GNP outpaced potential GNP by about 1.5 per cent. In the crucial memorandum to the President of 26 December 1965 (B24, reprinted in the Appendix), Ackley warns that "any GNP above $720 billion for 1966 had worrisome implications for price stability. We could stretch beyond that to some degree, but $729 seems to stretch too far." This acknowledges a $9 billion negative output gap, but most of the argument in favor of the tax increase was predicated on recent unexpectedly high growth rates in 1965–66 (e.g., B27). When GNP turned down slightly in late 1966 and created the mini-recession of 1967, the persuasiveness of the continuing negative output gap was nowhere to be found. This episode in policy making will be discussed in much more detail in Chapter 5.

CONCLUSION

The concepts of potential GNP and the output gap were critical developments in the early 1960s and their role in specifying the supply side of subsequent macro models has never been fully acknowledged or appreciated. What is more, publicizing the output gap in Chart 2.1 made the "missing demand" more dramatic and the tax cut more urgent than would have been possible with a business-cycle approach. Okun (1962; 1970, p. 314) put the matter in the following way:

> The evaluation of potential output can also help to point up the enormous social cost of idle resources. If programs to lower unemployment from $5\,1/2$ to 4 percent of the labor force are viewed as attempts to raise the economy's "grade" from $94\,1/2$ to 96, the case for them may not seem compelling. Focus on the "gap" helps to remind policy-makers of the large reward associated with such an improvement.

Nevertheless too much faith and not enough probing was put into the numbers that were generated for potential output. The use of 4 per cent unemployment as an optimal level and a growth rate of 3.5 per cent for potential GNP from 1955 onward were never subjected to rigorous testing. Furthermore the argument presented by the Council that structural unemployment had not risen, and was in fact likely to fall in the future, was the result more of wishful thinking than of hard-boiled analysis.

It would have been more truthful, but less appealing, if the Council had made its tax-cut proposal contingent on a range of values for the output gap in 1962 or 1963 based on "optimistic" or "pessimistic" numbers for crucial variables or parameters that were needed for its calculation. For example it could have stated, on the basis of its own and external research, that structural unemployment in the labor market may be as low as 3.5 per cent or as high as 5.5 per cent and that the Okun coefficient may be in the range of 2.5 to 3.5. With the current unemployment rate at about 5.7 per cent, the output gap would have been as high as 7.7 per cent or as low as 0.5 per cent. But the political process is impatient with such a conditional approach to economic policy; it wants simple and precise advice and no hedging with provisos. Heller and the other economic advisers would have made very little headway in persuading President Kennedy to consider a large-scale tax cut if he were presented with the possibility — remote as it was — that the output gap was virtually zero. The President would never have proposed tax-cut legislation based on uncertain macroeconomic contingencies and the Joint Economic Committee and Congress itself would never have acceded to that request. Understanding the requirement for simplicity Heller presented only one possibility for the size of the output gap: the largest one.[3]

Also no discussions seem to have been undertaken concerning a course of action in the event that the tax cut proved to be too large. No one at the Council asked the question: "Would taxes have to be raised a year after they were lowered or would certain expenditures have to be curtailed if aggregate demand exceeded potential output?" As we know from developments in 1966 and later, it proved impossible to raise taxes or to postpone the "Great Society" spending when the war in Vietnam made evermore pressing demands on the federal budget and on the macroeconomy as a whole. At that point the negative output gap had much less influence on stabilization-policy initiatives than the earlier positive gap. Finally, the Council had strong political incentives to disassociate the closing of the gap through a tax cut from inflationary pressures, even though they would have been initially quite weak. They needed to present a Pareto-improving proposal to Congress and the nation. One can only conclude that this novel and exciting economic concept of po-

---

[3] Schlesinger (1965, p. 623) believed that Kennedy was able to understand sophisticated economic reasoning, but Sorenson (1965, p. 394) recounts this charming anecdote: "He never mastered the technical mysteries of debt management and money supply. He once confided in his pre-Presidential days that he could remember the difference between fiscal policy, dealing with budgets and taxes, and monetary policy, dealing with money and credit, only by reminding himself that the name of the man most in charge of monetary policy, Federal Reserve Chairman William McChesney Martin, Jr., began with an 'M' as in 'monetary.'"

tential GNP and its role in improving stabilization-policy decisions was only partially successful and severely limited in its application.

DATA APPENDIX

Data for the estimation of the employment equation (2.6) are reproduced below to allow for accurate replication, especially since their original source, CITIBASE, is subject to revision. The regressions were performed on *MicroTSP*, Version 7.0.

$$n - 1948\text{--}95$$

10.9743528	10.9627103	10.9834547	11.0015459	11.0066299	11.0220041	11.0038747
11.0369920	11.0633897	11.0676507	11.0515718	11.0764102	11.0941390	11.0935277
11.1079854	11.1237201	11.1462202	11.1714248	11.1965417	11.2168865	11.2373428
11.2628593	11.2730016	11.2816801	11.3161211	11.3510103	11.3713912	11.3601264
11.3936071	11.4297313	11.4725837	11.5011081	11.5059347	11.5169134	11.5082063
11.5211086	11.5617418	11.5820226	11.6045980	11.6301689	11.6524620	11.6727199
11.6851606	11.6760015	11.6825666	11.6974000	11.7204685	11.7352743	

$$k - 1947\text{--}92$$

7.63882446	7.62958717	7.62963581	7.64482355	7.67457103	7.71801853	7.76429605
7.80065441	7.83735704	7.87180709	7.90551567	7.93329477	7.96443367	7.99550867
8.02662754	8.06041336	8.09440898	8.13185405	8.17692565	8.22793674	8.27272415
8.31749725	8.36014175	8.39550018	8.42428779	8.45175838	8.48621845	8.51753330
8.53728961	8.55527877	8.57713985	8.60522270	8.63739109	8.66568183	8.69262409
8.71063613	8.72607517	8.75145816	8.78210830	8.80718803	8.83011913	8.85249328
8.87551116	8.89731311	8.91154384	8.92560100			

$$w - 1948\text{--}95$$

5.27811479	5.31113481	5.35903596	5.37105655	5.39249038	5.43524932	5.44349956
5.49552774	5.52485513	5.52597093	5.52254056	5.56398391	5.56803894	5.58195352
5.61166715	5.62826824	5.64582061	5.67262411	5.68241405	5.68259000	5.69727516
5.70704078	5.69452571	5.71082162	5.75250911	5.75467634	5.71214485	5.67858982
5.69446706	5.70330762	5.70784378	5.67453670	5.61496973	5.60265970	5.58916616
5.60749197	5.61391878	5.60250949	5.60517358	5.59507703	5.58604955	5.57489109
5.55791807	5.54257631	5.54123401	5.54021072	5.54745006	5.54384183	

3

The CEA Model of Taxes
and Aggregate Demand

Despite bold assertions made by the proponents of the Kennedy–Johnson tax cut that it conformed to "modern economic theory," it is surprisingly difficult to find an official exposition of the macroeconomic model that provided the link between taxes and aggregate demand and output. Heller (1967, p. 72) suggests: "the rationale of the 1964 tax-cut proposal came straight out of the country's postwar economics textbooks." This textbook approach is summarized as follows: "On the basis of observed stable relationships between disposable income and consumption, together with not-so-stable investment relationships, the Administration spelled out how the proposed tax cut would multiply itself into an increment of GNP that could 'close or nearly close the gap between potential and actual output.'" Although ideas based on Keynesian countercyclical fiscal policies were discussed by President Kennedy's advisers as early as the pre-inauguration period in late 1960, it was not until early 1963 that a concrete proposal for a tax cut was put forward. Even then, in spite of the heavy burden that was being placed on the tax cut in the overall scheme to "get the economy moving again," the Council of Economic Advisers did not provide Congress, the economics profession, the public, or even itself with an explicit statement of a macroeconomic model that would support the urgent claims for the fiscal stimulus.

THE SEARCH FOR A MODEL

The earliest reference to a tax-cut model that I have been able to find is contained in (B5) and (B6), dating from November 1962. In the former, Ackley complains that "preliminary efforts to provide [economic

analysis of the tax cut] have produced only a debate among quite diver-
gent views as to (1) the appropriate multiplier plus accelerator which
should be used in making the calculation, and (2) the probable state
of the economy at the time the tax cut would be effective." To remedy
the situation, he illustrated savings and investment functions, with the
former more sensitive to income than the latter, to show the needed
shift in the savings function (which includes taxes) that would move the
economy from "present GNP" to "full-employment GNP." This view includes only the Keynesian multiplier model, in part because "Efforts to
calculate short run accelerators are ... bound to produce wide-spread
disagreement." In the second memorandum, David Lusher, a staff economist, attempted to provide quantititive information about this model.
He allowed for three scenarios, which differed largely as to investment
behavior. He wrote, "The basic assumption, here, is that with continued
full-employment, equilibrium growth and a concomitant capital/output
ratio, gross fixed investment would rise at approximately the same rate
as the over-all GNP growth rate." However, the move to full employment
and any other departures from a constant growth rate would subject the
US economy to dynamic instability as Samuelson's (1939) multiplier–
accelerator model will demonstrate later in this chapter. Nevertheless
Lusher calculated three multipliers, ranging in value from 2.4 to 3.4 and
requiring tax cuts from $6.6 billion to $10.3 billion using 1962:4 as the
starting-point. In any event, the Council's inability to decide whether
the multiplier model or the multiplier–acclerator model was the preferred link between the tax cut and the elimination of the output gap is
a continuing theme in this chapter.

The 1963 *Economic Report of the President* contains a section (pp. 45–
51) outlining the channels of influence of tax changes on total aggregate
demand and its main components, but it is neither rigorous in the development of behavioral relationships nor does it provide numerical predictions. Subsequently, two members of the CEA, Walter Heller and
Gardner Ackley, testified at the hearings of the Joint Economic Committee on 28 January 1963, presenting and defending their predictions
of the tax cut. Heller (1967, p. 182, fn. 13) later offered the opinion,
"In these hearings the CEA analyzed and charted in some detail the
expected stimulus of the tax cut through the workings of the consumption multiplier and investment responses." As the first witness, Walter
Heller read a prepared statement (*Hearings*, pp. 1–11) and Gardner Ackley then explained the two charts that were appended to the statement
(pp. 12–14); this "Explanation of Charts on Effects of Tax Reduction"
and the two charts are reproduced in the Appendix to this book. This
material contains an assumed $8.5 billion tax cut and a multiplier model

of consumption expenditures, but an unspecified investment response. After some questioning by members of the committee, the chairman, Senator Paul Douglas, abruptly asked Roy E. Moor, a staff economist, "to put on the board some charts which I asked him to prepare." (p. 17). For reasons that are now obscure, Senator Douglas was dissatisfied with the Council's presentation and stated, "I asked Dr. Roy Moor to prepare his estimates of what the multiplier would be, and to do so without consultation with the Council of Economic Advisers. I asked him to work this out arithmetically both for the multiplier, so far as consumption is concerned, and also consumption plus probable added investments or the stimulus to consumption from the additional investment created by the original increase in consumption." (p. 18). In a subsequent short but sharp exchange with Heller, Senator Douglas, who had been a member of the Economics Department at the Univerisity of Chicago and who would have welcomed a seminar presentation of the appropriate macroeconomic model, indicated he wanted more details on the investment response than the Council had provided. Unfortunately, Moor's charts (pp. 21–5) were not much more illuminating than the Council's, but they did elicit the following remark from Douglas: "What you call the second factor is generally known as the accelerator factor as distinguished from the multiplier factor, and the classic article on this was written in 1917, by J. M. Clark," to which Moor responded, "I was told that by the Senator. I didn't know." (p. 20). In his rebuttal, Ackley (p. 24) acknowledges, "We have been somewhat less bold than Mr. Moor in our willingness to attempt to estimate quantitatively the investment effects of the expansion of demand, but we have tried to indicate in an illustrative way the fact that rising demand would also lead to an increase in investment." The confusion does not end here. In Ackley's suggested response by President Kennedy (B8) to Senator Proxmire's letter (B7) about the multiplier analysis in the Council's JEC testimony, Kennedy is urged to write that, "it is possible to approach this question as you have done, in terms of multipliers, accelerators, and so on."

The most explicit development of the predictive model of the tax cut is contained in the *Joint Economic Report* that was published in March 1963, after the conclusion of the hearings by the Joint Economic Committee on the *Economic Report of the President*.[1] This document

---

[1] Much later, Okun (1968; 1970) put together an econometric exercise to show the difference between a hypothetical no-tax path for GNP in 1963–65 and compared it to the actual path. While this study had the requisite exposition in terms of equations of the model and parameter values, it was not available at the time that the tax cut was proposed.

comprises a majority report complete with legislative proposals, a short section entitled "Supplementary Staff Materials" and a minority report from the Republican members of the Committee. The middle portion (pp. 45–55), authored by Roy E. Moor and Gregory Guroff, sets out its purpose quite clearly: "The primary reason for tax reduction is to stimulate the economy. This stimulus will occur in large part through the so-called multiplier and accelerator principles. These concepts have been discussed at great length in the economic literature, but little attempt has been made to quantify them. This appendix is designed to summarize the concepts and to suggest some magnitudes that might be attached to the concepts." (p. 45). Nevertheless the Moor–Guroff analysis cannot be treated as the basis of the CEA's model since parts of it were privately repudiated. In a memorandum to the President summarizing the contents of this *Report* (K32, emphasis in original), Heller wrote, "The *accelerator* discussion, which deals with the problem of how investment responds to rising output and incomes, is technically unsatisfactory." This is certainly the case, but Heller did not provide his version of the multiplier–accelerator principle at this or any other time. That he had this model in mind is evident from an early article published in November 1962, in which he wrote, "By strengthening sales and pushing output closer to capacity, tax reduction spurs investment in inventories and in new equipment and new plants. This impact on investment is called the 'accelerator effect.' " (1962, pp. 40–41). But that is as far as he ventured down the path of explaining the accelerator principle and there are strong indications that he never really understood this concept and its dangers for a smooth landing after the tax cut.

Perhaps the most reliable source of information about the Council's model for the tax cut is contained in an anonymous, internal memorandum entitled "Notes on Economic Assumptions Underlying the President's Tax Proposals." It was written on 6 February 1963, a week after the Council's presentation at the Joint Economic Committee. It contains a discussion of how the US economy is expected to respond to the tax cut in terms of GNP growth, employment, unemployment and tax revenues, as well as numerical predictions for 1963–66. Although both the multiplier and "induced investment" are mentioned, the analytical content of this memorandum is of very low quality and there are relatively few calculations provided to justify the predictions. Specific criticisms of this document will be made as this chapter proceeds. The full text, referred to as (K28) in the bibliography, is provided in the Appendix.

The lack of leadership by the Council in putting forth and defending a well-articulated and specific model of the tax cut remains puzzling to this day and creates frustration for retrospective analysis since it forces one to search for a model specification that fits the prediction data. The only viable strategy at this point is to start the process by outlining a basic "textbook model" of the multiplier–accelerator (M–A) interactions as presented by Ackley (1961, pp. 485–7), especially since he was an active participant at the hearings and could have relied on this source to make his presentation.

THE MULTIPLIER–ACCELERATOR MODEL

The M–A model gained much of its prominence in the macroeconomics literature in 1939 with the publication of Samuelson's seminal article on the subject. Its main appeal was the ability to explain the dynamic properties of business cycles rather than as a means of overcoming them through countercyclical policy changes. Therefore a more obvious choice for a stabilization-policy model in 1963 would have been the IS–LM model, which allows one to shift the IS curve to the required extent through changes in government expenditures or taxes and has the added feature of allowing for interactions between the goods and money markets. This also would have been a "textbook" application to policy; it had been developed by Hicks (1937) and Hansen (1953) and was featured in the two most widely used and highly regarded textbooks by Dernburg and McDougall (1960, Chapters 10, 11) and by Ackley (1961, pp. 369–77). However, there was a dispute about the slope of the LM curve at this time and the Federal Reserve was at odds with the administration concerning the wisdom of expansionary policy. In that case avoiding any mention of the money market also circumvented any controversy about the appropriateness of the tax cut.

The Basic Model

The M–A model starts with a definition of national expenditure:

$$Y_t = C_t + I_t + G_t, \tag{3.1}$$

where C_t, I_t and G_t are consumption, investment and government expenditures. The consumption function is lagged one period:

$$C_t = a + bY_{t-1}. \tag{3.2}$$

The accelerator principle is involved in investment expenditures given by:

$$I_t = w + x(C_t - C_{t-1}), \tag{3.3}$$

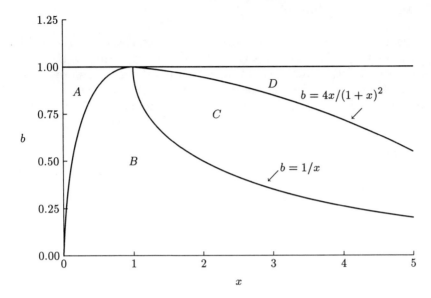

Source: Samuelson (1939, p. 78).

Figure 3.1 *Multiplier–accelerator interactions*

which, according to Ackley (pp. 486–7), "asserts that investment in any period will occur in an amount sufficient to supply the added capital goods required to produce any increment of consumer goods which has occurred since last period, plus a constant, w, which may be zero." In other words, firms in the consumer-goods sector have desired capital–output ratios that they try to maintain. The constant w could be interpreted as the investment necessary to cover depreciation.

By substitution of equations (3.2) and (3.3) into (3.1), we obtain the time profile of income, Y_t, after any exogenous change such as a tax cut. The solution for Y_t becomes a second-order difference equation:

$$Y_t = b(1 + x)Y_{t-1} - xbY_{t-2} + a + w + G_t. \qquad (3.4)$$

Depending on values of b and x, Samuelson found several possibilities for a path to a new equilibrium after some exogenous change in a, w or G_t: (A) a stable monotonic approach, (B) a damped cycle, (C) an explosive cycle and (D) an explosive noncyclical path. The combinations of b and x that create any of these four paths are shown in Figure 3.1, which is taken directly from Samuelson's article.

Deriving the Multiplier

The link between tax changes and income is established by the multiplier, but equation (3.4) does not show this directly. First, b, the parameter in equation (3.2) has to be derived from the marginal propensity to consume out of disposable income, c, which is the parameter on which consumption theory concentrates. Thus b is determined by:

$$b = c(1 - q)(1 - \tau),\qquad(3.5)$$

where q is the marginal deduction from GNP to arrive at personal income and τ is the marginal (and average) tax rate. The static multiplier is derived from:

$$Y = \frac{a + w + G}{1 - c(1 - q)(1 - \tau)},\qquad(3.6)$$

with the precise formula depending on the exogenous change: a, w, G or τ.

Ackley's Chart 2, presented at the hearings, gives some indications of the Council's estimates of the parameters in the multiplier formula. Corporate retained earnings are shown to be 10 cents in each dollar of GNP; thus $q = 0.1$. All levels of government take 36 cents of the remainder, but this is not restricted to personal taxes, so $\tau = 36/90 = 0.4$ is only an approximation. Finally, consumers save 4 cents out of disposable income, which creates $c = 0.92$. This leads to $b = 0.9 \times 0.6 \times 0.92 = 0.5$ and a muliplier of 2. In a subsequent staff memorandum (K28), the CEA gave some other indications of their estimates of the parameter values in equation (3.5). They assumed that $c = 0.94$ to 0.96 and $(1 - q)(1 - \tau) = 0.55$ and they also project the multiplier to have a value of 2 even though c is now larger. A third estimate is more direct. At the hearings in January 1963, the contemplated tax cut was estimated to increase disposable income by \$8.5 billion with \$8 billion spent initially; the total increase in consumption was predicted to be \$16 billion (Chart 1). At this point in the proceedings, the following exchange took place between Senator Douglas and Mr. Ackley:

> Chairman DOUGLAS. Mr. Ackley, this works out to the Kahn formula that the multiplier is equal to the reciprocal of the percentage of leakage; is that right? Mr. ACKLEY. One minus the marginal percentage [sic] to consume gross national product. Chairman DOUGLAS. So with the percentage of leakage of 50 percent, you have roughly the reciprocal of one minus five, and you get a multiplier of 2. Mr. ACKLEY. That is correct. (p. 15)

Later in the same day, Roy Moor presented a table (*Hearings*, p. 19), which also used a tax cut of \$8.5 billion and changed the parameters to: $q = 0.15$ and $\tau = 0.20$. In this case, $b = (1 - 0.15)(1 - 0.20)(1 -$

0.07) $= 0.632$. After his presentation, Chairman Douglas asked: "The total increase in consumption is approximately \$20 billion?" Mr. Moor replied, "Which would be about $2^1/_2$ times." Neither Ackley nor Heller challenged this estimate of the multiplier, despite their earlier testimony and despite the critical role played by this parameter in linking the tax cut to aggregate demand. Moreover, Senator Douglas, who presumably asked for the independent estimate of the multiplier effect to ascertain if alternatives should be considered, only commented, "Instead of two. What about the secondary effect [which dealt with investment]?" (p. 20).

Moor and Guroff provide another set of calculations in the *Report*. In their Table V, they indicate that 22.5 per cent of an increase in GNP goes to nonpersonal income (i.e., $q = 0.225$); the remaining 77.5 per cent generates 13 per cent in personal taxes (i.e., $\tau = 0.13$), which leaves the other 87 per cent as disposable personal income of which 7 per cent is saved (i.e., $1 - c = 0.07$). Thus, the marginal propensity to consume out of GNP, according to equation (3.5), is $b = (1 - 0.225)(1 - 0.13)(1 - 0.07) = 0.627$ and the multiplier is 2.68.

The tax cut was to be legislated as a reduction in personal-income tax rates, which would have increased b by reducing τ. Nevertheless almost everyone made the assumption that the tax cut was a lump-sum amount that increased disposable personal income and led to an initial increase in consumption and GNP. The Office of Tax Analysis at the Treasury Department provided calculations of the aggregate effects of tax changes that made such assumptions possible (K26). It started with six different adjusted gross income classes and the number of returns in each of these classes. Then it calculated the change in tax liabilities resulting from proposed rate changes, as well as from tax-reform measures, and estimated the total to be \$8.6 billion. No allowance was made for altered labor-supply behavior in the wake of the tax cut, except for a short comment by Ackley in the *Hearings* (p. 47) about "the incentive effects of tax reduction that you don't get from an expenditure increase." In other words, changes in federal revenues assumed a fixed base (i.e., $\Delta \tau Y$), and left out the other component that became important in the Reagan tax cut of 1982 (i.e., $\tau \Delta Y$). Moreover, without explanation, by May 1963 the projected tax cut was to be \$10 billion (K39).

From this presentation, there are now three distinct values of the multiplier: a value of 2 put forward by the Council, a value of 2.5 suggested by a staff member of the Committee and a value of 2.68, which is derived from calculations using predictions made by Moor and Guroff. Moreover the contemplated tax cut grew from \$8.5 billion to \$10 billion in just four months. Combining these two factors, the range of estimated changes in consumption expenditures and aggregate demand in the US economy is large: from \$16 billion to \$25 billion. Even more serious is the fact that nothing in the public record or the archives indicates any attempt at reconciliation of these disparate projections. Finally everyone's confusion about changes in the tax rate, τ, and lump-sum increases in disposable income contained in a in equation (3.6) made calculations of the multiplier even less trustworthy.

Another issue that was not resolved at the hearings or in other Council presentations is the speed with which the tax cut is translated into a new equlibrium value of output. Although Ackley's Chart 1 refers to "periods," their length is not defined. Later in the testimony, in response to a question from Senator Sparkman, Moor stated, "The initial problem, as Mr. Curtis indicated a few minutes ago, is how this \$8 billion initially begins to pump itself out. The Council has made an estimate, I believe, that 50 percent of the stimulus would reflect itself in 1 year. Another way to do this is to assume that these periods are quarter-years, at annual rates ... you might expect that the full effects might be felt in, say, 3 or 4 years." (pp. 20–21). Neither Ackley nor Heller responded to this assertion. We will return to the dynamics of the tax cut later when the Council's numerical predictions for GNP are presented.

Deriving the Accelerator

From equation (3.3) the crucial parameter in predicting investment expenditures is the capital–output ratio captured in x. In their testimony to the Joint Economic Committee both Heller and Ackley are deliberately circumspect in providing numerical forecasts for investment and in specifying the model that they prefer for such an exercise. In his evaluation, McLure (1972, p. 12, fn. 18) states that "The CEA's lack of quantification of the impact on investment reflects the state of empirical knowledge at the time." Nevertheless such limitations should not have prevented the Council from stating a hypothesis, assuming parameter values and later testing the predictions that emanate from this exercise. Although there are vague references to the accelerator principle in other places such as Heller (1962), (B3), (K32), (K66) and (K70), this model is never put forward as the basis for Ackley's Chart 1. Nevertheless, if the accelerator principle was the CEA's assumed model, we can make retrospective calculations of x from the information in that chart. After the initial increase in consumption expenditures of \$8 billion, investment expenditures rise by \$4 billion in the next period. According to equation (3.3), this would make the value of x equal to 0.5. From his Chart 3, which presents the same material in a somewhat different form, the total increase in consumption of \$16 billion results in higher investment of \$10 billion; here $x = 0.625$. These rather low values are in conflict with the empirical evidence of the time. The economy-wide capital–output ratio for 1962 can be calculated as $x = 1276.2/560.3 = 2.27$ from the same data sources as Chart 2.3. This discrepancy is difficult to eliminate, but it may be that the Council allocated the need for extra capital over the whole period of adjustment. If consumption is \$16 billion higher, it will take about \$36 billion more in capital to produce these goods, which could be the sum total of the red bars in Chart 1, the original version of which cannot now be found or reconstructed. The difficulty is that investment will *fall* to w in equation (3.3) once consumption settles at a new value and this causes output to fall as well, leading to the cycles described in Figure 3.1.

Alternatively the Council was not relying on the accelerator principle, but on a marginal propensity to invest. In (K28), the following statement is consistent with this view: "This higher ratio [10 per cent] of fixed investment to GNP is sustainable in an economy which is advancing at its full employment potential." Ackley's Chart 1, on the other hand, links investment demand to previous consumption expenditures, which might be captured by:

$$I_t = w + eC_{t-1}, \qquad (3.3')$$

as a new investment function. With equation (3.3') the solution for Y_t now becomes a first-order difference equation:

$$Y_t = b(1 + e)Y_{t-1} + a(1 + e) + w + G_t. \qquad (3.4')$$

The path to equilibrium is now stable if $b(1 + e) < 1$ and unstable if $b(1 + e) > 1$. With this model, which will be called the multiplier (M) model to distinguish it from the multiplier–accelerator (M–A) model in equation (3.4), both consumption and investment would be at permanently higher levels after the tax cut.

In retrospect it would have been strange indeed for the Council to rely on a full-blown M–A model to predict the effects of a tax cut. With $b = 0.6$ and $x = 2.0$ as reasonable and conservative values in equation (3.4), the economy would land in region C of Samuelson's chart, which is characterized by explosive cycles. Armed with such a prediction, the Republican opponents of the tax cut on the Joint Economic Committee would have been able to make a much stronger counterattack; even Democratic Senators such as Douglas and Proxmire, who were generally supportive and knowledgeable, would have balked at starting down such a dangerous path.

Predictions of GNP

In January 1963, Ackley sent a memorandum to Ted Sorensen (K27) outlining projections for GNP, the unemployment rate, and the budget, with and without a tax cut. Although he admitted that he was "rather sceptical of these numbers," this is an indication that the Troika, composed of the CEA, the Treasury and the Budget Office, made an effort to quantify an implicit macroeconomic model that related the tax cut to total aggregate demand.

These projections were updated in February and appended to a staff memorandum (K28). Although they are marked "Illustrative Figures for Internal Use Only," they must have been the basis of the tax-cut proposal, especially since no further projections were made until August 1963 in (K52).[2]

There are three "scenarios" that were contemplated. The first two assume no tax cut and differ with respect to assumptions about 3 per cent growth or a recession; the third assumes a tax cut. It should be remembered that even 3 per cent growth would not eliminate the output gap, since potential GNP was growing at 3.5 per cent. Data are presented for calendar years 1962–66, with the first year representing the base from which the three paths diverge. By comparing these calculations with those that would be generated by equations (3.4) or (3.4′) we may be able to deduce which macroeconomic model was closest to the Council's version.

Let us start with the model in equation (3.4′), using a one-quarter lag in the consumption function, as suggested by Moor and not refuted by Ackley. Assuming $b = 0.6$ and $e = 0.5$, we need to calculate the constant that would have forecast $Y = 553.6$ in 1962 and earlier, in order to replicate an equilibrium situation. This produces:

$$Y_t = 0.9Y_{t-1} + 55.36.$$

In (K28) the contemplated tax cut amounted to $9.5 billion, which is added to the constant, starting in the third quarter of 1963 to conform to the Council's assumption of "mid-year" implementation. These calculations are made for the period 1963:3 to 1966:4 and are shown in Chart 3.1 as deviations from the starting-point, $553.6 billion, thus indicating the effect of the tax cut.

For the M–A model in equation (3.4), the parameter values are assumed to be $b = 0.6$ and $x = 2.27$. The constant that would generate a

---

[2] There was another set of estimates in a memorandum from Okun to Heller (K66), but it was undated.

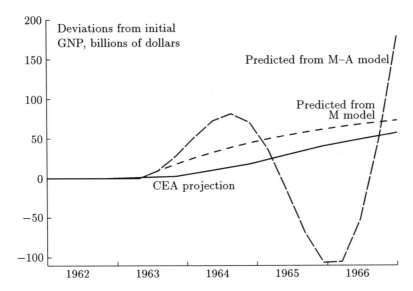

Chart 3.1 CEA and model projections of tax-cut effects, 1963–66

level of income equal to $553.6 billion is 221.44. Thus we start with:

$$Y_t = 1.962Y_{t-1} - 1.362Y_{t-2} + 221.44,$$

to which is added the tax cut of $9.5 billion in the third quarter of 1963. Similar calculations are made for the remaining quarters to 1966:4, which are also shown in Chart 3.1 as deviations from the starting-point. Finally the CEA projections are plotted here as the column marked, "Tax cut vs 3% growth."[3]

It is immediately obvious that the predictions from the M–A model are totally inconsistent with the projections supplied by the CEA. Within a year of its assumed implementation, the output gap would have been eliminated twice over. Then another massive tax cut would have been needed to prevent the disastrous fall in GNP. Even the multiplier model would need to have lower values for b or e than those that were chosen to coincide with the CEA calculations. No attempt is made here to provide an *ex-post* evaluation of the tax cut. Since it came into effect a year later and was larger than originally intended, it would be

---

[3] The staff memorandum assumed a 3 per cent real growth rate and a 4.5 per cent growth rate in nominal terms, implying a constant 1.5 per cent inflation rate. The table contains only nominal values of GNP, but the numbers show an annual increase that ranges from 3.9 per cent to 4.7 per cent (i.e., 553.6, 575.3, 602.5, 630.0, 657.5 for 1962–66).

fruitless at this stage to compare predictions with actual outcomes. This task will be postponed to Chapter 4 where an econometric model for the period will be constructed and simulated.

EVALUATION OF THE COUNCIL'S MODEL

Aside from the inconsistencies in the size of the multiplier and the convoluted link between investment and consumption, the Council's version of the macroeconomic model did not contain the postwar advances in consumption and investment theory that should have been available to and assimilated by its members and staff. As a consequence the predicted link between the tax cut and aggregate demand did not consider more sophisticated analysis of this relationship. It is not being suggested that the Council should have been aware of every esoteric macroeconomic model in existence at the time or to heed the criticism of their exclusive emphasis on aggregate demand that followed in the 1970s; instead the well-known and generally accepted models available in textbooks and mainstream journals should have been the basis for this exercise. First we can look at consumption theory as it existed in the early 1960s and then do the same for investment expenditures. In both cases the aim is to find alternative predictions for income from the time of the tax cut to a new equilibrium value.

The Consumption Function

The simplest of multiplier models requires an estimate of the marginal propensity to consume. The only evidence that the Council seemed to rely on is contained in (K28), which states, "Consumers have regularly saved between 6 and 8 percent of disposable income and spent the rest." This statement should be interpreted as an estimate of the *average* propensity to save and not the *marginal* propensity, which refers to the ratio of changes in savings to changes in disposable income. To verify rather than merely assert the stability of the marginal propensity to save, the Council should have used recursive least squares for a consumption or saving function such as Ackley's version, which is reported in equation (3.2). The results of such an experiment are reported in Chart 3.2. With data for personal saving and disposable income starting in 1953:1, to eliminate the Korean-war instability, the initial estimates of the marginal propensity to save continued to fluctuate wildly until the end of 1956; hence its value is reported only for 1957:1 to 1965:4. Also the

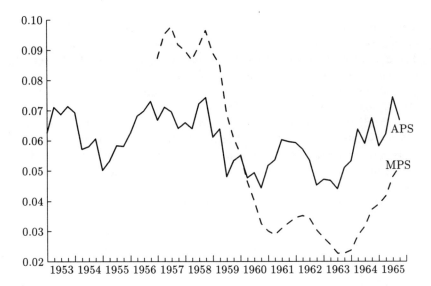

Source: US Department of Commerce (1977, Table 2.1, lines 24 and 29).

Chart 3.2 Average and marginal propensities to save, 1953:1 to 1965:4

average propensity to save, defined as savings divided by last quarter's disposable income, is plotted here.

Although the average propensity to save generally falls within the limits specified by the Council, the recursive estimates of the marginal propensity to save show a much different picture. During the years of sluggish economic activity in the late 1950s and early 1960s, MPS is falling from about 0.09 to 0.02 and then begins to rise again after the tax cut takes effect. This is evidence that consumers are taking expected life-time resources rather than quarterly or annual income as the constraint on their consumption behavior. In any case the Council seemed not to be aware of the dangers of variations in the parameter b in calculating the multiplier. If they had estimated a savings function at the end of 1962, they would have found that the marginal propensity to save was 0.023, and with $(1-q)(1-\tau) = 0.55$, the multiplier is now 2.15. Even if they were unwilling to rely on econometric techniques, there was also worrying evidence available from the Great Depression that the marginal propensity to save could fall during economic downturns.

Moreover Modigliani (1949), Modigliani and Brumberg (1954), Ando and Modigliani (1963) and Friedman (1957) had published their research that challenged Keynes's "fundamental psychological law" of a constant marginal propensity to save since it would be inconsistent with utility maximization in the face of changes in variables other than income. These were well-known publications; in fact, the March 1963 issue of the *American Economic Review*, which coincided with the publication date of the 1963 *Joint Economic Report*, contained an article by Ando and Modigliani on tests of the life-cycle model of saving and would have been fresh in the minds of economists involved in preparing the tax-cut proposal. Ando and Modigliani reported (p. 64) estimates of the marginal propensity to consume out of labor income, net of taxes, that varied between 0.51 and 0.87 for the years 1929–59, excluding 1941–46. They also concluded (p. 79) that "cyclical swings in income from its long-run trend will cause swings in the savings-income ratio in the same direction."

Even though the tax cut was presented as a one-time change in the tax law, its effect on consumption depends very much on the perceived permanence of the administration proposal. Writing in 1959, Farrell reviewed the new approach to consumption theory: "This serves to put trade-cycle theory on what one might call 'a fully expectational footing.' The recent orthodoxy has been an expectational theory of investment *plus* a mechanistic consumption function — now consumers can have their expectations too!" (pp. 694–5, emphasis in original). A few years later this new orthodoxy was still not the prevailing view at the Council. At the hearings, Representative Thomas B. Curtis of Missouri engaged Ackley in a debate about the model being used to derive the multiplier. The following exchange concluded the debate (*Hearings*, p. 16):

> Mr. HELLER. Mr. Chairman, may I note in Mr. Ackley's answer that when he said it was theory, it was a generalization from experience. It is grounded in the actual experience of what consumers do with additions to their income, from detailed studies of what they do with their additions to income. Representative CURTIS. Let me ask you this, Dr. Heller: In 1930, was that saving figure 3 percent? Mr. HELLER. Yes, in the thirties. Representative CURTIS. So you are assuming something, although you know it changed, beginning in 1957. We will get into that later. I just want to get these assumptions out in the open.

Although Representative Curtis was inviting the Council to consider that "permanent income" in the 1930s was higher than actual income and that consumption or saving decisions are based on permanent income at all times and not just in the Depression, Heller and Ackley did not take up the challenge offered by Friedman's view of consumption decisions.

In terms of Friedman's permanent-income hypothesis, if only a portion of the tax cut is thought to be a permanent addition to disposable income, the initial increase in aggregate demand will be correspondingly smaller. Instead of equation (3.2), the permanent-income hypothesis of consumption can be written as:

$$C_t = a + \theta b Y_{t-1}, \tag{3.2'}$$

where θ is the subjectively determined parameter that converts observed income into permanent income. Thus if $\theta = 0.5$, the initial increase in aggregate demand will be half of what it would be if $\theta = 1.0$. It is also possible that anticipations of the tax cut will affect savings and consumption. For example, if consumers believed that the tax cut was to be implemented in 1963, they may have increased their assessment of permanent income and increased consumption without waiting for the evidence in their pay-checks. The marginal propensity to save will decline and this is consistent with the MPS in Chart 3.2 being at its lowest level at that time. Then in 1964, when the tax cut was actually legislated, there was no further change in permanent income and savings rates rose. Such considerations would have made the link between tax cuts and aggregate demand much more tenuous and would have introduced an element of uncertainty about the size of the tax cut needed to close the output gap. But the Council's mission was to convince Congress and the public that the administration's recommendation for a tax cut had very predictable and beneficial effects; uncertainty would have hindered their salesmanship and was eliminated from their analysis. One is forced to conclude that the multiplier model used to analyze the tax cut was outdated in its theoretical basis and careless in its calculations.

The Accelerator Principle

The basis of the accelerator principle, as the name implies, is that firms want a relatively constant capital–output ratio. Therefore they will make investments when output increases, but they will also disinvest, to the extent possible by depreciation, when output falls. This relationship between the level of investment and changes in aggregate demand (i.e., consumption in the Ackley version) leads to the possibility of an unstable path for income. A tax-cut proposal that hinted at even the remotest chance of creating instability of the kind depicted in Chart 3.1 would have been rejected by Congress, even if the legislators did not understand completely Samuelson's elaboration of the interaction between the multiplier and the accelerator. Samuelson (1939, p. 78) wrote about region C: "A single impulse of expenditure or a finite number of expenditure impulses will result eventually in explosive oscillations around the level zero." It is interesting to note that Table 19-1 in the widely-used textbook by Dernburg and McDougall (1960, p. 214) shows a number of hypothetical levels of consumption and relates investment expenditures via the accelerator ($x = 1$ in this example). Here investment expenditures are very volatile even though any disinvestment is ruled out; while consumption varies from 17 to 29, investment varies from 0 to 11. The crucial column in the Dernburg–McDougall table is: "Required Machines." By avoiding any mention of a desired capital–output ratio for the US economy, the Council was also able to avoid having investment expenditures fall towards zero in their Chart 1.

Although there was great debate about the interest-sensitivity of investment at that time, the Council treatment of this issue is to assume that the interest rate will remain constant without specifying the need for a complementary role for monetary policy to make the tax cut work. Dernburg and McDougall (1960, pp. 97–100) take a more sophisticated view of the matter. It is worth an extensive quotation:

> There has been a great deal of discussion about the relationship between the rate of interest and the volume of investment spending per unit of time. Traditionally economists have been inclined to the view that investment was highly sensitive to interest-rate changes. Skepticism of this view, however, developed during the 1930s. Subsequent statistical investigation, though inconclusive, seems to corroborate the view that the interest rate is an unimportant determinant of the level of investment. The empirical investigations were conducted by asking businessmen to list the factors that determined their decisions to invest. The replies placed very little emphasis upon the cost of borrowing funds.... There are really two different questions to be answered. First, will businessmen invest more at a low rate of interest than at a high rate of interest, other things being equal? Second, why is it that business investment fluctuates so violently and is frequently so very small during periods of low interest rates? The first question has been answered above. If the interest rate is reduced, *ceteris paribus*, the volume of investment increases as additional projects, promising to yield a smaller return, are undertaken. But this is not inconsistent with an affirmative answer to the second question, because *ceteris paribus* is in fact an unrealistic assumption. The distinction is the familiar one between a movement along a given schedule and a shift of the schedule.

At the hearings William McChesney Martin, the Chairman of the Federal Reserve Board, was invited to comment on the President's proposal for a tax cut. Although not openly hostile, he did not offer to put monetary policy in a supportive role. He said:

> [I]n my judgment, the Open Market Committee of the Federal Reserve System would be derelict in its responsibilities were it — in the light of a large deficit — to add to bank reserves and to bring about substantial credit expansion solely to facilitate the financing of the deficit. It would

be improper to risk unsettling the balance of payments or to tempt banks to make imprudent investments through a sudden expansion of liquidity." (*Hearings*, p. 341)

This statement can be taken as evidence that Martin was convinced that easing of monetary policy would create too much investment. Later in the same session of the hearings, Senator William Proxmire commented to Chairman Martin: "Some experts predict the general level of interest rates will start climbing significantly in 1963. . . . Interest rates are generally expected to rise as an indirect result of the President's tax program and the big deficit budgets. If this is the case, it seems to me that the real steam and drive in the stimulation of the economy brought about by the tax cut will be dampened and absorbed. Certainly it will be reduced." (p. 354) Martin responded, "I don't think so. I think it would be a sign that the economy is making real progress. I have never seen a period, as I have said to you on a number of occasions, of really good business that has not been accompanied by slightly rising interest rates." Although Proxmire and Martin then disagreed about the stance of monetary policy, they did agree that interest rates rise in the wake of a tax cut and that would "crowd out" some investment. In other words they mentally deployed the IS–LM model in their discussion.[4]

If the Council of Economic Advisers thought it practical to rely on one boldly conceived diagram to show how the tax cut would change aggregate demand and income, they would have been better advised to replace Chart 1 in the *Hearings* with the IS–LM diagram from Dernburg and McDougall (1960, p. 121). They could have calibrated the original equilibrium to show output at $560 billion and the interest rate at 3 per cent. Then they could have shifted the IS curve to the right by the appropriate amount from the tax cut and finally indicated the predicted outcome for income and the interest rate. Since they were unsure of the interest elasticity of investment and of money demand, they could have drawn two versions of the IS–LM diagram, where the slopes differed by the range of values considered relevant for these two parameters to show the smallest and largest tax cuts necessary to achieve full-employment income. They could have quoted Dernburg and McDougall (1960, p. 124) to the critics of this approach: "We can now see that one of the virtues of the IS–LM model is that it shows that the crude multipliers of the past chapters implicitly assume monetary neutrality, i.e., that any change in government expenditures, taxes, or investment would not affect the rate of interest and therefore the level of investment." This line of reasoning

---

[4] Although the terminology is not used, Dernburg and McDougall (1960, p. 124) had a clear exposition of "crowding out."

would have had the additional advantage of putting more pressure on the Federal Reserve to increase the money supply. As it was, Chairman Martin was able to concentrate on the beneficial balance-of-payments effects of tight monetary policy, since the adverse investment effects were only hinted at by Senator Proxmire.

Walter Heller has claimed that the tax cut was not a radical departure from mainstream economic policy and that the predictions about the macroeconomic effects of the tax cut come from "textbook models." For reasons that should by now be clear, it seems that the Council chose the wrong model for this exercise. Put simply, the $IS–LM$ model would have made the predictive exercise more relevant than either the M–A model or the M model and, more importantly, it would have shown that the required tax cut was not a single figure, but a range of values, which in turn depended on assumptions about parameter sizes.

COUNTERVAILING ARGUMENTS

This retrospective criticism of the Council model of the tax cut relies not on macroeconomic theory as it has developed since 1963, but on received wisdom and practice as reported in the two most prominent textbooks available at that time. The claim here is that the Council's version of the model is not only virtually unspecified, but that the calculations involved in the exercise were careless and inconsistent. These predictions were widely circulated, first in a tentative way in the *Economic Report of the President* in January 1963, then more forcefully in the *Hearings* in late January and early February, and finally more coherently in the *Report of the Joint Economic Committee*, published in March. Surely someone in the economics profession must have spotted these problems during that two-month time span and volunteered to testify at the hearings, especially since the Chairman of the Joint Economic Committee sent letters of invitation to many groups and individuals to make submissions concerning the *Economic Report of the President*. That the hearings would have been an appropriate vehicle for debate on policy models is seen from the statement by Gerhard Colm, the Chief Economist of the National Planning Association (*Hearings*, p. 451):

> The committee [JEC] has regularly issued appraisals of the President's economic reports and has conducted very valuable studies of relevant topics. It has held hearings which gave academic and research economists, and representatives of business and labor, an opportunity to discuss current economic issues. Some of the reports have become valuable material for teaching and have helped to bridge the gap between an academic and a

more practical approach to economic policy. In all these respects the joint committee has made valuable contributions which have probably exceeded the expectations of the framers of the 1946 act.

The Professional Economists

In July a group of some 400 academic economists at more than 40 colleges and universities, led by Lester Chandler of Princeton University, signed a letter of support for the tax cut (K49). It said in part, "we believe that the Administration's program, as originally submitted to the Congress, represents a reasonable compromise. It provides tax reductions for both individuals and corporations. It should provide a significant stimulus to consumer's spending, and it should have a beneficial effect on private investment." Although one would not expect such a letter to contain a detailed discussion of the basis for these predictions, one could expect that the signers worked through the model presented by the Council and agreed with these conclusions. However this letter of support was not nearly as spontaneous or as impartial as it appears. In an earlier memorandum to the President (K38), Heller wrote, "This is the first draft of the letter the academic economists of the country are going to rally around. Although I provided the initial spark, it's now moving nicely on its own. If there are other points you would like to have the letter cover, we can still intervene as a friend of the court."

In the absence of public debate, one would still expect to see internal discussion and disagreement about the Council's model and numerical predictions. However a review of the Council's documents shows very little of this activity. In a confidential memorandum to Seymour Harris (K30), James Duesenberry worked through the tax-cut model and its assumptions and concluded that, "a return to full employment by 1966 is possible but the odds are against it." He found that a multiplier of two would mean that the "expansion would peter out," but he was also of the opinion that a multiplier value of three was "implausibly high." Although this memorandum found its way into the Council's files within a week, there is no record that it raised doubts or prompted a response from Heller.

Despite this successful attempt at silencing or ignoring criticism of the administration's tax-cut policy, there were other occasions on which dissenting views could have been expressed. On 5 and 6 February 1963, Senator Douglas scheduled two panel discussions, one devoted to fiscal policy and the other to monetary policy, with a group of academic economists as panelists. It is not evident on what basis the participants were chosen, but in retrospect, the appearance of some particular individuals would have changed the course of history. At this point I suggest that we engage in some counterfactual speculation to predict what might have happened if Franco Modigliani had testified that the tax cut would affect the life-time budget constraint of the average consumer in a very complicated way or if Milton Friedman had testified that the tax cut would affect permanent income in a way that depended on the consumer's expectations. Together they might have pointed to the difficulty of arriving at a truly reliable value for the multiplier and that a range of values of consumption effects should be considered. Then Paul Samuelson could have explained how the "true" accelerator principle operates and having brought his chart of the values of b and x (Figure 3.1 above) he could have indicated that $b \approx 0.6$ and $x \approx 2$ would have put the economy in region B or C, both of which were characterized by cyclical activity. Finally, Tom Dernburg or Duncan McDougall could have argued that the IS–LM model of the macroeconomy would predict rising interest rates and faltering investment in the wake of the tax cut, unless fiscal and monetary policy were co-ordinated.

Based on such evidence, the prediction that I am prepared to make is that the tax cut would never have made it out of Committee. The concerns and uncertainty about the link between taxes and aggregate demand would have been overwhelming and members of the Council of Economic Advisers, even with their most persuasive performance, would not have been able to bring that tax cut back to life. We know that such evidence was not presented and we cannot be sure that the hypothetical panelists would have made the points that I have forced them to utter, but we do know that their own research produced these conclusions.

Even less far-fetched is the question: why did Gardner Ackley, having written a textbook that included a cogent presentation of the accelerator, not clear up the confusion about investment expenditures in the wake of the tax cut that is so evident in the testimony? It is true that the members of the CEA did not use the term "accelerator" in their testimony, but there are references to this concept in Heller (1962) and internal memoranda (B3), (K32), (K66) and (K70). Neither Heller nor Ackley took the opportunity to indicate exactly what their view of investment demand was. The simple truth is that Heller did not understand the operation of the accelerator and Ackley, who certainly did, found it impossible to correct that situation. As a result the Council's muddled and unfocussed view of investment expenditures prevailed.

During the hearings there was some professional dissent to the prevailing view of the accelerator. Louis J. Paradiso, Assistant Director of the Office of Business Economics in the Department of Commerce, submitted a long statement, part of which is as follows (*Hearings*, pp. 246–7, emphasis added):

> Since we are initially interested in the effects over the next 2 or 3 years, there is some question whether the accelerator principle in its direct form is entirely applicable. With many industries operating at less than capacity there is no apparent reason why an increase in output should call for additional investment. ... It is, of course, true that if we assume that output continues to rise, forces will be at work to bring investment in plant and equipment in line with the long-run relation with output. These are long-run effects, and it is difficult to approximate the timing of such changes. Under these conditions for a given expenditure, the combined effect of the multiplier and a version of the accelerator, which makes investment responsive to the *level* of output rather than to the rate of *change* of output, will show considerable variation, depending on the particular combination of psychological, economic, political, and international forces prevailing at the time. If we assume that the secular relationship is operative, a multiplier of 2 would be changed to about $2^{1}/_{2}$, but for reasons regarding capacity utilization already referred to it is questionable whether a relatively high value such as this is appropriate in the short run.

Although Senator Douglas had asked for this statement to allow for comparisons to previous testimony, as he had asked Roy Moor to perform the same function noted earlier, he once again did not pursue the point of accelerator generated instability and went on to ask Secretary of Commerce Luther Hodges about *The Trade Expansion Act.*

The Politicians

With only modest countervailing views being expressed by professional economists at the hearings, it was inevitable that the model as presented by Heller, Ackley and Moor would be accepted as the basis for translating the tax cut into increased aggregate demand and income. However the 1963 *Joint Economic Report* was not unanimous in its recommendation of the Administration proposal. In addition to the minority objections which relied in part on Paradiso's statement (pp. 72–3), Senator Proxmire, a member of the majority, wrote a dissenting view, part of which is as follows (pp. 38–40):

> The tax cut may have little or no stimulative effect on the economy. After only four of the nine tax cuts in the past 40 years did business significantly improve. There were times it actually got worse. This doesn't prove the so-called stimulative multiplier didn't appear; it does show it can be washed out by other factors. ... Dr. Meltzer, of Carnegie Tech, argued that the stimulative effect (multiplier) of the tax cut would depend almost entirely on the degree of monetary tightness ... The heaviest and most consistent support for the tax cut came from those who argued that

it was necessary to stimulate investment ... One distinguished Senator re-marked as the committee hearing opened that the 1954 tax cut seems to have had a long-term adverse effect on the economy because it stimulated investment between 1955 and 1957 to such an extent that the economy has been characterized by idle investment facilities, overbuilt plant capacity, unemployment, and slow growth ever since.

Although Senator Proxmire did not use the terms "life-cycle consump-tion decisions" and "desired capital–output ratios," he is expressing the kinds of concerns that should have come from professional economists about the modified M–A model.

At some point at the hearings, the tax cut became a partisan issue and the underlying model was attacked or defended depending not on one's understanding of macroeconomic theory, but on one's ability to score political points. The following exchange (*Hearings*, p. 249) is indicative of this situation:

> Senator MILLER. Mr. Secretary, getting back to the multiplier problem, as I understand it, we have been given roughly a $2\frac{1}{4}$ multiplying factor. If this is valid, I am wondering why we would be proposing an $8 billion tax cut. Why not a $16 billion tax cut or a $24 billion tax cut? Secretary HODGES. Senator, you could reach either absurdity or political unrealism on how much you put out. I don't think you could afford psychologically, economically, or politically a tax cut of that proportion at one time. Senator MILLER. Where would you draw the line, though? Secretary HODGES. I would draw the line where we have it. We are standing at that line. Senator MILLER. I wonder if it would be feasible to have your people, when they come up with these figures that Senator Douglas asked for, test this out to try to come up to a, let us say, point of diminishing returns on this multiplier effect. I recognize you could carry it on to absurdities. But offhand I just would like to have some basis for picking $8 billion rather than $9 or $10 [the amount actually chosen later] or $16 billion. There ought to be some solid basis for that. If they could come up with some kind of a factoring to show us where the point of diminishing returns would be, I think it would be very helpful to us. Secretary HODGES. We will do whatever we can, Senator Miller. But I have to point this out to you in all realism. You simply cannot measure in statistical form psychological reaction or political reaction or anything else. You have to make a choice somewhere along the line. The Treasury experts and the rest have picked these figures. We will do whatever we can on it.

Later, in a statement appended to the minority report (*Report*, p. 107), Senator Miller became doctrinaire and jingoistic in his condemnation:

> So much reliance has been placed by the majority on the "multiplier" theory that I believe a little more refutation is in order. The supplementary ma-terials (p. 45) appended to the majority report sets forth the theory of the "multiplier" and so-called "accelerator." In a completely regimented coun-

try, where the government controls wages, prices, profits, raw materials, etc., the theory might work. In a capitalistic economic country like the United States, deeply involved as it is in world trade, the theory will not work — at least to any measurable degree.

The Moor–Guroff version of the model now becomes associated with the views of the majority members on the Joint Economic Committee, which the minority is duty-bound to oppose. With such an adversarial approach to establishing the macroeconomic effect of the proposed tax cut, finding the best model to make the predictions becomes secondary to accusing opponents of muddled thinking, but it does have the advantage of forecasting the outcome: the majority wins.

A MODEL OF PARETO-IMPROVING TAX CUTS

It is inconceivable that members of the Council and staff economists at the Joint Economic Committee were not aware of the severe modifications that they made to the standard M–A model to arrive at the predictions for the tax cut. It is also inconceivable that they were unaware of the IS–LM model as a suitable alternative to predicting tax effects on aggregate demand. Then how does one explain the choices made and the strategy followed by the proponents of and spokesmen for the tax cut? It will be remembered that the US economy was not in 1963 or even in 1964 in a recession; therefore, the tax cut could not be considered an "emergency remedy" as might have been the case in 1960. A balanced budget or even a surplus was thought to be the appropriate fiscal stance by most politicians and the public. A deliberate deficit, caused by a $10 billion loss of tax revenue, in order to push the economy to potential output was not a convincing argument to the public unless it could see some direct benefits.

It will be argued here that the "textbook model" was essentially irrelevant to the task of shifting public opinion in favor of the tax cut; it acted only as a crutch to support the necessary macroeconomic projections. The truly critical element in the tax-cut model was that it had to conform to Pareto optimality. This means that most of the major groups in the economy had to perceive a gain in their economic welfare without any other group fearing a loss. In that light, it was not sufficient to show that the output gap would be closed, but that income for all identifiable groups would rise. As Stein (1988, p. 99) remarks, "the idea of change was put forward with no suggestion that there would be any cost. No one would have to give up anything." It became paramount in convincing Congress and the public to show that economic theory would predict benefits to all but costs to no-one.

Even Heller admitted that the tax cut represented the first stage of rather dramatic changes in fiscal strategy that became "more activist and bolder. Feeding fiscal stimulus into a briskly rising economy ... is now seen as a prudent response to the needs of an expanding economy that is still operating well below its full potential." (1967, p. 68). This may have been accepted wisdom in 1967, but it was not in 1963 when President Kennedy still had rather conventional pre-Keynesian views on fiscal policy. Stein (p. 102) believed that, "A little persuasion would be required to get him to recommend a tax cut when the federal budget was already in deficit. Moreover, his administration had to consider that the Congress and the public might be even more conventional in this regard than the President, so that a move to increase what already seemed a worrisome deficit might be politically unwelcome." But Schlesinger (1965, p. 647) reports that, "Lacking doctrinaire belief in the sanctity of balanced budgets or of unregulated markets," Kennedy was receptive to Keynesian countercyclical policies. In the June 1962 Yale commencement address, the President took the opportunity to comfort his audience: "What is at stake is not some grand warfare of rival ideologies which will sweep the country with passion but the practical management of a modern economy."

In the fall of 1962, Kennedy was obviously preoccupied with the Cuban missile crisis, but Heller must have known that he would be able to get the President's support for a tax-cut stimulus if he could do so without creating a divisive and prolonged debate in the press and in Congress. In a memorandum of 16 December 1962 (K24), Heller reported to the President that "the Treasury proposals are superbly conceived to provide something for everyone, and in a way that is solidly defensible on economic grounds." A few days later, in another memorandum to the President (K25), Heller listed a number of influential groups such as *Life Magazine* and the AFL–CIO that endorsed the tax cut. To overcome any resistance to the planned tax cut, Heller and his colleagues had to prevent any effective lobbying against it for "conventional" fiscal or other reasons. Senator Hubert Humphrey wrote to the White House (K29) that, "Unfortunately, the tax reform provisions have resulted in considerable opposition from segments of business and industry that were for the President on tax reductions." Not surprisingly, Heller advised the President (K42), "to get a tax bill out of Ways and Means that will meet minimum standards of equity and political acceptability, even after most of the reforms are either stripped out, watered down, or converted into new loopholes."

Therefore the economic model for the tax cut had to concentrate on Pareto improvements, not on macroeconomic forces. The 1963 *Economic*

Report of the President (p. 45) spells out all the "beneficiaries" of the proposed legislation: "Tax reduction will directly increase the disposable income and purchasing power of consumers and business, strengthen incentives and expectations, and raise the net returns on new capital investment." Even state and local governments would have additional revenues from higher GNP "to meet their pressing needs."

Unfortunately both the M–A model and *IS–LM* model of aggregate demand make producers of capital goods potential losers from any policy change that increases total demand for goods and services. As pointed out earlier, almost any realistic combination of the parameters b and x will lead to only short-term increases in investment spending, with subsequent declines and then to an uncertain cyclical path. Such an outcome would have an even more magnified effect on the profitability of firms producing these goods. Heller, despite his inability to predict the effects of the tax cut on investment expenditures, was quite certain that profits would rise. He wrote (1962, p. 41), "Tax reduction thus strengthens the incentive to invest in two ways: Businessmen have money available to undertake the risks of new investment. And there is the prospect of larger after-tax returns to be earned on new productive facilities." In a speech in May 1963 (K39), he promised, "increased profits and profitability through direct tax benefits to investment and $2½ billion of corporate tax reduction." Heller was aware of the stormy passage of the 1962 tax-credit legislation that affected this same group. Sorensen (1965, p. 401) reported that, "Businessmen were suspicious of a Democratic administration doing them favors. Labor leaders had to be persuaded not to oppose it ... [Treasury Secretary] Douglas Dillon told of explaining the bill's merits at length to a businessman on a plane who then said, 'Wonderful, wonderful. Now would you tell me again why I'm against it?' "

In these circumstances it was imperative that the CEA modify the M–A model to obtain a sufficiently small value for x to bring the combination of b and x into Samuelson's region A. This could not be done with any plausible value for the capital–output ratio and thus the emphasis switched to an empirical connection between the level of output (or consumption) and the level of investment that could be interpreted as a marginal propensity to invest, e, with a value of only 0.5. Although all the proponents admitted that this relationship was tenuous or "more difficult to predict than the induced effects on consumption" (1963 *ERP*, p. 49), the calculations of the multiplied effect of the tax cut proceeded to show consumption, investment and total income all rising smoothly to new higher levels. At the same time, claims were made that these projections would lead to a healthier and more buoyant business climate and to greater consumer confidence, a task that would have been impossible if the standard model of the multiplier and accelerator were deployed for this exercise. Although Paradiso pointed this out in his testimony, he also seemed to argue that for short-run analysis of the tax cut, the CEA approach was acceptable. Therefore we can conclude that despite the incorrect application of the "true" model by the participants, no serious challenge was raised, no prominent economist pointed out the error and no alternative model of aggregate demand was suggested as being more appropriate. The need to show that a Pareto-improving tax cut would work became the over-riding imperative.

Despite the efforts of Allan Meltzer and Senator Proxmire to point out the importance of the money supply in determining aggregate demand, no attempt was made to show the interaction of fiscal and monetary policies in an $IS–LM$ model. Even if tax cuts have predictable effects on income by shifting the IS curve to the right, this model would have been uncomfortable to its proponents, since there would also be some "crowding out" of investment expenditures through higher interest rates and once again a Pareto improvement could not be claimed. Just like the capital–output ratio in the M–A model, projected interest rates in the $IS–LM$ model would have raised doubts among the beneficiaries that all the promises made to them could not be fulfilled.

To the disappointment of John Kenneth Galbraith, the macroeconomic stimulus was to be through tax-relief and not through extra government demand. This choice could not be made on the basis of the M–A model since it does not matter whether a or G_t in equation (3.4) is raised, but it can be made with a view to Pareto optimality. Increased government expenditures will be spread unevenly throughout the economy and the "trickle-down" effect through the multiplier would be difficult to envisage by the average worker or business owner. On the other hand a direct increase in take-home pay through a tax cut would improve the economic welfare of all workers and their families. Thus the tax-cut route stood a much better chance of having self-identification of beneficiaries compared to higher government expenditures. Galbraith's (1958) celebrated argument that the electorate should want to substitute public goods for private goods at the margin would imply that increased expenditures by the government would also be a Pareto improvement, but the CEA may not have been convinced or decided it could not find the kind of public goods — except perhaps for space exploration — that had widespread support from the electorate. Charles Schultze, the Director of the Bureau of the Budget, made that point very clearly in a speech in May 1963 (K37).

Neither the proponents nor the opponents of the tax cut had a compelling, well-articulated economic model of the link between taxes and the important macroeconomic variables of output, unemployment, interest rates and prices. Despite the superiority of the *IS–LM* model of macroeconomic behavior to anything else available at the time, no government agency involved in the debate could muster the intellectual resources to present the theoretical and empirical predictions of this model. Instead the combatants either made extravagant claims for the employment and output benefits of the tax cut or pointed to the mortal dangers of budget deficits and inflation as direct appeals to interest groups. All of the participants were more concerned with counting votes than calculating the value of *b* or *x* or the slope of *IS* or *LM* curves.

CONCLUSION

Politicians make promises and economists make predictions. It is important, but not always possible, to tell the difference between these two activities. In the oral-history project (Hargrove and Morley, 1984, pp. 185–7), Heller was asked to "describe how the Council develops political resources to work in this rough world and be effective?" In a lengthy and detailed response, the former Chairman of the CEA said:

> The idea was to get all of these people to understand that we knew what we were talking about, that Kennedy would make better policy if he listened to us, that they ought to be clued in on what we were trying to do in spite of the fact that this was an arcane subject to a bunch of lawyers. In that sense, the first job was to become an accepted part of the inner circle.

Since lawyers would not understand a second-order difference equation, the temptation to simplify the theoretical model to the point of corrupting it must have been strong. Even more crucial to a politically-attuned lawyer would be an explanation of a policy that predicted widespread benefits and no identifiable losses. Heller and other economists in the White House did not have an audience of graduate students, but a group of politicians and bureaucrats who could count votes in committees, but who could not stand a mind-numbing lecture on macroeconomic theory. As Arthur Burns, a former Chairman of the Council, pointedly remarked, "Although the Council consists of economic experts, it is also a political body. The Council cannot discharge its primary responsibility of assisting the President and at the same time express views that diverge significantly from the President's public position. At best, the Council's pronouncements are destined to be punctuated by silence on matters that justify the eloquence of candor." (quoted in 1964 *Hearings*, p. 213).

The CEA had to convince the President, not a seminar group at a prestigious university, and its approach was guided by this changed environment. In the oral history (p. 187), Heller was asked, "what the conditions are that cause the CEA chairman to be influential with the president on a given policy question?" The response was: "First, you have to establish that you're right. Second, facts have to be facts. Nor could you afford constantly to put the brightest face on the facts. Third, I'd say the rationale must be plainly understood." Based on the historical evidence dealing with the tax cut, I would judge that Heller failed on all three counts, yet he was very successful and admired in the corridors of power, precisely because he could translate economic predictions into political promises.

DATA APPENDIX

The time series for the marginal propensity to save in Chart 3.2 was derived from recursive least squares of an equation, $S = \alpha + \beta Y_{d_{t-1}}$, that adds one quarterly observation and reports the value of β. The first observation is 1953:1. The data for the two variables follow.

$$S - 1946:1\text{--}1965:4$$

16.3 15.0 11.6 10.8 8.1 2.2 5.7 3.9 6.3 10.0 13.7 12.7 8.7 6.3 6.6 5.5 15.4 10.8 4.3 12.5
8.0 17.6 16.9 16.3 15.6 14.4 18.3 15.4 15.3 17.6 17.3 18.0 17.5 14.5 14.7 15.5 13.1 14.1
15.8 16.1 17.6 19.4 20.2 21.4 20.0 21.5 21.3 19.9 20.5 19.9 22.6 23.8 19.9 21.1 16.2
18.0 18.8 16.5 17.3 15.6 18.2 19.0 21.7 21.8 22.1 21.6 20.5 17.5 18.4 18.5 17.6 20.7
22.0 27.0 25.7 29.9 26.1 28.3 34.6 32.1

$$Y_d - 1946:1\text{--}1965:4$$

152.0 156.0 161.5 165.0 165.8 163.7 170.9 173.2 178.7 186.1 192.7 192.6 187.5 186.8
186.5 188.0 200.8 200.2 207.6 213.2 219.3 224.2 226.0 229.2 229.8 232.6 238.9 243.9
247.3 251.5 251.9 252.1 253.5 253.0 255.5 260.6 264.4 270.7 276.8 281.2 284.4 288.8
292.7 299.0 302.0 305.8 310.1 310.3 310.5 312.6 320.1 325.2 329.6 336.7 337.1 341.1
345.7 349.7 350.8 351.2 354.3 359.7 365.2 372.4 377.5 382.8 385.8 389.5 394.5 398.9
405.0 412.7 422.5 435.1 442.2 448.3 455.0 464.1 479.2 490.2

4

The Macroeconomic Effects
of the Tax Cut

The previous chapter concentrated on the *ex-ante* predictions of the tax cut; here the emphasis is on the *ex-post* evaluation of how this policy influenced the important macroeconomic variables in the US economy in the middle and late 1960s. What would have happened to output, employment, prices and interest rates in the absence of this stimulus to aggregate demand? In order to answer a question such as this, we need to have an econometric model of the US economy that would allow us to predict retrospectively the path of these variables with an assumption that the tax cut did not take place. The difference between the historical forecasts of the model and the values from this counterfactual exercise would show the effects of the policy.

Arthur Okun (1968; 1970) undertook such a task in the summer of 1965. He reported (Table 2, p. 356) that by 1965:2, GNP was $24.4 billion higher than it would have been in the absence of the tax cut. This extra demand came from $16.3 billion in consumption expenditures, $4.8 billion in business fixed investment and $3.2 billion in inventory investment. At the time the output gap was thought to be in the vicinity of $30 billion and Okun concluded (p. 345) "that the tax cut of 1964 carried us a giant step toward full employment." However, as soon as the research was completed, Okun began to worry (p. 345) that his analysis did not make allowances for changes in monetary policy at the time and that he ignored the inflationary consequences of the extra aggregate demand, especially since the ultimate increase in GNP was expected to be around $36 billion (p. 358) and would create a negative output gap. He must have been aware that higher interest rates would have "crowded out" some of the tax-cut effects on the demand for goods and services and that predictions of higher nominal GNP would not have been translated into higher real GNP and employment as inflationary pressures rose.

THE APPROPRIATE ECONOMETRIC MODEL

Okun realized that concentrating on aggregate-demand equations was not sufficient to capture the full effects of the tax cut and in retrospect he would have used a more sophisticated model for this exercise. From the vantage point of today, what is the appropriate econometric model with which to judge the tax cut of 1964? Diebold (1998) provides a selective review of macroeconomic models of the postwar era. On the one hand, it is possible to rely on the Brookings Model (Duesenberry et al., 1965), which was published at the time of the tax cut and represents the collective wisdom of a generation of experienced econometricians. It is an elaborate and detailed model of over 150 equations, but mostly dealing with demand behavior. An alternative, smaller model is by Thurow (1969), which appears to be tailor-made for the purpose at hand because it concentrates on fiscal-policy evaluation. However, despite its supply-demand orientation, it is not a price-adjustment model and the inflation rate is exogenous (p. 46). On the other hand, one could deploy a very modern real-business-cycle model (Stadler, 1994) that relies on equilibrium being maintained in all markets despite productivity shocks to the economy. None of these choices is appealing.

Instead the IS–LM–AS model, consisting of only four behavioral equations, will be estimated. It concentrates on the crucial macroeconomic variables of the inflation and interest rates as well as output; it also allows for monetary policy to have independent effects on aggregate demand; finally, it pays equal attention to demand and supply factors in the macroeconomy. The equations of the model are as follows:

$$y = a_0 - a_1(i_l - \pi^e), \tag{4.1}$$

$$\mu - \pi = a_2 y - a_3 i_s - (m - p)_{-1}, \tag{4.2}$$

$$\pi = \pi^e - a_4(y_e - y), \tag{4.3}$$

$$i_l - i_s = a_5 - a_6 \Delta i_s + a_7(i_l - i_s)_{-1}. \tag{4.4}$$

The four equations determine y = natural log of output, π = the inflation rate, i_s = the short-term interest rate and i_l = the long-term interest rate. The parameters, $a_1 \ldots a_7$, are to be interpreted as elasticities. The exogenous variables are: π^e is the expected inflation rate, μ is the growth rate of nominal money balances, $(m - p)_{-1}$ are real money balances existing at the end of the previous period and y_e is potential output. Equation (4.1) is the IS curve, with a_0 representing the natural log of exogenous "injections" (i.e., exports and government demand) minus "withdrawals" (i.e., imports and taxes) from the expenditure stream. The *LM* curve is given by equation (4.2) once it is recognized that $m - p = (m - p)_{-1} + \mu - \pi$. The *AS* curve is provided by equation (4.3) in that a deviation of y from y_e implies disequilibrium in the labor market and requires an adjustment in real wages. For example, if $y < y_e$, real wages will fall and this requires that nominal wage growth linked to π^e be less than π. Finally, equation (4.4) is the yield curve and links the two interest rates in the model; this version was suggested by Mankiw (1986, p. 62).

Expected inflation is exogenous to the model only in the sense that there is no equation to explain π^e. In a rational expectations framework, to the extent that a change in some other variable is predictable, it should lead to equal changes in π and π^e; only unpredictable events leave π^e unaffected. In practice it is virtually impossible to think of predictable policy changes. Even the timing and size of the tax cut of 1964 was in doubt until it actually occurred, despite the lengthy discussion of its implementation starting in 1962. From that viewpoint, adaptive expectations are rational in that the past inflation rate incorporates all the information that is available at the time that decisions have to be made.

Estimating the IS–LM–AS Model

The first decision that has to be made concerns the time period for which the model will be estimated. It was decided to use 1953:1 to 1972:4, for a total of 80 observations. Earlier quarters were eliminated to avoid special considerations during the Korean-war period and later observations were discarded because the first oil-price shock and world food shortages had independent effects on inflation and output starting in late 1973. Individual regressions will have somewhat fewer observations because of unavailablity of some data.

The estimating technique involves TSLS with autoregressive-error correction. The list of instruments is provided in the Data Appendix at the end of this chapter. Also polynomial distributed lags were used for some of the variables. These procedures were probably not readily available to most empirical researchers in the mid-1960s, but the Cochrane–Orcutt iterative process for autocorrelation was published in 1949, Johnston (1963, pp. 258–60) presents the TSLS estimation procedure, and Almon (1965) is the source for polynomial distributed lags. Of course the ease with which econometric work is done today cannot be compared to the time-consuming calculations that were required at the time of Okun's research.

The IS equation

To allow for a direct comparison of the endogenous variables with and without the tax cut, a_0 in the IS equation is decomposed into two parts: (1) exogenous expenditures, captured in a_0, are defined as government purchases and net exports of goods and services; (2) the tax component, labelled τ, is defined as the natural log of personal income tax payments (only a small proportion of which went to state governments in the 1960s) deflated by the GNP price index. The relevant nominal interest rate is the Baa corporate bond rate. Expected inflation is defined as the average of the inflation rate experienced over the previous four quarters. For both τ and $i_l - \pi^e$, a second-degree polynomial distributed lag (PDL) structure with near and far ends constrained to zero was employed; for a_0 the PDL is first degree with only a far-end zero constraint. The regression results for the IS equation, which uses a second-order autoregressive error correction, were as follows:

$$
\begin{aligned}
y = \ & 0.0932\ a_0 + 0.0746a_{0-1} + 0.0559a_{0-2} + 0.0373a_{0-3} + 0.0186a_{0-4} \\
& (3.703) \\[4pt]
& -\ 0.0166\ \tau - 0.0298\tau_{-1} - 0.0397\tau_{-2} - 0.0464\tau_{-3} - 0.0497\tau_{-4} \\
& \ \ (7.077) \\[4pt]
& - 0.0497\tau_{-5} - 0.0464\tau_{-6} - 0.0397\tau_{-7} - 0.0298\tau_{-8} - 0.0166\tau_{-9} \\[4pt]
& -\ 0.00057\ (i_l - \pi^e) - 0.00103(i_l - \pi^e)_{-1} - 0.00139(i_l - \pi^e)_{-2} \\
& \ \ (3.963) \\[4pt]
& - 0.00165(i_l - \pi^e)_{-3} - 0.00180(i_l - \pi^e)_{-4} - 0.00185(i_l - \pi^e)_{-5} \\[4pt]
& - 0.00180(i_l - \pi^e)_{-6} - 0.00165(i_l - \pi^e)_{-7} - 0.00139(i_l - \pi^e)_{-8} \\[4pt]
& - 0.00103(i_l - \pi^e)_{-9} - 0.00057(i_l - \pi^e)_{-10} \\[4pt]
& +\ 1.3429\ \epsilon_{-1} - \ \ 0.3417\ \epsilon_{-2}, \\
& \ \ (11.99) \quad\quad\ \ (3.045)
\end{aligned}
$$

nobs = 77 (53:4–72:4), $\bar{R}^2 = 0.998$, SEE = 0.0087, D.W. = 1.95.

Individual t values are shown for only some coefficients since the lagged variables of a_0, τ and $i_l - \pi^e$ have the same value as those reported. Both the tax variable and real interest rates have relatively long lags. With respect to the former, consumers incorporate increases in their disposable income from tax cuts into their permanent income over approximately two years. The long-run elasticity of real GNP with respect to tax payments is 0.364; in 1965, the ratio of taxes to GNP was 0.095, thus the partial-equilibrium tax multiplier is equal to 3.83, a number substantially larger than predicted by the Council at the time of the tax cut. Many years later, in Hargrove and Morley (1984, p. 205), Heller is quoted as saying: "A pure consumption multiplier of about two buttressed by further investment and consumption effects would bring the total multiplier — we called it the 'gross accumulator' — to about three." Also the tax elasticity is much larger than the government expenditure elasticity which takes a value of 0.280 in the long run, but it is not possible to test whether this difference is significant in the absence of a calculated covariance between them.

The LM equation

Normally the *LM* curve is estimated as a demand-for-money equation, but here the short-run interest rate will be treated as the stochastic variable since it is being determined by the interaction of supply, $m - p$, and demand, $a_2 y - a_3 i_s$. The adjustment process suggested by Hendry and Ericsson (1990) is adapted for this purpose.

$$\ln i_s = -\; \underset{(6.674)}{2.3491} + \underset{(2.166)}{3.5601} \; \Delta y_{-1} - \underset{(3.108)}{0.0574} \; (\mu - \pi)$$
$$+\; \underset{(10.02)}{2.6493} \; (y - m + p)_{-2} + \underset{(9.387)}{1.1194} \; \epsilon_{-1} - \underset{(4.808)}{0.5204} \; \epsilon_{-2},$$

nobs $= 77$ (53:4–72:4), $\bar{R}^2 = 0.907$, SEE $= 0.153$, D.W. $= 1.84$.

All the parameters, which are significant at the 0.05 level or higher, are elasticities with respect to the short-term interest rate. A positive change in real income or a higher velocity will raise the interest rate, but increases in real money balances (i.e., $\mu > \pi$) in the current quarter will reduce the interest rate. In the long run, when nominal money increases are exactly matched by inflation, the income elasticity of the demand for money is automatically equal to one and the interest elasticity is equal to -0.3781, both of which are within the requirements of the Baumol–Tobin inventory rule with integer constraints.

The AS equation

Here the expected inflation rate was estimated as a first-degree polynomial distributed lag. Also, despite misgivings expressed in Chapter 2, potential output is calculated in the same way as recommended by Okun (1962; 1970). Even if we now adjust y_e downward by an arbitrary percentage, it would not influence the estimated results of the *AS* equation except for the constant term. The slope coefficient would only be changed if a different growth rate to potential output were applied. The regression estimates are the following:

$$\pi = 0.6741 + 0.3471\ \pi_{-1} + 0.2603\pi_{-2} + 0.1735\pi_{-3} + 0.0868\pi_{-4}$$
$$\quad (3.028)\quad (13.71)$$

$$-\ 9.8472\ (y_e - y) + 0.1990\ \epsilon_{-1},$$
$$\quad (3.251)\qquad\qquad (1.683)$$

nobs = 78 (53:3–72:4), $\bar{R}^2 = 0.843$, SEE = 0.560, D.W. = 1.99.

Not only are all coefficients for the lagged inflation rate significantly different from zero, but their sum is significantly different from one ($t = -2.01$). This, plus the constant term, imply the absence of a long-run vertical AS curve. It should be noted that the relationship between the ouput gap and π is contemporaneous. If the output gap is one per cent (i.e., 0.01), actual inflation will fall below expected inflation by 0.098 per cent in the first period. This suggests a very flat short-run aggregate-supply curve and policy errors that cause the economy to deviate from potential GNP do not have large inflationary consequences, as long as these errors are not perpetuated.

The term-structure equation
The link between long-term and short-term interest rates is provided by the yield curve, which is estimated as follows:

$$i_l - i_s = 0.1977 - 0.7575\ \Delta i_s + 0.9281\ (i_l - i_s)_{-1} + 0.5035\ \epsilon_{-1},$$
$$\quad (3.191)\quad (15.06)\qquad (34.56)\qquad\qquad (4.449)$$

nobs = 78 (53:3–72:4), $\bar{R}^2 = 0.985$, SEE = 0.123, D.W. = 2.12.

For this equation all coefficients are significantly different from zero. The long-run implications of these estimates are that the long rate will exceed the short rate by $0.1977/(1 - 0.9281) = 2.75$ per cent. Also, if the short rate is rising, the spread between the long and short rates is falling by about 0.75 per cent per quarter. A one-time increase in the short rate will mean that the long rate will take many quarters to adjust to a new final value, as is obvious from the large coefficient attached to $(i_l - i_s)_{-1}$.

Simulations of the Model

Each of the equations provides a very good prediction of the dependent variable, but a historical simulation of the entire model may not do as well, as errors in one equation are transferred to another. For instance if $\hat{y}$ is the prediction from the IS equation:

$$\hat{y} - y = \epsilon_y,$$

and ϵ_y would be approximately 0.87 per cent on average as seen from the standard error of the estimate. Then in the AS equation:

$$\pi = \pi^e - a_4(y_e - \hat{y} - \epsilon_y) + \epsilon_\pi$$

and

$$\pi - \hat{\pi} = a_4 \epsilon_y + \epsilon_\pi,$$

where $\epsilon_\pi = 0.560$ on average. By adding 9.847×0.0087, the average-sized error would now be 0.646 per cent, which is larger than the error from the AS equation alone. This problem would be mitigated if positive ϵ_ys occurred at the same time as negative ϵ_πs, or vice versa; however, the correlation between these two errors is only 0.084. Also errors may become cumulative even though they are randomly distributed within each equation. This becomes obvious in terms of the expected inflation rate. If we simplify the AS equation to:

$$\pi = \pi_{-1} - a_4(y_e - y) + \epsilon_\pi,$$

then the error in predicting the lagged inflation rate will increase the size of the error to

$$\pi - \hat{\pi} = a_4(\epsilon_{y_{-1}} + \epsilon_y) + \epsilon_{\pi_{-1}} + \epsilon_\pi.$$

Only if there are alternating positive and negative residuals in each of the IS and AS equations will the cumulative error become smaller. But serial correlation of residuals is required to be zero, not negative.

To ascertain the predictive quality of the whole IS–LM–AS model, root-mean-squared errors were calulated for y, π and i_l for the period 1964:1 to 1966:4 (12 observations). The RMSEs were as follows: for y it was 0.79 per cent; for π it was 0.243 percentage points against a mean value of 2.32 per cent; for i_l it was 0.321 percentage points against a mean value of 5.12 per cent. From these results one can conclude that the model has very good forecasting abilities, at least on a historical basis. However many of the remaining errors are not random; a tendency to over- or underpredict carries on for many quarters.

THE NO-TAX-CUT EXPERIMENT

The aim of the exercise is to show what different path the important macroeconomic variables would have taken in 1964–66 if the tax cut had not been implemented. Okun (1968; 1970, p. 348) has estimated the reduction in personal tax payments that were involved in *The Revenue Act of 1964* for 1964:1 to 1965:4. To lengthen the period of comparison somewhat, it will be assumed that in each of the quarters of 1966,

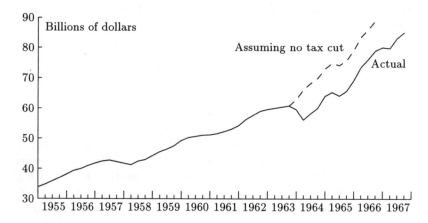

Sources: US Department of Commerce (1977, Table 2.1) and Okun (1968; 1970, p. 348).

Chart 4.1   Personal tax and nontax payments, 1955–67

the $10 billion difference found for 1965:3 and 1965:4 will continue. The path of personal tax payments is shown in Chart 4.1. As can be seen the tax cut took effect in 1964:1 and caused a sharp downturn in tax payments at that point, but they rose quickly thereafter. The hypothetical case of "no tax cut" would have meant that the upward path of these payments would have been undisturbed. It is not safe to assume that the divergence between these two streams would have remained at $10 billion after 1966, since other changes occurred in the meantime. Thus the comparison is made only for the 12 quarters of 1964–66.

In addition to reductions in personal income taxes, the legislation also lowered corporate taxes. Okun (p. 348) estimated that for 1964 this amounted to $1.8 billion and in 1965 it was $3 billion; however the changes are not allocated on a quarterly basis. Concerning beneficiaries of the tax cut on corporations, Okun stated, "Without great conviction, I assume that there was no shifting in the short-run period covered by this paper." Essentially this amounts to treating it as a "pure profits tax," in which case it should not cause firms to make any different decisions with respect to output and factor inputs. For that reason the reduction in the corporate tax rate does not play an independent role in determining aggregate demand for goods and services.

The Counterfactual Experiment

In the *IS* equation, the higher value of τ is introduced in 1964:1 and in every subsequent quarter all the relevant values of τ_{-i} are also altered. Then the model is solved once more and the endogenous variables are calculated. The outcome of this counterfactual experiment for the path of $y_e - y, \pi$, and i_l is shown in Chart 4.2 for this time frame.

The operative comparison is between the "predicted" path and the one marked "hypothetical no tax cut." Okun (p. 357) compares the latter with actual output and consumption, but this is invalid since the difference between them includes prediction error. The most important observation concerns the output gap. In early 1964, it was forecast at around 4 per cent and the tax cut resulted in its virtual elimination by 1966; in the absence of the tax cut, the economy would have remained virtually stagnant. Despite increasing potential output during this time, the tax cut created sufficient aggregate demand to allow real income to grow by 14.9 per cent in the two years. In 1966:4, predicted real GNP was \$983.4 billion, which is \$54.5 billion higher than without the tax cut. This allows us to calculate an all-inclusive multiplier of 5.5, if both induced consumption and investment are counted. However this process took time as the reduction in personal taxes was incorporated into permanent income rather slowly. At the end of 1964, the change in real GNP was only \$16.0 billion, which produces a multiplier as small as 1.6. To allow for direct comparisons with the quantitative predictions made by the Council, we note that they projected GNP to be \$40.5 billion higher in 1965, which is the third year since the intended tax cut of \$9.5 billion (K28). This produces a multiplier with a value of only 4.3.

Furthermore Chart 4.2 shows that GNP increased not only through the direct effects of the tax cut but through lower real interest rates stimulating investment expenditures. During 1964–66, real rates were predicted to fall from 3.48 per cent to 3.25 per cent, but in the absence of the tax cut, they would have risen to 3.95 per cent. One would expect that expansionary fiscal policy would lead to crowding out of investment expenditures through higher real interest rates, but the dynamics of the model are such that inflation adjusts faster than nominal interest rates. This can be seen in the last two panels in Chart 4.2.

Nevertheless the planners of the tax cut would have been pleased with its very limited inflationary effect, at least in the first three years after its implementation. Although the inflation rate was rising, the additional effect attributed to the tax cut is only about 1.5 per cent at the end of 1966. As discussed in the previous section, the short-run AS curve was quite flat during this period and the elimination of the output gap, or the increase in real output of over \$50 billion, may have been an acceptable trade-off against an inflation rate that would have

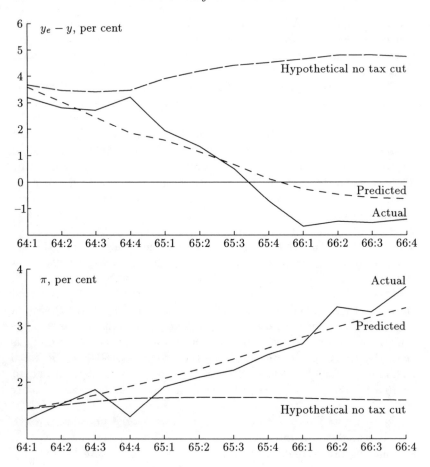

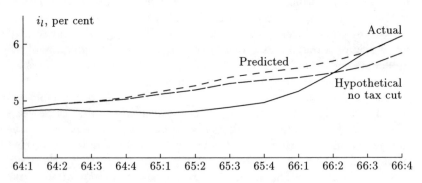

Chart 4.2   Predictions of the effects of the tax cut

settled at about 3 per cent. Only when Vietnam war expenditures and other influences made the actual output gap negative did inflation rise significantly in 1966, but according to the simulations of the model, the blame for this cannot be placed at the door of the tax cut. At this stage all that can be said is that the difference between the two paths in Chart 4.2 includes unspecified changes in other policies that are not part of the counterfactual exercise.

After this review of the evidence, one can conclude that the tax cut had mostly beneficial effects on the operation of the macroeconomy and that it can be judged to be an overall success. Especially noteworthy is the fact that the *size* of the tax cut was almost exactly correct. The aim was to increase aggregate demand to the point where actual GNP reached its potential and by the end of 1966 the predicted output gap was virtually zero. Of course the tax cut was to be implemented at least a year earlier according to the plans of the Council and Joint Economic Committee. At that time the output gap was larger: in 1963:1 it was 5.4 per cent.

In spite of the CEA's faltering analysis of how the tax cut would affect output and the decision to avoid any discussion of its inflationary side effects, the outcome is very much in conformity with "textbook analysis" as Heller had claimed; however the *IS–LM–AS* model is superior to the multiplier–accelerator model. Parts of this model represent developments in macroeconomic theory and estimation since 1964, making it difficult to criticize the Council for not relying on it for their projections, but the appearance of the elaborate Brookings Model in 1965 and Okun's retrospective analysis of the same year does suggest that a more deliberate econometric approach to the forecasting exercise in 1962 and 1963 would have paid handsome dividends. Even as late as 1984, Heller was defending the *ad hoc* and oversimplified approach taken twenty years earlier. He said (Hargrove and Morley, 1984, p. 205):

> With appropriate charts, Gardner Ackley and I spelled out for the first time in history for a congressional committee just how the multiplier was going to work. Fortunately, as Art Okun's retrospective analysis later showed, the tax cut operated virtually on the schedule that we had projected in that analysis. Of course, one can't isolate economic cause and effect all that precisely. But Art's analysis is pretty persuasive.

Moreover one is left with nagging concerns that the tax cut actually pushed the economy beyond its true potential. From Chart 4.2, we see that the hypothetical path of the output gap would have remained in the vicinity of 4–5 per cent after having fallen from about 7 per cent in 1961. One interpretation of this evidence is that the inflation rate would have stabilized at about 1.5 per cent and output would have grown at

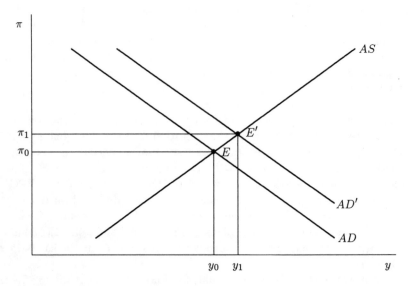

Figure 4.1   The tax cut and inflation

the same rate as potential GNP, namely 3.5 per cent per annum. In turn
this would make a measured output gap of 4–5 per cent consistent with
equilibrium in the labor market and lead to an upward bias to the time
series for y_e used here. In other words the natural rate of unemployment
may have been higher than assumed by Okun in his calculation of potential GNP. To test this proposition, however, is virtually impossible since
one is unable to predict short-run differences in the important variables
based on variations in y_e. This can be seen with the aid of an AD–AS
diagram in Figure 4.1. The AD curve combines equations (4.1), (4.2),
and (4.4), while equation (4.3) represents the AS curve.

Starting from π_0 and y_0, the tax cut shifts the AD curve upward
and from the short-run AS curve we can predict that inflation will rise
to π_1 and income will increase to y_1. Although y_e helps to determine
the horizontal intercept of the AS curve, its slope depends only on the
value of a_4. Hence the value of y_e is irrelevant in predicting the short-
run inflationary effects of the tax cut, if π_0, y_0 and a_4 are known. The
model used here was not constructed with long-run predictions in mind;
therefore, it cannot settle the issue and indicate the long-run inflation
rate with and without the tax cut.

Alternative Fiscal Measures

An alternative stimulus to the economy that was being considered was

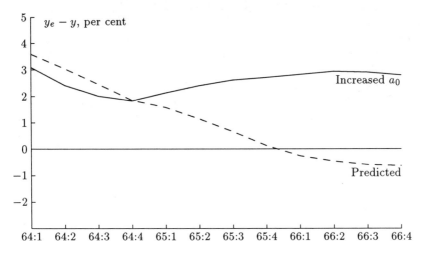

Chart 4.3   Predictions of the effects of an increase in a_0

larger government spending programs, but this plan was rejected at the time as having little political support. One of the benefits of this proposal would have been that it worked its way into the economy much faster. According to the IS equation, an increase in government demand takes four quarters to raise aggregate expenditures, but a tax cut takes ten quarters to be fully effective. If, instead of a $10 billion tax cut, this amount is converted into an equal increase in a_0, then we add $13.835 billion in 1972 dollars to the actual amount for the 12 quarters between 1964:1 and 1966:4. The effects of this experiment on the output gap are shown in Chart 4.3.

In addition to the predicted path that is repeated from the first panel of Chart 4.2, there is also the forecast output gap if the tax cut is replaced by an equal increase in government expenditures. Because the elasticity of output with respect to a_0 is lower than the elasticity with respect to τ, higher government expenditures have much smaller effects on the output gap and on inflation and interest rates. In this exercise the output gap falls somewhat faster in the first year, but at the end of 1966 it has stabilized at about 3 per cent. From that perspective the absolute increase in government expenditures should have been $37.7 billion instead of $13.8 billion to get the same results in 1966:4 as the tax cut that was implemented. From this comparison the Council chose the right fiscal instrument, not only politically but from a macroeconomic point of view as well.

ACCOMMODATING MONETARY POLICY

The Council of Economic Advisers was much more ready to rely on a fiscal stimulus to "get the economy moving again" than on persuading the Federal Reserve Board to follow a policy of easy money. Nevertheless Congress and especially the Joint Economic Committee were not reluctant to put direct pressure on the Fed to follow an expansionary policy. In the 1963 *Joint Economic Report* (p. 20) the criticism of the Fed is not subtle:

> We recommend that the monetary authorities follow a policy of assuring that the money supply expands in line with the rising needs of an expanding economy. Such a policy will reinforce the proposed fiscal policies and at the same time spare the Federal Reserve System their perennial explanations of why monetary policy is blameless in the face of a lagging economy.

At the time the generally accepted view was that fiscal policy was more effective as a stabilization-policy tool than monetary policy. This was in line with mainstream Keynesian thinking. For example, Ackley (1961, p. 167) wrote, "the emphasis is on fiscal measures in securing economic stabilization." But to Congress, expanding the money supply and lowering interest rates to generate extra investment expenditures seemed to be less costly to the public purse than raising total aggregate demand through larger budget deficits. William McChesney Martin, the Chairman of the Fed, was neither openly hostile to the idea of the tax cut nor enthusiastically supportive in his testimony to the Joint Economic Committee in February 1963, but perhaps secretly he wanted the tax cut as a possible scapegoat in the event that the economy became overheated and inflation replaced economic slack as the primary concern. He could then declare himself and his colleagues blameless for the fiasco.[1]

The JEC was clearly irritated by the Fed's refusal to submit to its demands. It pointedly reminded the Fed that it was "a direct servant of the Congress. It acts solely as the agent of Congress in carrying out its functions of controlling the money supply. This power is given to Congress by the Constitution and the Federal Reserve authorities merely act for Congress under delegated powers." (*Report*, p. 25). In

---

[1] The Council and the Fed often had a stormy relationship. In July (K50, emphasis in original), in a draft memorandum to Heller "RF" wrote, "Chairman Martin ... testified yesterday before the House Committee on Banking and Currency. The stenotype record runs 94 pages. Chairman Martin did not deliver 94 words (or syllables) of support for the tax cut ... Martin was *not* asked about the tax cut in so many words and studiously avoided *many* opportunities to say a kind word for it. *But* once he came close and his response get's [sic] an 'F'."

recommending the tax cut, the Committee wanted to coerce the Fed into an important accommodating role in this exercise. They wrote:

> This shift in emphasis which has pushed fiscal policy to the forefront in current policy discussions in no way eases, however, the responsibility of the Federal Reserve authorities to do more than in the past to restore the desired growth pattern. Indeed, if there has ever been any uncertainty as to the force of the public mandate in calling upon the monetary authorities for stimulative measures, vigorously pursued, that uncertainty can no longer exist. The widespread demands for stimulative tax reductions are by the same token demands for stimulative monetary action. Monetary policy must now help fiscal policy to do the stimulative job which, unfortunately, the monetary authorities have not done. (p. 20)

In their *Report* the Committee had both a specific complaint and a recommendation for future action. Perhaps persuaded by the expert testimony of Allan Meltzer at the hearings on 6 February 1963 (pp. 595–601), the JEC used the evidence of the secular rise in the velocity of money as a clear indication that monetary policy had been too tight. In summarizing this evidence they wrote, "at the end of 1954 the money supply was called upon to support a gross national product 2.8 times its size. Eight years later it was called upon to do one third more; that is, the gross national product was 3.8 times the money supply." (p. 21) A year earlier in their 1962 *Report* (p. 8) they saw the cause of this upward trend in velocity by commenting, "Federal Reserve authorities have shown a stubborn propensity to tighten credit and force up interest rates during each recovery period, notwithstanding the fact that each recovery has begun from a higher plateau of interest rates (and a money supply relatively smaller) than the previous recovery."

According to modern monetary theory, the velocity of money is not a constant, but varies with interest rates and can rise rapidly during a period of hyper-inflation. However Congress was concerned with the secular rise of the velocity of the commonly used monetary aggregate, composed of currency and demand deposits. It was not convinced by the Fed's suggestion that a broader concept of money, that included other liquid assets, had a much smaller increase in velocity.

As a complement to the tax cut, the Joint Economic Committee formally recommended that "the monetary authorities provide the basis for secular increases in the money supply as the economy grows." (*Report*, p. 23). This can be interpreted as a command to the Fed to keep the velocity of money constant and according to the definition of velocity would require a growth rate of nominal balances according to the following equation:

$$\mu = \pi + y - y_{-1}. \tag{4.5}$$

The higher is the rate of inflation or the rate of growth of GNP, the larger is the indicated growth rate of money. This makes the Fed's role much more passive and would require them to validate any inflation that came in the wake of the tax cut, but it is nevertheless a useful exercise to assume that the Fed followed this policy beginning in 1964:1, at the same time as the tax cut became effective. It is possible to make another counterfactual simulation of the econometric model to see how output, inflation and interest rates would have behaved differently had velocity been forced to remain at its level in 1964:1, namely 4.02. This will replace the actual value for $y - m + p$ in the LM equation and equation (4.5) will allow for the calculation of the required growth of nominal money to achieve constant velocity. The model is simulated once more for 1964:1 to 1966:4 and the results for the output gap, the real interest rate and the growth of money are shown in Chart 4.4.

Congressional critics of the Fed would have been unpleasantly surprised by the effects of their hypothetical demand for the Fed to keep velocity at the value it had in 1964:1. The difference in the output gap is minute over this 12-quarter period. The two paths for $i_l - \pi^e$ are shown in the second panel of Chart 4.4; until the half-way point of the simulation period, the real interest rate is almost the same, thus no extra investment expenditures are stimulated. In the last panel of the chart, it can be seen that until 1965:3, the actual growth rate was about 1 per cent higher than if the Fed's mandate were to keep the real supply of money growing at the same pace as income. Only in 1966:4 was the actual value of μ lower than the required value.

During 1964–66 the Fed's policy was in fact quite permissive, despite Martin's reputation as an advocate of tight money. The growth rate of money was sufficiently large to allow the velocity of money to fall by about 0.5 per cent in the last two quarters of 1964, before starting its relentless upward path again in 1965–66, but by then it had very little impact on output. Given the long and variable lags in the operation of monetary policy, the starting-point of the experiment is crucial to its outcome. If velocity had been stabilized at an earlier date and at a lower value, the required growth rate of money would have been larger in 1964–66 and the stimulus to demand would have been more apparent. In any case one cannot accuse the Federal Reserve or its Chairman of sabotaging the tax cut by following a deliberately tight monetary policy. Furthermore the fact that this difference in growth rates of the money supply had no measurable effect on the output gap is another indication that monetary policy was much less effective than fiscal policy as a stabilization instrument, at least in the 1960s.

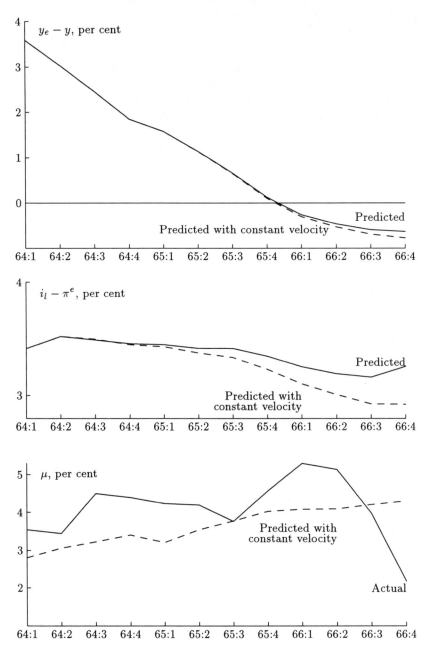

Chart 4.4   Predictions of the effects of constant velocity of money

CONCLUSION

Retrospective evaluation of the tax cut with the aid of a simple macro-econometric model based on the IS–LM–AS equations for 1953–72 reveals that the tax cut was a stunning success and that alternative routes to full employment and potential output were less likely to achieve the same goals. Nevertheless, Walter Heller's claims that the results followed the Council's predictions closely are exorbitant. The most revealing evidence in support of this assertion is a comparison of the actual multiplier with the various values that were put forward in 1963. This comparison is shown in Chart 4.5. In each case both the consumption and investment effects of the tax cut are compared after the passage of sufficient time to consider these effects to be close to their "equilibrium" values. The multiplier, calculated from the differences in the real GNP projections in Chart 4.2 and a \$10 billion cut in taxes, shows it rising from near zero to slightly above five. The highest estimate made in 1963 comes from the CEA's internal memorandum (K28) which shows a \$54.1 billion increase in real GNP arising from the tax cut which at that time was projected to be \$9.5 billion. On the other hand, at the JEC hearings in January 1963, Moor predicted an increase of \$32 billion from the original tax-cut proposal of \$8.5 billion. Ackley's Chart 3 at the same hearings was too evasive to calculate a multiplier. Heller later referred to a "gross accumulator" with a value of 3 (Hargrove and Morley, p. 205), which in turn is at the low end of a range for a long-run expenditure multiplier between 3 and 4, mentioned in (J6) in 1963. Finally, from the CEA's 1967 version of an internal econometric model (J75), Saul Hymans calculated expenditure multipliers for eight quarters; the dynamics are different from Chart 4.2 here in that the multipliers are larger in the early period but smaller later on. Not only are there large divergences among the predictions, but none of them is close enough to the calculated *ex-post* value to justify Heller's claim.

The Council was essentially lucky in three respects: (1) it picked the right instrument and the right size for the tax cut despite its inaccurate forecast of the multiplier effects; (2) it avoided crowding out investment because of easy monetary policy despite ignoring its consequences; and (3) the inflationary effects were minimal but not completely absent as was assumed. Admittedly with the benefit of hindsight, these three elements of good fortune can be explained more readily than at the time the tax cut was implemented. To take the last point first, inflation did not seriously worsen in 1964–66 because the AS curve was quite flat at that time. This may have been a temporary phenomenon as the public was learning about the effects of inflation only after experiencing them.

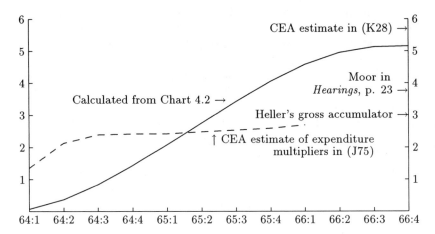

Chart 4.5   Values of the tax multiplier, 1964:1 to 1966:4

By avoiding any discussion of inflation, the CEA could argue that it knew in advance the flat slope of the *AS* curve or the Phillips curve. The staff memorandum (K28) noted that:

> Increases in GNP which do not carry it beyond potential should not put undue pressures on our resources of manpower or industrial capacity. Hence the kinds of GNP increases expected to result from the tax cut, when fully effective, are not too large to be accommodated within the Nation's capacity. In turn, this means that the increases in GNP are not expected to strain against resource ceilings.

However they assumed an invariant 1.5 per cent inflation rate,[2] which Chart 4.2 indicates could only be sustained in the absence of the tax cut. The model used in this chapter, on the other hand, predicts the inflation rate to be more than double this value within three years of the tax cut, an outcome that would be inconsistent with the position taken in the staff memorandum. The Heller Council was fortunate that short-term inflation did not ruin macroeconomic performance during their watch. That came later, when Great Society spending and the Vietnam war created an unsustainable boom and inflationary pressures worsened. The difficulty of persuading the President and Congress of the need for a symmetrical tax increase in 1966–68 is the argument to be developed in the next chapter.

---

[2] Actually, the memorandum stipulates a 5.8 per cent real and 7.4 per cent nominal growth rate for 1962–66 after the tax cut; thus inflation would be 1.6 per cent. Calculations of the nominal growth rate vary from 4.4 per cent to 8.1 per cent in their table.

Continuing in reverse order, Heller and Ackley in their testimony before the Joint Economic Committee in 1963 did not specify any assumption about interest rates or monetary policy in making their multiplier predictions. They could not have known that monetary policy was very accommodating to the tax cut and that there would be no adverse influences on investment spending. The multiplier–accelerator model that was the starting-point of the Council's "textbook model" would have contributed to a lot of volatility in investment expenditures as firms tried to maintain their optimal capital–output ratios. In retrospect the *IS–LM* model would have been a better choice, but only after the fact could one see that both the *IS* and *LM* curves shifted to the right in 1964, leading to higher output and approximately the same real interest rate in the subsequent 12 quarters. Heller and his Council colleagues tried to take credit for co-ordinating fiscal and monetary policies. After leaving the CEA, Heller (1967, pp. 85–6) stated:

> During most of the expansion monetary policy had played a largely permissive role. Constrained by the balance-of-payments problem, it nonetheless served the cause of expansion by meeting the growing credit needs of the economy at no more than gently rising long-term borrowing costs. Close and friendly co-operation between monetary and fiscal authorities was the order of the day in the 1961–1965 expansion. [*pace* (K50)] But in December 1965, as overexpansion increasingly threatened, the Federal Reserve Board slipped out of the harness of monetary-fiscal coordination to raise the rediscount rate and touch off a wave of interest-rate increases. The Administration, although wincing at the timing and the "go-it-alone" nature of the action, did not seriously contest its substance.

Not only was Heller unaware that the real cost of borrowing was actually falling because inflation was rising more quickly than interest rates, but he also failed to indicate that monetary policy was not assigned any role in the *ex-ante* predictions made in 1963 in the *Economic Report of the President* (pp. 45–51) or in the *Hearings* (pp. 1–11). Subsequent appraisals of this period have in fact reversed the order of importance of monetary and fiscal policies. Stein (1988, p. 111) wrote:

> The trend of thinking in the years since the 1964 tax cut has been to emphasize the monetary contribution, and particularly to emphasize that the effect of the tax cut is likely to be quite temporary, whereas an increase in the continuing rate of growth of the money supply can cause a permanent increase in the growth of demand. But in 1964 and 1965, after the tax cut went into effect, it was considered to be the main cause of the expansion. The good performance of the economy was considered to be the complete demonstration of the validity of the Keynesian theory.

Lastly it must be reiterated that the $10 billion tax cut was just right for eliminating the output gap in terms of its size and in terms of the instrument. But it must be remembered that the Council had several suggestions for the amount of the tax cut, anywhere from $8 billion to $16 billion. Of course the right amount depends on the size of the output gap which decreased as time went on; but there were different multipliers that were being proposed, without any resolution to the dispute. Moreover the choice of a tax cut instead of expenditure increases was entirely political in nature and not based on differences in multipliers or in benefit–cost ratios. When asked, "Wasn't there also the fear of the Nixon criticism — of being branded as a big spender, irresponsible?" Heller replied (Hargrove and Morley, 1984, p. 195), "The fear of Nixon was more on the spending and deficit side (though that's hardly unrelated). A tax cut fitted in better than expenditure increases."

To sum up, many have hailed the 1964 tax cut as the best single example of successful demand management in postwar history. Even a long-time critic of macroeconomic-policy decisions such as Herbert Stein (1996b, p. 19) concedes that the Kennedy–Johnson tax cut was "the Oscar on the shelf of the CEA." In view of the monumental change required in political decision making to incorporate modern macroeconomic thinking in the 1960s, it may seem somewhat churlish to demand greater precision and sophistication in the models presented by the Council to Congress and to suggest that potential costs be indicated as clearly as anticipated benefits. Nevertheless the members of the Council are, first and foremost, economists who have spent decades honing their analytical and predictive skills. They have a comparative advantage in these activities, not in the art of political persuasion. Perhaps history would be prepared to give even more accolades to the Kennedy–Johnson Council of Economic Advisers if part of its legacy included a well-specified and estimated model of how the macroeconomy was to react to the tax cut.

DATA APPENDIX

Data were taken from sources that were approximately contemporaneous to the end of the sample, 1974:4. The major sources of data are: *National Income and Product Accounts of the U.S., 1929–74: Statistical Tables* published in 1977, referred to as *NIPA*; *Federal Reserve Bulletin (FRB)*, various issues; and Prachowny (1969).

y natural log of GNP, billions of 1972 dollars, seasonally adjusted at annual rates. Source: *NIPA*, Table 1.2, line 1.

y_e natural log of potential GNP, in billions of 1972 dollars, seasonally adjusted at annual rates. It is calculated by assuming $y_e = y$ for

1955:3 and applying a quarterly growth rate of 0.875 per cent both forwards and backwards.

p natural log of GNP price deflator, 1972 = 100, seasonally adjusted. Source: *NIPA*, Table 7.1, line 1.

π year-over-year inflation rate, calulated as $(p - p_{-4}) \times 100$.

a_0 natural log of government purchases and net exports of goods and services, billions of 1972 dollars, seasonally adjusted at annual rates. Source: *NIPA*, Table 1.2, lines 21 and 18.

τ natural log of personal tax and nontax payments, in billions of 1972 dollars, seasonally adjusted at annual rates. Source: *NIPA*, Table 2.1, line 23 for current-dollar values and Table 7.1, line 1 for GNP deflator.

m natural log of currency plus demand deposits, in billions of dollars, seasonally adjusted, end of period. Sources: *FRB*, December 1970, pp. 895–8 and later issues.

μ year-over-year growth rate of the money supply, calculated as $(m - m_{-4}) \times 100$.

i_l yield on corporate Baa bonds, per cent, average of monthly observations. Sources: Prachowny (1969, pp. 139–40) and *FRB*, various issues.

i_s market yield on 3-month Treasury bills, per cent, average of monthly observations. Sources: Prachowny (1969, pp. 139–40) and *FRB*, various issues.

The following variables were included as instruments in the first stage of the two-stage least-squares regressions: $a_0, m, y_e, \pi_{-1}, \pi_{-2}, \pi_{-3}, \pi_{-4}, r_{l_{-1}}, r_{l_{-2}}, \Delta y_{-1}, (i_l - i_s)_{-1}, \tau_{-1}, \tau_{-2}$, plus a constant.

To allow for accurate replication of results in this chapter, the primary data are reproduced below. They are also available from the author in machine-readable form. The regressions and simulations were performed with *MicroTSP*, version 7.0.

$$y - 1947{:}1\text{--}1974{:}4$$

6.13988447	6.14739942	6.14846849	6.16057443	6.16814517	6.18620872	6.19603681
6.20637416	6.19624042	6.19215774	6.20132017	6.19277143	6.23734760	6.26358890
6.29600381	6.31824731	6.33221340	6.35123491	6.37109899	6.37280750	6.38232326
6.38367557	6.39409208	6.41754913	6.43326139	6.43966960	6.43358278	6.42389631
6.41033935	6.40621948	6.42064619	6.43950986	6.46318531	6.47820234	6.49269437
6.50278997	6.49843263	6.50353956	6.50413846	6.51574897	6.52268075	6.52341556
6.53029441	6.51722812	6.49737834	6.50458765	6.52854251	6.55407571	6.56625032
6.58796310	6.57730484	6.58782529	6.60759592	6.60516262	6.60082244	6.59564399
6.60204505	6.61873912	6.63160657	6.65531158	6.66962480	6.68248462	6.68997240
6.69183540	6.70134592	6.71380662	6.73197221	6.74158287	6.75821065	6.77078962

6.78048992 6.78434419 6.80572271 6.82045316 6.83765459 6.85856485 6.87688350
6.88376998 6.89304780 6.90052938 6.90213966 6.90905427 6.92126369 6.92902755
6.93867254 6.95597410 6.96772098 6.97044849 6.97988986 6.98434591 6.98785972
6.98239898 6.97877264 6.97923851 6.98656654 6.97672128 6.99878358 7.00606107
7.01301574 7.02153015 7.03983545 7.05875825 7.07157325 7.09190845 7.11289787
7.11346769 7.12003993 7.12359237 7.11371183 7.10430860 7.09854078 7.07901573

$$y_e - 1947{:}1{-}1974{:}4$$

6.19519567 6.20394563 6.21269559 6.22144556 6.23019552 6.23894548 6.24769544
6.25644540 6.26519536 6.27394533 6.28269529 6.29144525 6.30019521 6.30894517
6.31769514 6.32644510 6.33519506 6.34394502 6.35269498 6.36144495 6.37019491
6.37894487 6.38769483 6.39644479 6.40519475 6.41394472 6.42269468 6.43144464
6.44019460 6.44894456 6.45769453 6.46644449 6.47519445 6.48394441 6.49269437
6.50144433 6.51019430 6.51894426 6.52769422 6.53644418 6.54519414 6.55394411
6.56269407 6.57144403 6.58019399 6.58894395 6.59769392 6.60644388 6.61519384
6.62394380 6.63269376 6.64144372 6.65019369 6.65894365 6.66769361 6.67644357
6.68519353 6.69394350 6.70269346 6.71144342 6.72019338 6.72894334 6.73769330
6.74644327 6.75519323 6.76394319 6.77269315 6.78144311 6.79019308 6.79894304
6.80769300 6.81644296 6.82519292 6.83394289 6.84269285 6.85144281 6.86019277
6.86894273 6.87769269 6.88644266 6.89519262 6.90394258 6.91269254 6.92144250
6.93019247 6.93894243 6.94769239 6.95644235 6.96519231 6.97394227 6.98269224
6.99144220 7.00019216 7.00894212 7.01769208 7.02644205 7.03519201 7.04394197
7.05269193 7.06144189 7.07019186 7.07894182 7.08769178 7.09644174 7.10519170
7.11394166 7.12269163 7.13144159 7.14019155 7.14894151 7.15769147 7.16644144

$$p - 1947{:}1{-}1974{:}4$$

3.88094496 3.89182019 3.90921902 3.94002723 3.95680522 3.96840333 3.98508763
3.98024225 3.96991443 3.96062278 3.95947885 3.95966958 3.95661377 3.96499490
3.99452424 4.01023817 4.04111957 4.04620409 4.04655408 4.05698871 4.05508375
4.05421686 4.06044292 4.07158756 4.07295083 4.07550144 4.07889270 4.07431173
4.08664846 4.09000205 4.08782339 4.09267663 4.10165119 4.10693168 4.11382055
4.11903715 4.12761831 4.13580656 4.14709520 4.15528297 4.16682004 4.17084264
4.18006324 4.18113374 4.18494653 4.18707561 4.19283151 4.19584751 4.20439434
4.21138668 4.21508598 4.21877193 4.22566509 4.22756338 4.23134899 4.24763774
4.23193025 4.23671197 4.24103879 4.24262094 4.25092077 4.25433540 4.25703001
4.26310253 4.26717662 4.26787757 4.27081584 4.27763795 4.28054761 4.28400039
4.28950023 4.29155492 4.29973125 4.30487537 4.31160402 4.31642103 4.32651376
4.33820533 4.34406518 4.35324144 4.35914182 4.36284399 4.37248134 4.38389968
4.39666891 4.40818166 4.41739368 4.43129301 4.44206285 4.45492839 4.47049522
4.48277664 4.49769639 4.50987005 4.51895856 4.53249216 4.54754114 4.56153154
4.56985378 4.57862091 4.59269285 4.59965515 4.60806608 4.61946773 4.63511705
4.65243530 4.67030239 4.69143962 4.71474170 4.73865175 4.76813888 4.79950284

$$a_0 - 1947{:}1{-}1974{:}4$$

4.51852226 4.53796148 4.54009819 4.48863649 4.46245384 4.50534963 4.54542016

4.58904075 4.63472890 4.66908359 4.67656040 4.63666868 4.63860511 4.61413002
4.57779884 4.65300750 4.78080272 4.90156412 5.00595760 5.05815458 5.08202505
5.10594558 5.11499547 5.10655117 5.13990783 5.14516639 5.14633083 5.15962982
5.10108518 5.06638526 5.05879020 5.05369472 5.05560874 5.03304910 5.05433320
5.04535865 5.04857301 5.07329702 5.07141685 5.09742450 5.13049030 5.13226270
5.13285303 5.12396383 5.12634229 5.14458322 5.16020393 5.17784309 5.14923715
5.14166355 5.14691305 5.14107847 5.15329170 5.17614984 5.19462203 5.21003246
5.23537778 5.23164319 5.23962831 5.27043199 5.27862453 5.29129266 5.30181121
5.29881715 5.30479621 5.31123352 5.32884645 5.34376859 5.36410522 5.36504077
5.36223077 5.36457300 5.34567785 5.37712860 5.39362764 5.41610050 5.42406845
5.43546724 5.46510219 5.48852443 5.51504039 5.52664756 5.53930091 5.53457450
5.54283094 5.56413745 5.56490325 5.55295944 5.54478693 5.54517745 5.54165554
5.53930091 5.53575801 5.52385807 5.52823781 5.52385807 5.52465581 5.50288963
5.52266025 5.51584529 5.51504039 5.51664924 5.52305984 5.52863502 5.54829740
5.54556798 5.56068181 5.58199119 5.60837221 5.59953260 5.59768104 5.60211896

$$a_0 \text{ (in lieu of tax cut)} - 1964{:}1{-}1966{:}4$$

5.42686462 5.42774343 5.42510414 5.42730426 5.40956783 5.43910074 5.45461559
5.47577285 5.48328113 5.49402809 5.52200078 5.54414176

$$\tau - 1947{:}1{-}1974{:}4$$

3.75917816 3.75787234 3.75934195 3.77420401 3.77950191 3.67651605 3.62080240
3.63061070 3.61078524 3.57840442 3.54160308 3.51339936 3.55545735 3.60028028
3.63593697 3.78128480 3.82981014 3.89828801 3.94976329 4.00133848 4.04355907
4.07141399 4.08278369 4.09178352 4.10737037 4.10201406 4.09298944 4.09474134
3.99976181 3.99023556 3.99241399 4.00292205 4.02693414 4.04785585 4.07208728
4.09705114 4.12038755 4.14312982 4.14695453 4.16345930 4.17124605 4.18383169
4.18164491 4.16882371 4.15311956 4.13895702 4.16184282 4.17052268 4.19176054
4.21369123 4.22953653 4.24923086 4.27742910 4.29561185 4.29974699 4.29131698
4.30897951 4.31198024 4.32112741 4.33472633 4.34877347 4.38152933 4.40339708
4.42129898 4.42732524 4.43330240 4.43699789 4.43676567 4.41395473 4.35008668
4.38127231 4.41128778 4.46588325 4.48081684 4.45556926 4.47536945 4.51710128
4.56560993 4.59315347 4.62137651 4.63055181 4.62310218 4.65393638 4.66509723
4.68470096 4.71332740 4.81568622 4.84296083 4.89226341 4.90984821 4.88047599
4.88114309 4.86364698 4.86258935 4.81359958 4.81325292 4.77344560 4.78421306
4.79406547 4.83302640 4.93464565 4.94858503 4.95152187 4.96656608 4.94678688
4.94520616 4.96987056 4.98200559 4.97864198 4.99286079 5.00353002 4.99249458

$$\tau \text{ (no tax cut)} - 1964{:}1{-}1966{:}4$$

4.46616888 4.51385021 4.53957986 4.56496381 4.59726715 4.61644840 4.60033035
4.61684751 4.65189456 4.69300842 4.71661472 4.74056529

$$m - 1947{:}1{-}1974{:}3$$

4.70320415 4.71939134 4.72738790 4.72827243 4.72384166 4.71849870 4.72028303
4.71402454 4.71133041 4.71222925 4.70862913 4.71133041 4.72295331 4.73707532
4.74666976 4.75531291 4.76728916 4.77575635 4.79081964 4.80974245 4.81866741

4.82831382 4.83945131 4.84733152 4.85203027 4.85592889 4.85670709 4.85826063
4.86136150 4.86676502 4.87443351 4.88507223 4.89485025 4.90082025 4.90527486
4.90675497 4.91044664 4.91265487 4.91412448 4.91925048 4.91925048 4.91925048
4.91851997 4.91191911 4.91632461 4.93014812 4.93806457 4.94946908 4.96144485
4.96842336 4.96842336 4.96004343 4.95300626 4.94805049 4.95441770 4.95371198
4.96144485 4.96842336 4.97397136 4.98360681 4.98907136 4.99111270 4.98838949
4.99788761 5.00796508 5.01794195 5.02453804 5.03435182 5.04342508 5.05241680
5.06953287 5.07829380 5.08574295 5.09436368 5.10715675 5.12396383 5.13873529
5.14574861 5.14691305 5.14574861 5.16249752 5.17897081 5.19794416 5.21003246
5.22467088 5.24807596 5.26579427 5.28523206 5.29881715 5.31024599 5.31222009
5.31615734 5.33078479 5.34329080 5.36035299 5.36877584 5.39226293 5.41832017
5.42758989 5.43022251 5.45318222 5.46594810 5.48728370 5.54322242 5.54751825
5.57291412 5.57367372 5.60396194 5.61749792 5.63371753 5.63764286

$$i_l - 1950{:}1{-}1974{:}4$$

3.24 3.26 3.25 3.21 3.18 3.41 3.50 3.56 3.54 3.50 3.51 3.53 3.54 3.76 3.86 3.77 3.61
3.48 3.49 3.45 3.47 3.50 3.56 3.60 3.59 3.72 3.93 4.26 4.48 4.53 4.83 5.04 4.72 4.61
4.69 4.88 4.87 4.95 5.12 5.27 5.31 5.25 5.10 5.10 5.06 5.02 5.11 5.11 5.06 5.01 5.05
4.96 4.89 4.86 4.84 4.84 4.83 4.85 4.82 4.81 4.78 4.82 4.89 4.97 5.17 5.49 5.87 6.14
5.88 5.98 6.33 6.72 6.83 7.02 6.86 7.03 7.24 7.59 7.92 8.37 8.76 8.98 9.41 9.28 8.53
8.61 8.70 8.41 8.23 8.22 8.17 7.99 7.97 8.09 8.47 8.44 8.61 9.11 9.81 10.49

$$i_s - 1953{:}1{-}1974{:}4$$

1.98 2.15 1.96 1.47 1.06 0.79 0.88 1.02 1.23 1.48 1.86 2.34 2.33 2.57 2.58 3.03 3.10
3.14 3.35 3.30 1.76 0.96 1.68 2.69 2.77 3.00 3.54 4.23 3.87 2.99 2.36 2.31 2.35 2.30
2.30 2.46 2.72 2.71 2.84 2.81 2.91 2.94 3.29 3.50 3.53 3.48 3.50 3.68 3.89 3.87 3.86
4.16 4.60 4.58 5.03 5.20 4.51 3.66 4.29 4.74 5.04 5.51 5.20 5.58 6.09 6.19 7.01 7.35
7.21 6.67 6.33 5.35 3.84 4.24 5.00 4.23 3.44 3.77 4.22 4.86 5.70 6.60 8.32 7.50 7.62
8.15 8.19 7.36

5

The Inflationary Aftermath

At the beginning of 1967 the Council of Economic Advisers was under the spell of a euphoric sense of achievement. Keynesian economics had been thoroughly vindicated by the success of the tax cut and *Time* magazine celebrated the promise of full employment without inflation by naming Keynes as its Man-of-the-Year for 1965. Walter Heller, the chief architect of the tax cut had resigned from the Council in late 1964, but Gardner Ackley, the new Chairman, had the pleasure of seeing the results that he and Heller had predicted in early 1963. In the 1967 *Economic Report of the President* (p. 42), the Council claimed that:

> A major economic accomplishment of 1966 is that the United States made essentially full use of its productive potential. Gone were the chronic underutilization of resources, general excess supply in the labor markets, and wastefully idle industrial capacity that had blemished the performance of the economy for a decade. Because of the excessive unemployment and idle capital in previous years, the Nation sacrificed the opportunity to consume and invest a large amount of the output that it was capable of producing. At the trough of the recession in the first quarter of 1961, the "gap" between actual and potential GNP amounted to $57 billion (1966 prices). From 1958 to 1965, the cumulative gap totalled $260 billion.

The combination of identifying and calculating potential GNP and then designing the tax cut to lift aggregate demand to this point were the twin sources of this achievement. Nevertheless there were ominous signs that this state of bliss would not endure and that analytical decisions and policy advice in the period of 1966–68 suffered from the momentum of success experienced in 1964–65. There were essentially three problems in the later period that will be addressed in this chapter: (1) an unwarranted increase in the estimate of potential GNP that failed to give the appropriate warning of inflationary pressures, (2) the inability to "sell" a tax increase in the wake of the Vietnam war expenditures and the resulting lack of symmetry in Keynesian policy advice and (3) the absence of an analytical framework for the wage-price guidelines that would expose voluntary compliance as an unreliable basis for the fight against inflation. The point to be made here is that the overall evaluation of the tax-cut episode needs to take into account that *negative* output gaps, where $y > y_e$, require as much attention and forceful policy initiatives as *positive* ones. The Johnson Administration's failure to deal with the imperatives of symmetry is as much a legacy to be comprehended by succeeding generations as the immediate success of the 1964 tax cut.

ADJUSTMENTS TO POTENTIAL OUTPUT

The analytical history of potential GNP was provided in Chapter 2. Okun's great insight was to bring supply considerations to the same level of importance as Keynesian demand factors. He also suggested an innovative production-function approach to its estimation. Unfortunately both Okun and his followers soon began to make *ad hoc* calculations of this crucial time series. Even with this rather cavalier approach, the 3.5 per cent growth rate that was initially applied to potential GNP proved in retrospect to be a good estimate, in the sense that inflationary pressures were weak when $y < y_e$, but they became much stronger once the macroeconomy experienced excess demand with $y > y_e$.

By 1965, however, the Council had decided that potential GNP was in fact higher than was previously thought. Although the 3.5 per cent growth rate still applied to the period 1955:3 to 1962:3, from 1962:4 the growth rate was raised to 3.75 per cent. In 1967, another upward adjustment was made: from 1965:3, the growth rate of potential GNP was 4 per cent. The results for the output gap are shown in Chart 5.1. As is easily observed the use of the original estimate of potential GNP leads to a negative output gap by the middle of 1965 that remains until the end of 1968. On the other hand the potential output path with higher growth rates results in a virtual coincidence of y and y_e for 1965–66, after which excess supply appears again.

Although one is tempted to suggest that the Council adjusted potential GNP to a trend of actual GNP — a possible procedure discussed in (J20) — to make the performance of the economy under their watch appear optimal, there are in fact justifications offered for the higher estimates. The Council was convinced of changed circumstances. They argued in the 1967 *Report*, "The growth of potential stems from three principal determinants: the rise in the labor force; changes in annual average hours worked per man; and the growth of average output per manhour — that is productivity." (p. 44).

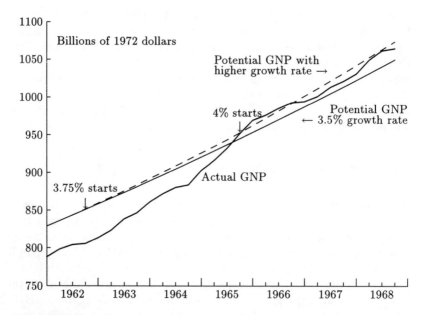

Source: US Department of Commerce (1977, Table 1.2).

Chart 5.1   Actual and potential Gross National Product, 1962–68

Growth in Supply Factors

Repeating the "adding-up" equation (2.5) derived from a production function produces:

$$dy_e = \alpha dk^* + \beta(d\ell^* + dh^*) + d\rho^*, \qquad (5.1)$$

where starred values represent sustainable and long-run growth rates of the relevant variables: y is output, k is the capital stock, ℓ is the supply of workers, h is the hours that they work and ρ is a productivity factor, all in natural logs. To justify $dy_e = 4$ per cent, the Council presented the following estimates (p. 44): $d\ell^* = 1.75$ per cent, $dh^* = -0.25$ per cent and $\rho^* = 2.5$ per cent. However this last factor, which measures output per manhour, applies only to labor productivity and not to total factor productivity; therefore, it should be multiplied by β, which is the share of labor in total output. The only way to obtain the correct result requires the assumption that $\beta = 1$. Although this is not explicitly stated, the fact that capital-stock growth is not mentioned adds to the impression that there existed in the mind of the Council members a one-to-one relationship between changes in the labor input and output. It is hard to imagine a realistic aggregate production function that would be consistent with that view. It is also ironical that inclusion of capital-stock growth in equation (5.1) would have led to the same conclusion reached by the Council. During 1962–66, the capital stock increased, as shown in Chart 2.3, at an annual rate of slightly more than 4 per cent; therefore the relative size of α and β does not matter as long as they add to one, in which case, $dy_e = 4$ per cent.

The Changing Natural Rate

Nevertheless equation (5.1) does not capture the possibility that the natural rate of unemployment is changing. The Council was convinced that 4 per cent unemployment remained as the best estimate of the natural rate in 1967. They "judged that an unemployment rate near 4 percent would (with the existing structure of labor markets) yield approximate balance between the supply and demand for labor.... In 1966, labor markets were generally in balance, although there were shortages of certain labor skills and a few remaining pockets of unemployment." (*ERP*, 1967, pp. 42–4). Gordon (1993), who has calculated a long time series for the natural rate, estimates that it was 5.6 per cent in 1966. The actual rate of unemployment that year was 3.8 per cent. If the Council's version of the natural rate is used in the Okun equation:

$$y_e - y = 3.2(u - u_e), \qquad (5.2)$$

the output gap for 1966 is about −0.6 per cent. If, on the other hand, Gordon's estimate is used, $y_e - y = -5.8$ per cent. If the latter is closer to the mark, this suggests that the Council's potential output figure should be adjusted downward by the difference between −5.8 per cent and −0.6 per cent, namely 5.2 per cent. If this were done, despite higher growth rates of factor inputs, potential output would be lower in Chart 5.1 than the path indicated by a growth rate of 3.5 per cent. It is not being argued that Gordon's data for the natural rate are intrinsically superior to those of the Council. In fact there continues to be uncertainty about the true value of the natural rate in the 1960s and 1970s. Adams and Coe (1990) support the Council's estimate of 4 per cent in 1966, but have a rising rate shortly thereafter. Gordon (1997) has recently revised his estimates of the natural rate and found it to be rising from about 5.5 per cent in 1960 to 6.2 per cent in 1970. He believes that, "The late 1960s were a time of labor militancy, relatively strong unions, a relatively high minimum wage and a marked increase in labor's share in national income." (p. 30). The point of my argument is that useful calculations of potential GNP depend not only on accurate growth rates of productivity and factor inputs from some starting-point, but also on labor-market developments that may have changed the unemployment rate consistent with equilibrium.

Thus, on the basis of very sketchy evidence and a questionable analytical framework, the Council made the fateful decision to raise potential GNP by about $25 billion dollars in 1968:4, which had the advantage of making the extra demand for goods and services derived from war expenditures at that time appear to be filling a gap. In fact in that last quarter shown in Chart 5.1 output was $10 billion shy of the new version of potential GNP, as well as $15 billion above the old one.

THE NEED FOR TAX INCREASES

As early as December 1965, Ackley was concerned about the surging macroeconomic performance and contemplated a tax increase. He reported to President Johnson (B24, reproduced in the Appendix) that GNP for 1966 would be about $9 billion above potential output and with the enactment of current tax proposals, this negative output gap would be reduced by only $2 billion. He therefore urged Johnson to consider an increase in individual and corporate tax rates. In other words the CEA was prepared to reverse course quite sharply, within a year of *The Revenue Act of 1964*, even though most of the prior predictions indicated that it would take two or more years to be fully effective. This change of direction in midstream is evident in the Council's ambivalence between economic urgency and political embarrassment. In a 12 March 1966 memorandum to the President (B26), all three CEA members again recommended a tax increase, but wrote (emphasis in original):

> Obviously, the *Administration cannot do a 180-degree turn overnight*. But you laid a good basis for further tax action with strong statements about the need for flexibility in your State of the Union Message, Budget, and Economic Report. *We could build on this foundation by gradually indicating an increased determination to take action before inflation takes hold.*

Despite the claim of "flexibility," there was a lack of symmetry and continuity in 1966–68 compared to the actions taken in 1963–64 in two respects. First, the CEA was not nearly as persuasive in recommending a tax increase when inflation was the major problem as it had been in promoting a tax cut when unemployment was the chief concern. Second, it became less certain of its own position in an environment of delicate "fine-tuning" compared to the earlier situation of a large and obvious output gap.

Contradictions in the Historical Record

Almost everyone involved in the *débâcle* surrounding the tax surcharge enacted in 1968 has attempted to deflect criticism by leaving a historical record that places the blame elsewhere. Even after comparing their contemporaneous private papers with their subsequent recollections or public statements, there remain many unresolved contradictions which need to be reviewed before embarking on an analysis of the Johnson Administration response to an overheated macroeconomy.

The accepted view, expressed by Stein (1996a, p. 525), is that from late 1965 the Council held a steadfast and unshakable position that aggregate demand was growing too strongly and that a tax increase was needed at the first opportunity; however, President Johnson was opposed to this move until early 1967 which meant that a whole year was wasted in internal debate. In 1973, Okun recollected (J96, reproduced in the Appendix) that, "during 1966 economic policy veered substantially off my preferred course. Starting in December 1965, the Ackley Council urged a tax increase upon President Johnson ... I felt that professional responsibility called for staying in the political battle to get fiscal policy back on course." Perhaps by then Okun had forgotten that he wrote to the President in May 1966 (J40):

> I think the outlook now is for continued growth with reasonable price stability. I think we need that growth. If we increase taxes now, we risk the disruption of that growth. Unless someone shows me some more definite reason for being afraid of too much expansion, I am unwilling to take the risk of bringing our long economic expansion to an end.

In the oral-history project (Hargrove and Morley, 1984, p. 251), Ackley is quoted as stating, "I don't know all of what went through LBJ's mind in reaching his decision [against a tax increase] which was against the unanimous advice of his presumably principal advisers in this area: the Treasury, Council and Budget Bureau." In explaining Johnson's opposition, Ackley speculates on the link between the needed tax increase and the political repercussions concerning support for the Vietnam war. He put the following words in Johnson's mouth (p. 252): "If we make people pay for this, then they'll change their view of how important it is to pursue it." Kearns (1976, pp. 295–6) makes the same point. Johnson also contributes to the historical confusion. In his autobiography he wrote (1971, p. 450), "At the time I was pleading for the tax bill, several newspapers increased our difficulties by speculating that I did not really want a tax increase, that deep down I hoped it would fail." Yet, according to Kearns (1976, pp. 300–301), he told his cabinet, "If I were a dictator and didn't have to be concerned with the city council or the legislative body and could just write my own ticket, I would add to the budget instead of taking from it and I wouldn't have a ten percent surcharge either."

The irony here is that President Johnson did not have to rely on his dictatorial instincts for his reluctance to incur the political costs of a tax increase, but instead could have blamed the wavering advice that he received from his Council of Economic Advisers. The source of his defense could have been the mini-recession that started in late 1966 and continued until early 1967. As Chart 5.1 demonstrates, real GNP was trapped between the old and new versions of potential output, leading to mixed macroeconomic signals that the Council never managed to resolve. In fact, unlike their argument in favor of the tax cut in 1963, there is no mention of an output gap or its size in the memoranda that circulated in 1966–67. Instead they reverted to the earlier NBER-style of business cycles and the policy goal became (J51), "maximum advance in production and income that is consistent with an improved price performance." For most of 1966, the Council advocated fiscal restraint through tax increases in its advice to the President (e.g., B26, B27, B30, J38, and J41). However hesitation begins to creep into a 14 October 1966 memorandum from Joseph Califano to the President which stated (J47), "Gardner Ackley says that several economists are now coming to the conclusion that no tax increase will be necessary. While he does not now share this view, he said his own sights on the size of a tax increase are lower than they were a few weeks ago." A little later, Ackley again recommended a tax increase in order to allow for easier monetary policy. He wrote (J50), "In restraining demand, tight money has acted as a substitute for a big tax increase. Its over-all effect is as large as could be expected from a tax hike of roughly $10 billion." In late November Ackley wrote (J52): "All told, there is no fundamental change in the situation since early September when you decided to make the budget cuts. The only reason the economy looks healthier today is because your program is having precisely the effects that you intended it to have." Then abruptly on 2 December 1966, Ackley wrote to the President (B31):

> Overly strong demand no longer appears to be the number-one threat to the health of the U.S. economy. Fiscal and monetary actions to cool things off have done their job for the present. . . . *In terms of pure economics*, the prescription for policy seems fairly clear. A tax increase would be put on the shelf until and unless the private economy bounced up strongly again, or McNamara had to add significantly to his spending.

In a Troika memorandum to the President (J57) a postponement of a tax increase until 1 July 1967 is recommended because an earlier date "would endanger the health of the economy in the first half year when the economy will already be seriously weakened by inventory adjustments." In fact the Troika was now proposing a complete reversal of stabilization policy. They stated (J58), "No additional net restraint on demand is needed, now or in the near future. Indeed, for the coming months we need new stimulus, both from fiscal and monetary policy, to minimize the risk of a dangerous stall." Faced with this new information, President Johnson could easily persuade himself that his economic advisers were mistaken in their earlier urgent appeals to raise taxes. Their recommendations amounted to fine-tuning the economy and the claimed economic benefits did not outweigh the political costs. In the end the President needed to accept less, and the Council more, of the blame for this fiasco than has traditionally been allocated.

Fine-Tuning

A close examination of Chart 5.1 shows the difference in the problems faced by policy makers in 1963 and in 1966. Despite uncertainty about the location and growth rate of potential GNP, it remains true that a major boost to aggregate demand was needed in 1963 to close the output gap, but that only a much smaller cut in demand was needed in 1966. However the very success of the tax cut caused the Council of Economic Advisers to make bolder use of its Keynesian framework. From now on, fiscal policy could eliminate even the slightest departure from potential GNP and it could do so quite quickly.

While economic analysis suggests that there is a monotonic relationship between the size of the output gap and the size of the required tax change to close it, the legislative process recognizes that there are fixed political costs that have to be paid every time that tax laws are changed. Hence there is a conflict between the costs of intervention and the costs of nonintervention, which dictates an optimal course of action that reduces the extent of fine-tuning. Eizenstat (1992, p. 70) put the matter in the following way:

> [E]conomists should concentrate less on tinkering with the economy and more on identifying broad trends. ... The economy has many natural self-correcting mechanisms which economists should emphasize. ... Presidents and their political advisers are under tremendous pressures to change policy with every temporary change in the economic environment. The CEA must help the President resist such temptations unless the economic realities have changed profoundly and permanently.

Essentially, Eizenstat was pointing to the importance of the costs of intervention to counter the exclusive focus on the costs of nonintervention by Keynesian macroeconomists of the 1960s.

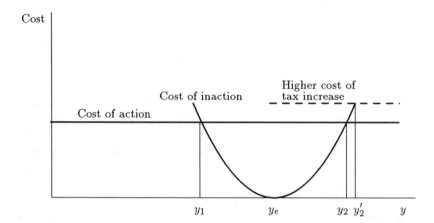

Figure 5.1   Policy maker's decision rule

In Figure 5.1 the tension between these two costs is shown. Any departure from potential GNP, y_e, imposes economic and political costs;
these are shown as quadratic and hence symmetric "costs of inaction."
On the other hand the cost of intervention is assumed to be linear. For
instance, if the House Ways and Means Committee scheduled hearings
on a tax bill, it would be overwhelmed with lobbyists arguing for some
special exemption for the group that they represent and whose costs
would not be related to the size of the tax change. As a consequence,
policy makers who are trying to minimize these costs should take no
action if output falls between y_1 and y_2. During the early 1960s, output
was probably below y_1 and the decision to legislate a tax cut imposed
lower costs than did further inaction, but by 1966, when $y_e < y$, the gap
was smaller than could justify the need to incur the costs of implementing a tax increase.

The area of inaction, or absence of fine-tuning, is between y_1 and
y_2, but this gap may change over time for a variety of reasons. For
example, the CEA may have thought that the success of the 1964 tax cut
indicated that the political costs of changing taxes frequently had fallen
and this would make smaller departures from y_e easier to overcome.
Alternatively the cost of inaction may have increased, as the public
expected the federal government to expand its stabilization role. This
would make the U-shaped curve in Figure 5.1 steeper and also reduce the
area of inaction. Probably the best explanation for the lack of symmetry
between the tax cut of 1964 and the needed tax increase in 1966 lies in
the fact that the height of the "cost-of-action" line is unlikely to be
symmetrical. In Figure 5.1 there is a higher cost that has to be paid for

implementing a tax increase than for a tax cut. This issue of asymmetry will be raised again in Chapter 7.

Moreover, the difficulty with this optimizing behavior by policy makers is that they are unable to make predictions whether recent events are permanent or short-lived. If the Vietnam war expenditures were only temporarily higher, it would not seem necessary to increase taxes in order to reduce aggregate demand in the economy. If, however, it would take years to eliminate the need for war-time financing, then a tax increase should have been instituted at the first opportunity. In 1966 the solution was not clear; Eizenstat's advice to economic policy makers does not allow for such uncertainty and is of little practical relevance. During the 1970s, the debate concerning stabilization policy was enlarged as Keynesian and neoclassical macroeconomists argued whether there was any room for intervention in the face of rational expectations, without a clear victor as the costs of both action and inaction seemed to rise. In any case, Hamilton (1992, p. 62) quotes Heller as admitting that, " 'Fine tuning' should join the 'Puritan Ethic' in the gallery of gaffes in economic-policy semantics."

The Effects of Higher Taxes

Fine-tuning a macroeconomy involves not only making small adjustments to small deviations from optimality but also requires quick responses to these deviations before they get worse. Since it took approximately two years to plan, legislate and implement the 1964 tax cut, the Council of Economic Advisers had hoped to be able to move more quickly the next time that such action was needed. In the end the tax increase also took from 1966 to 1968 from conception to implementation.

The initial proposal was a 6 per cent surcharge on personal and corporate income taxes in January 1967; by August of that year Johnson was forced to request legislation that contained a 10 per cent surcharge for most of 1968 and the first half of 1969. However, because fiscal years ended in June, the predicted extra receipts were $3 billion in fiscal year 1968 and $13 billion in fiscal year 1969. As a result the contractionary effect on the economy was essentially delayed another year. Moreover *The Revenue and Expenditure Control Act of 1968* was in doubt until its final passage in June of that year; therefore it could not have any anticipatory influence on aggregate demand, while its explicit temporary nature made certain that permanent-income calculations were left essentially unchanged. If there was to be any weakening of aggregate demand, it came from the accompanying requirement that $6 billion in expenditures be cut from the next budget.

After a lengthy discussion of fiscal policy since the 1930s in the 1968 *Economic Report of the President* (pp. 62–71), there is a section (pp. 86–87) predicting the macroeconomic effects of the surcharge. Unlike the 1963 multiplier–accelerator model used for the tax cut which completely omitted any mention of inflation, the analysis here has an implicit *AS* equation. The Council stated (p. 68):

> [A] tax cut enacted when there are ample idle resources as in 1964, has its main expansionary effect on output, with only a minor impact on prices. Under present circumstances, however, with rapidly expanding demands and essentially full employment, the main restraining impact of the tax increase will be on prices, and secondarily on output.

The first part of this assertion was borne out by the evidence produced in Chapter 4, where it was found that the tax cut stimulated real output, but had only minor initial effects on inflation. The second part, which claims that the *AS* curve was very steep by 1966, can now be subjected to empirical testing.

Using the econometric model estimated in the previous chapter, we can perform an experiment that hypothetically increases taxes sufficiently to eliminate the negative output gap within three years. The tax increase is assumed to be implemented in 1966:1. Various values of τ were tried in an attempt to create a zero output gap by 1968:4 and it was found that a 5 per cent increase from the actual value produced this result. In 1966:1, this would have meant $4.66 billion in 1972 dollars more in tax revenue. When the model was simulated for twelve quarters, 1966:1 to 1968:4, the results are shown in Chart 5.2 for the output gap, $y_e - y$, the inflation rate, π and the long-term interest rate, i_l.[1]

The appropriate comparison in all three parts of Chart 5.2 is between the predicted path of the variable which is based on the actual value of τ and the path marked "higher taxes," which allows τ to be 5 per cent higher. As planned, the effect of this hypothetical tax rise is to eliminate the negative output gap gradually. At the same time the inflation rate is reduced but only marginally. In the first quarter of 1967, π is only 0.13 percentage points lower and by the end of the simulation, the difference is only 0.5 percentage points. Also of concern is the observation that the long-term interest rate is virtually the same.

To reverse the inflationary trend that had become established would have required a much larger tax increase. Without knowing the Council's desired value of π or the target date for its achievement, it is not possible

---

[1] For this period the root-mean-squared errors were somewhat larger than for 1964:1 to 1966:4: 0.0112 for y, 0.7321 for π which had a mean value of 3.507 per cent, and 0.4661 for i_l which had a mean of 6.277 per cent.

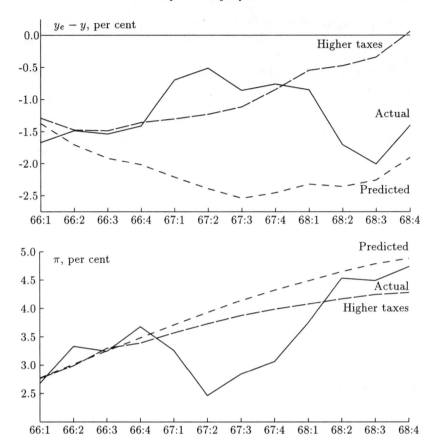

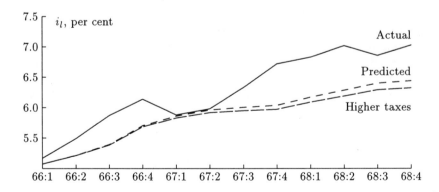

Chart 5.2   Predictions of the effects of a tax increase in 1966

to indicate the size of the needed tax increase, but it is certainly more than 5 per cent. Contrary to the Council's claim that the ratio of gap changes to inflation changes — sometimes called the sacrifice ratio — had improved between 1964 and 1966, the situation had in fact worsened. Comparing the results in Charts 4.2 and 5.2 shows this clearly: in 1968:4 the 2 per cent difference in the output gap resulted in a reduction in the inflation rate of 0.5 per cent for a sacrifice ratio 4.0; earlier in 1966:4, the difference in the output gap was 5.4 per cent and in the inflation rate it was 1.5 per cent for a ratio of 3.6. The government now had to pay a high price to bring inflation under control, requiring overwhelming contractionary policies that it was not prepared to implement. The claim of a steep *AS* curve and a small trade-off by the Council was wishful thinking; its aim was to remove any threatening predictions of the effects of the tax increase. Like the war in Vietnam the fight against inflation would be more painful and protracted than anticipated at this time.

Simulating the Surcharge

When the tax surcharge was finally passed in 1968, it failed to rein in the inflationary trend in the economy and it made a positive output gap even worse. This assertion can be verified by another counterfactual experiment that eliminates the effects of the surcharge and the reduced government expenditures that President Johnson accepted as part of his agreement with Congressman Mills. According to *The New York Times* on 31 May 1968, the surcharge would produce an extra $7 billion in calendar year 1968 and another $5 billion in 1969. Therefore, to obtain a time series for τ that assumes an absence of the surcharge, $7 billion was subtracted for 1968:3 and 1968:4, which are calculated at annual rates, and $5 billion was subtracted from 1969:1 and 1969:2, after which the surcharge expired. Also $6 billion was added back into a_0 starting in 1968:3, the first quarter of the 1969 budget year. With these hypothetical values, the model was again solved for twelve quarters, from 1968:3 to 1971:2.[2]

The results are shown in Chart 5.3. Once more the important comparison is between the values that were predicted by the model and the values marked "without surcharge." By the middle of 1969 the economy was predicted to move into a recession as defined by the output gap, but the absence of the surcharge would have reduced the size of this gap by about 1 per cent at the end of the simulation. From that perspective the

---

[2] The root-mean-squared errors now are: 0.0113 for y, 0.9033 for π which had a mean value of 4.994 per cent, and 0.9983 for i_l with a mean of 8.215 per cent.

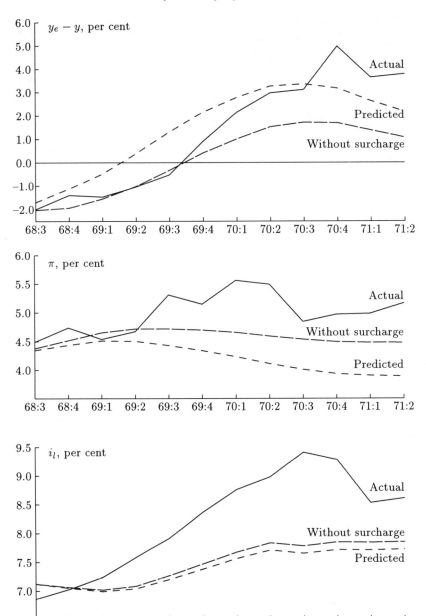

Chart 5.3   Predictions of the effects of the 1968 surcharge package

surcharge was in fact a procyclical policy initiative and reinforces the view that such action should have been taken in 1966 and not two years later. During the same period the inflation rate was expected to fall, although the actual rate continued to rise. The surcharge, therefore, had only a small effect on the inflation rate: about $1/2$ per cent by 1971:2. The same is true of the long-term interest rate, which would have been only marginally higher if the surcharge were not implemented.

THE WAGE-PRICE GUIDEPOSTS

In the absence of fiscal restraint, inflationary pressures in the US economy increased in 1966 and continued to worsen thereafter. The aim of the wage-price guidelines was to improve the trade-off between inflation and unemployment, allowing the government to reach lower levels of unemployment before inflation accelerated.

The genesis of the wage-price controls was the dramatic confrontation in 1962 between President Kennedy and US Steel which resulted in previously announced price increases being rescinded. This victory led to the mistaken belief that persuasion applied to other influential industries could keep down the inflation rate at the same time as the output gap disappeared.[3] Although the AS curve was relatively flat, as shown in Chapter 4, the Council was convinced that direct pressures on business and union leaders to minimize wage and price increases would make the AS curve even flatter. Needless to say, macroeconomists in the 1960s did not use the AS curve in their analysis, but their reasoning would generate such implications.

Starting in 1962 the Council began a series of statements in the *Economic Report of the President* about ways to preserve price stability. These guideposts were aimed at both unions in their wage demand and firms in their price setting. According to the guideposts in the 1962 *Report* (p. 188), wages were to rise by "the trend rate of over-all productivity increase" and individual goods prices were to fall "if the industry's rate of productivity increase exceeds the over-all rate" in productivity. Because these groups had economic power to set prices and wages, controlling their behavior in the public interest would reduce inflationary pressures.

---

[3] In a letter to Heller (J8) Barbara Berman of Brandeis University asked: "Can anyone point to a single can of beans that sold for a cent cheaper or to a worker who worked for a cent less thanks to the [guideposts'] influence? ... What of the steel serial? The last episode — the piece-meal price rises — left the President looking ridiculous and impotent, which is, of course, exactly what he was." There is no record of a response.

In opposition to Friedman's view that inflation was a monetary phenomenon, Ackley argued that market power has dynamic features that allows inflation to take place. He wrote (1966, p. 71):

> My model of price-making can be sketched somewhat as follows. A plausible theory of oligopolistic-pricing behavior suggests that the margin over costs that producers in strategic industries can attempt to earn varies with the strength of demand in their markets. . . . Thus as the economy expands, producers in these industries attempt to raise their margins over costs by lifting their prices. In the absence of effective downward flexibility in other prices and in wage rates, the average level of prices is thereby raised. But the higher prices in turn affect the general level of costs . . . Prices will consequently be raised again in these industries, and in others, in an effort to restore the desired and competitively feasible margin, even without any further increase in the overall degree of utilization in the economy, and without any increase in industrial concentration. And then we can be off to the races.

Ackley's uncritical acceptance of downward price rigidity is weakened by earlier statements by the Council. They wrote in the 1962 *Report*, "Developments in the steel industry in 1961 were propitious for the continuation of price stability. Steel prices at the end of the year were slightly *below* the level of the end of 1958." (p. 180, emphasis added). More than a theory of inflation, Ackley's argument points to a deeply held belief that raising prices is tantamount to unsocial behavior. Rising excess aggregate demand triggered by the 1964 tax cut and Vietnam war expenditures did not, in Ackley's view, make price and wage increases mandatory if firms and labor unions could be persuaded to behave in the national interest. He reported to the President in July 1965 (B17, emphasis in original): "In my speeches to business groups, I have been making a strong pitch about *the responsibility of businessmen to reduce prices wherever possible, and to avoid unnecessary price increases.*" However, he went on to admit, "I never was sure that it did any good."

Also Ackley's assertion that general excess demand for goods could not explain the current inflationary pressures was not consistent with his advice to President Johnson throughout most of 1966 that taxes had to be raised. In March 1966, a month before the conference in Chicago where he provided his justification for the guideposts, he warned the President (B26, emphasis in original) "that *a further tax increase is needed* to counter inflation ... *A continuation of the recent pace would mean general shortages by mid-year* ... This means that the needed tax increase may get larger the longer we wait ... guideposts can't be expected to carry the major load in an overheated economy."

There was a wide gap between Ackley's private and public views on the sources of inflation. As long as President Johnson had not committed himself to a tax increase, Ackley was forced to deny the existence of general excess demand and to rely on irresponsible behavior on the part of business and unions to explain rising prices. After the administration officially backed the tax surcharge in January 1967, the Council had to rationalize the need to reduce aggregate demand for goods and services by forecasting that the main effect would be on inflation, a proposition that is not consistent with the experiments in Charts 5.2 and 5.3.

Improving the Trade-off

Only retrospectively can the wage-price guideposts be put into an appropriate macroeconomic model, a process to which we now turn. The Administration wanted to change the trade-off between inflation, π, and the output gap in the AS curve, written as:

$$\pi = \pi^e - a_4(y_e - y) \tag{5.3}$$

to achieve both full employment and price stability. To see if this is possible requires that the derivation of the AS equation pinpoint the influence that macroeconomic policy might have on this trade-off. From a production function, output changes from one period to the next according to:

$$y - y_{-1} = \beta(n - n_{-1}), \tag{5.4}$$

where β is the output elasticity of the labor input, n. In a Cobb–Douglas production function with constant returns to scale, it also measures the share of labor in total output. In this case capital and other factors of production are treated as fixed factors. Next using a labor-demand relationship where the marginal product of labor equals the real wage:

$$n - n_{-1} = -\gamma(\omega - \pi), \tag{5.5}$$

where γ represents the inverse of the slope of the demand curve and indicates how quickly the marginal product of labor falls for every increase in employment; it is also the wage-elasticity of labor demand. Furthermore ω is the growth rate of nominal wages; if $\omega > \pi$, the real wage is rising and firms will reduce employment. In a situation where firms have some market power, they will equate the marginal revenue product of labor to the nominal wage and although this changes the quantity of labor demanded, it does not affect the value of γ. Finally, in a contractual setting, the growth of nominal wages will be determined according to:

$$\omega = \pi^e + g, \tag{5.6}$$

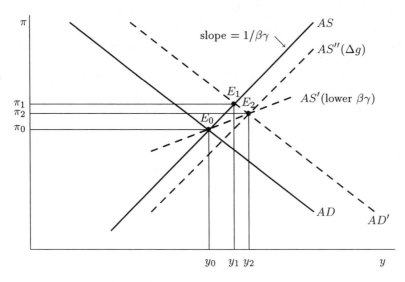

Figure 5.2   The effects of wage-price guidelines

so that expected real wages could rise by the factor g, which will be determined in the process of bargaining between workers and firms. Substituting equations (5.5) and (5.6) into (5.4) produces:

$$\pi = \pi^e + g - \frac{1}{\beta\gamma}(y_{-1} - y), \tag{5.7}$$

which can be compared directly with equation (5.3), where $g = 0$, $y_{-1} = y_e$ and $1/\beta\gamma = a_4$.

In order to allow the economy to increase output with an inflation rate that is mitigated by guidelines, it would be necessary to lower the values of β, γ or g in equation (5.7). These possibilities are shown in Figure 5.2. Starting from y_0 and π_0, the 1964 tax cut and Vietnam war costs shifted the AD curve to the right, and based on the AS curve, output would rise to y_1 and inflation would move to π_1. The role of guidelines would be to allow an even larger increase in output, to y_2, but with a lower inflation rate, π_2. This could be achieved if the AS curve became flatter, as with AS', or if it shifted downward to AS''. The former requires that either β or γ fall in value. But both of these parameters are essentially technical in nature and seem to be impervious to policy initiatives, especially if the guidelines involved only voluntary compliance. For example, the guidelines could be interpreted as an attempt to reduce market power of firms, but as pointed out above, this does not affect the value of γ. Moreover it is impossible to change the labor intensity of total output in the short run; therefore it would be fruitless to argue that the guidelines could lower the value of β. In fact the guideposts announced in the 1962 *Economic Report of the President* (p. 188) assumed "no change in the relative shares of labor and nonlabor income."

However the adoption of the guidelines on wages could reduce g from what it would have been otherwise. According to equation (5.6), g is a measure of productivity improvements that allows the real wage to rise over time. If negotiators have an inflated view of these productivity increases, wage settlements can shift the AS curve upward. An imposed lower value of g could bring about the desired result. For example, according to Table 12 in the 1965 *Economic Report of the President*, total compensation per manhour increased by 3.8 per cent in 1964 at a time when the trend rate of productivity increases was only 3.2 per cent. Therefore, if the guideposts were successfully applied, the AS curve would shift down by 0.6 per cent and inflation would also be lowered to a smaller extent. But the situation actually deteriorated rather than improved during the period of the guideposts. In the 1967 *Economic Report of the President* (p. 85), the Council is forced to admit that, "During the first half of 1966, unit labor costs rose at a rate of about 2 percent, but then accelerated to an annual rate of nearly 5 percent in the second half of the year." In other words the AS curve shifted upward by 2–5 per cent during 1966 which made the inflation–output trade-off worse rather than better.

In the labor market, real wages that are growing at a lower rate because of the guidelines would increase employment compared to the absence of this type of intervention. In Chart 2.4 in Chapter 2 which plots a static version of equation (5.5) for 1948–70, one can see how a falling real wage, adjusted for productivity changes, caused employment to rise substantially in 1964–68, compared to 1960–63. Successful guidelines would involve moving down the labor-demand curve faster than in their absence as real wages grew less than productivity increases. Nevertheless, despite Ackley's warning (1966, p. 72), that "wage increases in excess of productivity gains raise costs and therefore prices, and in the end do labor no good," one should resist judging the guidelines as a Pareto improvement; although they allowed more people to have jobs, they also lowered the welfare of those who already had jobs.

That the guidelines were essentially unsuccessful is indicated by the continuing rise in the inflation rate during the late 1960s. By the end of 1968, the inflation rate was almost 5 per cent. The deteriorating inflationary performance of the US economy starting in 1964 is the result of overly aggressive increases in aggregate demand from a combination of Great Society programs, the Vietnam war and the 1964 tax cut. The

Council believed that it was possible to get more output and employment at lower inflation rates by relying on the guideposts. Ackley (1966, p. 72) argues that they forced the participants into a new understanding of the public interest:

> The larger influence of the guideposts is ... indirect. For five years we have been hammering home some fairly simple arithmetic about the relations among wages, productivity, and costs; and between individual actions and overall results. ... As a result of this educational effort, the labor unions, at least in many cases, are bringing a different attitude to the bargaining table.

Nevertheless educating the public about the externalities of wage bargaining does not in any way eliminate or internalize their effects. There was nothing in the guidelines that was likely to change bargaining behavior, especially since Ackley (pp. 74–5) was adamant that no coercion beyond "ear-twisting" was applied to those firms or unions that breached the guideposts. It is not surprising that union leaders who are elected by their membership had strong reasons to ignore the guideposts. Ackley believed that labor's welfare is augmented by lower wages because they increase job opportunities. But those workers who are "secure" in their jobs, want *higher* wages to allow for greater goods consumption; only "marginal" workers are prepared to sacrifice wage increases to protect their jobs. Since the former outnumber the latter by a large margin, union bosses are almost always pushing for higher wages.

Although almost every economist has been exposed to Adam Smith's pronouncement that individuals following their private interest will also contribute to the public good, Ackley and the other proponents of the wage-price guideposts were prepared to argue that powerful economic groups that paid attention to the national interest would also prosper individually. Perhaps Ackley was convinced that inflation was a negative-sum game, similar to the prisoner's dilemma, and that a cooperative solution would make everyone better off. By demanding smaller wage and price increases, both profits and labor income could rise because of increased output and employment at y_2 in Figure 5.2, instead of y_1.

An alternative rationale for the guideposts relied on the idealism and altruism that was spawned by the Kennedy election. In his inaugural speech, Kennedy uttered the now famous words: "And so, my fellow Americans, ask not what your country can do for you; ask what you can do for your country." Although the President could not use that occasion for a detailed prescription of the requirements for self-denial, the fact that "the torch had been passed to a new generation of Americans" made it possible to have a new balance between private greed and public needs. What Ackley failed to realize is that the initial public-spirited enthusiasm for the "New Frontier" in 1961–63 had been worn down by the harrowing experiences of the Vietnam war. This made cooperation among competing groups impossible; the reappearance of self-interest and survival instincts was so well captured by the student slogan against the military draft: "Hell no, we won't go!"

The Distraction Effects of the Guideposts

Although the economics literature of this era concentrated on the direct effects of the guideposts on the inflationary experience of the period, my real concern is that they became a mind-numbing, bureaucratic exercise that siphoned the time and talents of the Council from more fruitful activities. We may never be able to answer the question: how much better would the Council's advice have been if there were no guidelines? Nevertheless it is worthwhile exploring the recorded evidence to see how many resources were diverted to microeconomic management of individual prices. An especially glaring example involves shoe prices in February 1966. In a memorandum to Joseph Califano, a White House aide at the time, Ackley recommended (B25) "that we can and should intervene to forestall" price increases that would range from 3 per cent to 7 per cent. He acknowledged that the "principal cause of this rise has been a great increase in cattle hide exports." He then suggests that

> [A]ny meaningful intervention on our part hinges upon our willingness to impose export restrictions ... Commerce should simultaneously proceed to draw up the export restriction order. Such an order would presumably limit each exporting firm to a fixed percentage of its actual exports during an appropriate base period, quotas to be applied on a quarterly basis, and an appropriate escape clause provided.

Export controls were in force between March and November 1966, which the hide industry blamed for a sharp decline in their prices. Okun in turn had to reply to Califano who was concerned about Congressional criticism, this time on behalf of hide producers. Okun wrote somewhat defensively (J76):

> The present low price in the hide market cannot validly be attributed to the 1966 quotas. ... Export quotas did affect prices while they were in effect. They stopped speculation almost immediately and that was their purpose. Hide prices dropped approximately 35 percent during the quota period, but remained well above levels of 1962–64.

Most importantly for the issue at stake here, the resources expended to deal with shoe and hide prices are totally incommensurate with the claimed beneficial effect that intervention could have on the overall inflation rate.

If this intervention were an isolated example, it could be treated as idiosyncratic, but as time went on, the Council spent more and more resources on reporting and trying to counter individual price increases. By 1967 Ackley was sending a "Weekly Price Report" to the President. In addition James Duesenberry, another member of the Council, received "Early Price Warnings" and "Weekly Stockpile Reports" from staff economists. Since the Consumer Price Index was available only on a monthly basis, Ackley resorted to tracking individual firms' price announcements (J26) and the latest farm prices to fill out his weekly report to the President. In one report (B51), he wrote, "Choice steer prices were steady; prices of utility cows were down." Why the President should be interested in cattle prices, except for the fact that he owned a ranch, is impossible to answer. In another report (B54), Ackley indicated that the price of "bulked filament nylon carpet yarn" had been increased. This information was not only incomprehensible to the President but it should have been totally irrelevant to him as well. There are many more examples of trivial information that was brought to the President's attention (e.g., B40, B41, B43, B44, B45, B46, B48 and B51–55). Nevertheless some of these items were bait for Johnson's belligerent instincts. In a 12 March 1966 memorandum to the President (J33), Ackley reported that Canadian firms were about to increase newsprint prices by 7 per cent. In a rare handwritten note Johnson wrote, "Shame Pearson," referring to the Canadian prime minister. In an appended note entitled "Checklist on our Marching Orders from the President," Ackley wrote "Leak that we will shame Pearson on Canadian newsprint prices." One can only imagine the countless hours that were devoted to this futile and vindictive exercise.

Not only were these reports a total waste of precious resources and talent, members of the Council, together with other administration officials, spent considerable time meeting with businessmen who were about to announce price increases in a useless exercise to dissuade them from these intentions. For example Okun, as acting chairman, reported to the President (B54, emphasis in original):

> Sandy Trowbridge and I *met with officials of the rubber products industry*. This was another of the series of meetings at which the general economic outlook and major economic problems of the industry are discussed. The industry people complained about unions and the high first year cost of their new wage contract. They were not at all apologetic about their price increases.

It seemed that the less successful these efforts were in bringing inflation under control, the greater the intensity with which the Council pursued them. Instead of abandoning its futile attempts to "micromanage" the economy and concentrate on improvements in macroeconomic performance, these activities had a vigorous life of their own. As is so often the case in Washington, urgency crowds out importance in competition for attention. Without realizing the transformation, the Council had slipped into the harness of a command economy, in which every private economic decision was measured against some unspecified notion of public responsibility. One example is a news release (J32) which stated, "Chairman Ackley said that [Bethlehem Steel] price increases were a poor service to the 200,000 Americans risking and giving their lives for freedom in Vietnam." One has to be grateful in retrospect that by their training and instinct the members of the Council showed their ineptness in these activities.

CONCLUSION

The major difference between the macroeconomic performance in 1964–66 and in 1967–68 is the asymmetrical approach to stabilization policy. In general, it seemed much more difficult to legislate and implement contractionary policy initiatives in the latter two years than to bring about expansionary policies in the former period.

Successful stabilization policy required the ability to move the level of aggregate demand to the point where actual and potential GNP coincide. But the Council of Economic Advisers could not resist the temptation to increase their estimate of potential GNP and therefore failed to rein in aggregate demand. In a debate with Milton Friedman, Solow (1966, p. 63) wondered about the policy dilemma that the Council faced. He wrote, "In other words, in Milton's own phrase, the normal level of unemployment in this sense is too high for comfort, and the normal degree of excess capacity in the economy is too big for comfort. The question is: What do you do then?" In retrospect the answer is that the Council should have done more careful analysis of equilibrium unemployment and potential output and should have educated the public about the limits of macroeconomic policy to achieve "full employment." The fact that the Council urged a tax increase in 1965–66 indicates that they instinctively knew that the output gap had become negative at that time, but when their advice was ignored because of political considerations, they reverted to showing a positive output gap and the need for guideposts to stem the inflationary tide. The analytical basis for the tax cut presented by Heller, Ackley, Moor and Guroff in 1963 was weak and inconsistent but the theoretical foundations for policy in 1966–68 were almost nonexistent and what was put forward was contradictory. It is not that the Council failed to understand the relationship between aggregate demand and inflation. In the 1967 *Economic Report of the President* (p. 47), they stated, "The surge in demand for goods and labor created pressures on prices in many areas. ... All in all, the economy exceeded reasonable speed limits in the period from mid 1965 through the first quarter of 1966." Instead of reconciling themselves to the trade-off between low inflation and further reductions in the unemployment rate, the Council began to think in terms of achieving both "full employment" and price stability, by using Keynesian expansionary policies for the former goal and wage-price guideposts for the latter. The failure of this combination of policies to reach these goals had important repercussions for many years afterward, especially on the disappearance of a cyclically-balanced budget and its stabilization properties, a topic to be taken up in the next chapter.

DATA APPENDIX

In addition to the data provided in Chapter 4, the new variable required for Chart 5.1 is the higher value of potential GNP, reported in the 1967 *Economic Report of the President*, p. 43. It is written in natural logs of billions of 1972 dollars. Also the hypothetically higher values of τ for the simulation in Chart 5.2 and the values of τ and a_0 for the surcharge in Chart 5.3 are listed.

$$y_e' - 1962{:}4{-}1972{:}4$$

6.74702453 6.75635623 6.76568746 6.77501869 6.78434991 6.79368114 6.80301284
6.81234407 6.82167530 6.83100652 6.84033775 6.84966945 6.85961961 6.86956977
6.87952041 6.88947057 6.89942073 6.90937137 6.91932153 6.92927169 6.93922233
6.94917249 6.95912313 6.96907329 6.97902345 6.98897361 6.99892425 7.00887441
7.01882505 7.02877521 7.03872537 7.04867601 7.05862617 7.06857633 7.07852649
7.08847713 7.09842729 7.10837745 7.11832809 7.12827825 7.13822889

$$\tau + 0.05 - 1966{:}1{-}1968{:}4$$

4.56710149 4.61561014 4.64315368 4.67137672 4.68055202 4.67310239 4.70393659
4.71509744 4.73470117 4.76332761 4.86568643 4.89296104

$$\tau \text{ minus surcharge} - 1968{:}3{-}1971{:}2$$

4.744806 4.775040 4.847089 4.866058 4.880476 4.881143 4.863647 4.862589 4.813600
4.813253 4.773446 4.784213

$$a_0 \text{ plus \$6 billion} - 1968{:}3{-}1971{:}2$$

5.587623 5.575949 5.567963 5.568345 5.564903 5.562603 5.559142 5.547518 5.551796
5.547518 5.548297 5.527045

6

Fiscal Drag and the
Burden of the Debt

As the first Keynesian Chairman of the Council of Economic Advisers, Walter Heller proposed the 1964 tax cut, not only for its immediate boost to aggregate demand, but also as the initial experiment in an increasingly aggressive and assertive fiscal policy. Through the Council's educational role, Heller (1967, pp. 36–7) was able to claim that the Kennedy and Johnson administrations "were largely free of the old mythology and wrong-headed economics which had viewed government deficits as synonymous with inflation; government spending increases as a likely source of depression that would 'curl your hair'; and government debts as an immoral burden on our grandchildren."

One of Heller's intentions was to warn Congress and the public of the dangers of what came to be called "fiscal drag." He explained its effects as follows:

> [I]n a growth context, the great revenue-raising power of our Federal tax system produces a built-in average increase of $7 to $8 billion a year in Federal revenues (net of the automatic increase in transfer payments). Unless it is offset by such "fiscal dividends" as tax cuts or expansion of Federal programs, this automatic rise in revenues will become a "fiscal drag" siphoning too much of the economic substance out of the private economy and thereby choking expansion. (p. 65)

While the two previous chapters recounted the effects of fiscal-policy decisions on macroeconomic performance, here the emphasis will be on two related issues: (1) the threat of fiscal drag and (2) the elimination of the burden of the federal debt. Until the early 1960s, deficits were accepted by the public only as the inescapable outcome of recessions; surpluses were considered desirable. In the Kennedy–Johnson Administration, surpluses were to be deliberately eliminated by further planned tax cuts as part of an overall macroeconomic strategy to keep aggregate demand at potential output. To overcome the conventional dogma, the CEA began calculating a full-employment budget surplus to show that tax rates were too high and expenditures too low when the economy reached its optimal position. Moreover, to make prolonged deficit spending more appealing, the CEA and other Keynesian economists put forward the position that the accumulating debt created by deficit financing had no harmful economic effects.

THE FULL-EMPLOYMENT BUDGET

To comprehend fiscal drag and the need for continuing fiscal dividends, the 1962 *Economic Report of the President* featured a discussion of a new concept, "the full-employment surplus." It was defined as the outcome of a chosen budget program in terms of tax rates, expenditure and entitlement programs, evaluated at potential GNP. This would differ from the actual balance whenever an output gap appeared. For example, in 1960 their Chart 6 shows that with a 5 per cent output gap the actual federal surplus was 0.4 per cent of potential GNP, but would have risen to almost 2 per cent if the output gap had been eliminated.

Defining Budget Balances

The connection between these two ways of measuring the surplus can be established by starting with a definition of the surplus as:

$$S = \tau Y - G - i(1 - \tau)B_{-1}, \tag{6.1}$$

where S defines the nominal amount of the budget surplus, τ is the assumed average and marginal tax rate, Y is income or output, G are federal government expenditures on goods and services as well as transfers except for $i(1 - \tau)B_{-1}$ which are net interest payments on the debt, B, accumulated from past deficits (i.e., $S < 0$). For their Chart 6, the CEA divided all of these magnitudes by potential GNP, Y_e, which then produces ratios designated by lower-case letters:

$$s = \tau[1 - (y_e - y)] - g - i(1 - \tau)b_{-1}. \tag{6.2}$$

In equation (6.2), $y_e - y$ is the output gap, measured as a fraction, since $Y/Y_e = 1 + (Y - Y_e)/Y_e = 1 - (Y_e - Y)/Y_e$. Thus if the output gap is 5 per cent, $Y/Y_e = 0.95$. The full-employment surplus ratio involves assuming that $y = y_e$, hence:

$$s^* = \tau - g - i(1 - \tau)b_{-1},$$

which differs from s only because of the elimination of the output gap. No consideration was given to the possibility that the interest rate on government debt, i, or the debt ratio, b, might differ between the two situations.

The Threat of Fiscal Drag

On the basis of these calculations the Council stated (p. 80):

> The full employment surplus rises through time if tax rates and expenditure programs remain unchanged. Because potential GNP grows, the volume of tax revenues yielded by a fully employed economy rises, when tax rates remain unchanged. Full employment revenues under existing laws are growing by about $6 billion a year. With unchanged discretionary expenditures, a budget line drawn on Chart 6 would shift upward each year by about 1 percent of potential GNP.

At hearings before the Subcommittee on Fiscal Policy of the Joint Economic Committee in 1965 (*Hearings*, p. 5), Gardner Ackley essentially made the same point. He stated, "A constant set of tax rates and a constant level of Government expenditures exert an increasingly restrictive influence as time passes. In short, fiscal policy tightens by standing still in a growing economy." In both of these quotes, Heller and Ackley are making unwarranted assumptions about what should be treated as exogenous. By pretending that tax revenues will grow over time, but that public expenditures will not, they raise the specter of an unbalanced economy, much the same as would happen if the capital stock remained constant in an economy with a growing population.

The budget lines in Chart 6 of the 1962 *Economic Report* are explicitly represented by equation (6.2), with s on the vertical axis and $1-y_e-y$ on the horizontal axis. Therefore the vertical intercept is $-g - i(1 - \tau)b_{-1}$ and the slope is τ.[1] The full-employment budget surplus ratio, s^*, is a particular point on the budget line where $y_e = y$. For the budget line to shift upward over time and give rise to fiscal drag requires that g falls, which is consistent with "unchanged discretionary expenditures" only if G is constant while Y_e is growing at the assumed 3.5 to 4 per cent a year or if $i(1 - \tau)b_{-1}$ is getting smaller over time.

---

[1] Although the CEA does not indicate its evaluation of the slope, by substituting the values for two points, A and F, it was possible to calculate the slope as 0.3. This is higher than the average federal tax rate at that time. DeLeeuw *et al.* (1980, Table 3) report federal receipts to be about 19 per cent of GNP; hence some elements of expenditures must be assumed to be countercyclical, but the *Economic Report* does not address this point.

The assumption by Heller and Ackley of "unchanged discretionary expenditures" or "a constant level of Government expenditures" was contrary to the evidence that should have been available to them. Between 1955 and 1964 federal expenditures almost doubled and even increased as a percentage of GNP. Of course they would not have been able to make the case for fiscal drag if they assumed that g in equation (6.2) would remain constant instead of G in equation (6.1). In a submission to the Subcommittee on Fiscal Policy of the Joint Economic Committee in 1965, Raymond Saulnier, a former chairman of the CEA, was aware of this very issue. He wrote, "advocates of the full-employment budget surplus concept have no cause for anxiety over our having a large surplus in the Federal budget. On the contrary, it is presently estimated officially that there will be a deficit in the fiscal 1965 budget (administrative) of \$5.7 billion." (*Statements*, p. 110).

Alternatively fiscal drag could occur and s could be rising over time if the tax rate is nonlinear. For example, if tax revenue is generated by a progressive tax system dictated by τY^2 then equation (6.2) is replaced by:

$$s = \tau Y[1 - (y_e - y)] - g - i(1 - \tau)b_{-1}, \qquad (6.2')$$

where the growth rate of Y dictates the path of s over time. However this assumption would be inconsistent with the straight budget lines in their Chart 6; if equation (6.2') were used, the slope would be τY which would make the budget lines convex from below.

Nevertheless Kermit Gordon, the Director of the Bureau of the Budget, appearing before the Joint Economic Committee in 1963, seemed to argue that the federal tax system was nonlinear. He said (*Hearings*, p. 75):

> As economic activity responds to the successive steps of tax reduction and reform, the advance in output and incomes toward full employment levels will be accompanied by a more than proportional increase in Federal revenues. ... Within a few years after enactment, total revenues will be larger than those which would have been yielded by the existing tax structure.

No indication is given by Gordon as to the degree of nonproportionality of the federal tax system.

Thus the concept of fiscal drag is subject to obfuscation because the CEA was unable to make clear how the intercept and slope of the budget lines in their Chart 6 were to be determined. In other words proponents of fiscal drag move back and forth between equations (6.1) and (6.2) as if they were interchangeable in their argument. Moreover there is not enough explanation of the slope of the budget lines in terms of assumed tax rates and the cyclical behavior of expenditures to make a reliable case for fiscal drag.

Nevertheless, if Heller and Ackley were able to convince the public and Congress that fiscal drag was something to worry about, the proposed tax cut would have greater assurance of acceptance. Not only was it needed to stimulate aggregate demand in 1963–64, but if it became only a first instalment of continuing tax cuts, it would prevent tax revenues from rising too quickly and make it easier to maintain potential output and full employment in future years. Since opponents were unlikely to understand that fiscal drag relied on a nonlinear tax system or a falling ratio of government expenditures to potential GNP, the CEA simplified the problem by drawing linear budget lines which inexorably shifted upward through a process that was left deliberately vague. It is also noteworthy that when tax increases were needed in 1966–67, the concept of fiscal drag disappeared from the Council's lexicon of economic evils.

The Optimal Full-employment Budget Surplus

Not only was fiscal drag a bogus threat to the performance of the macro-economy but the Council failed to specify that $s^* = 0$ was the optimal policy to follow in the long run. Instead they wrote in the 1962 *Economic Report of the President*, "If the full employment surplus is too large, relative to the strength of private demand, economic activity falls short of potential." (p. 81). This, of course, is not a valid point concerning the choice of s^*; given enough time for adjustment, all output produced at Y_e will be sold because potential GNP is supply constrained not demand determined. By specifying s^* only in terms of missing private aggregate demand, the CEA discounted the effects of surpluses and deficits on the accumulation of debt and the required interest payments that have to be financed far into the future. In other words they optimized s^* for one period instead of over many periods. To understand this distinction we can first define the process of debt accumulation as:

$$b = b_{-1} - s, \tag{6.3}$$

which means that b is falling over time if $s > 0$. A continuing surplus means that a falling tax rate will support a given value of g over time as interest payments decline. If $s = s^*$ because the economy remains at potential GNP:

$$b = [1 + i(1 - \tau)]b_{-1} - \tau + g. \tag{6.3'}$$

Thus, even if the primary surplus (i.e., $\tau - g$) is zero, the debt ratio will grow at the rate dictated by the after-tax interest rate which may itself be rising to account for the increasing risk of government debt. If, on the other hand, the primary surplus is positive and large enough to cover interest payments, b will fall over time. Finally if b is stabilized,

$$\tau = \frac{g + ib}{1 + ib},\qquad(6.4)$$

which falls with a lower value of b because $g < 1$. For example, assume that $g = 0.2$ is the optimally chosen ratio of public-goods provision and compare the required tax rate for two debt ratios, $b = 0.5$ and $b = 1.0$. Although the default-risk differs between the two situations it will be assumed that $i = 0.07$ for both. In the first case $\tau = 0.227$ while for the second case $\tau = 0.252$.

In an inflationary environment budget calculations are said to be biased; they reflect the requirement that governments must pay higher interest rates but not the fact that the inflation tax reduces the real value of the debt over time. To make this correction $[i(1 - \tau) - \pi]b_{-1}$ should replace $i(1 - \tau)b_{-1}$ in equation (6.2). This does not make the tax system inflation-neutral, since the inflation premium is typically not tax deductible. In turn the required tax rate to keep b constant over time in equation (6.4) becomes:

$$\tau = \frac{g + (i - \pi)b}{1 + ib}.\qquad(6.4')$$

To the extent that inflation is fully predictable, the *ex-post* real interest rate should not be affected and τ remains the same as i and π increase equally. If, however, the *ex-post* real interest rate increases with the inflation rate, the required tax rate is also higher.

In general the tax rate that will support a desired level of g is not independent of past surpluses or deficits and by the same reasoning it is not possible to fix τ strictly on the basis of current aggregate-demand requirements. Countercyclical fiscal policy *does* allow for changes in τ or g to keep aggregate demand closer to potential output, but this requires symmetrical adjustments for positive and negative output gaps and it requires that $s^* = 0$ on average over a business cycle. In 1963–64, the CEA argued in favor of tax cuts to stimulate consumption and investment demand; by 1966–67, when the output gap had been closed and inflation was the major threat, the Council members accepted the political impracticality of tax increases.

Countercyclical Fiscal Policy

It was not until 1980 that a thorough discussion of the full-employment budget surplus appeared in the *Survey of Current Business*. The article by deLeeuw *et al.* (1980) indicated not only the methodology behind the renamed "high-employment budget," but also provided historical data

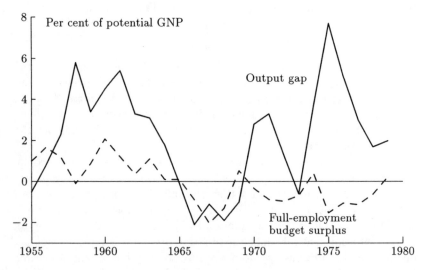

Source: deLeeuw *et al.* (1980, p. 17, Table 1, column 6 and p. 24, Table 3, last column).

Chart 6.1   The output gap and full-employment surplus, 1955–79

for the period 1955–79. These data are shown in Chart 6.1, together with the output gap as measured at that time, instead of the CEA estimates used in Chart 5.2, to allow for greater consistency.

Countercyclical fiscal policy requires that taxes and expenditures be adjusted so that a high-employment surplus appears in a boom period and a deficit in a recession. The "actual" budget would not give the needed indication of fiscal-policy changes because tax revenue will automatically rise and fall with economic activity, while some components of expenditures and transfers are also countercyclical. For present purposes the movement of the output gap and the budget ratio in the period 1963–68 is of particular interest, but the entire 1955–79 period is shown for historical perspective. It is immediately obvious that fiscal policy was not successful in eliminating output gaps. While the tax cut in 1964 generated enough extra aggregate demand to wipe out the positive gap by 1965, there followed a negative gap until 1970. During those years, a full-employment budget surplus should have appeared but instead the deficit reached 2 per cent of potential GNP in 1967. Instead of moving in opposite directions, the two lines move together in 1963–69. In contrast, during the turbulent 1970s that witnessed two oil-price shocks, fiscal policy is at least moving in the right direction at the right

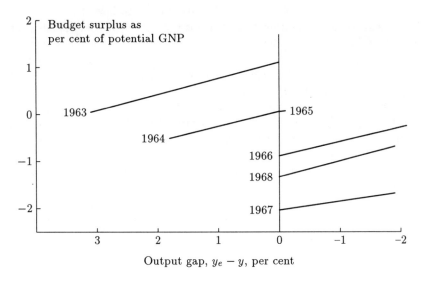

Source: Same as Chart 6.1.

Chart 6.2 Budget lines for 1963–68

time.

This evidence supports the contention in the previous chapter that the Kennedy–Johnson Administration's tax policy lacked symmetry. By 1966 or at the latest by 1967, taxes should have been increased and/or expenditures should have been curtailed when the Council realized that inflationary pressures had strengthened substantially. However the fixation with the threat of fiscal drag was enough of a counterpoise that their advice on tax increases lacked the last ounce of commitment that was needed to persuade President Johnson and Chairman Mills of the House Ways and Means Committee.

Another way to show that countercyclical policy in this crucial period lacked symmetry is to draw the budget lines for the years 1963–68 that originated in Chart 6 of the 1962 *Economic Report*.[2] These are shown in Chart 6.2. Budget lines for 1963 and 1964 are moving down, as they should, in an attempt to stimulate aggregate demand when the output gap is positive. On the other hand the budget lines for 1965–68 should be moving up each year as the output gap is now negative; instead, each budget line is lower than the previous one, except for 1968.

---

[2] The slope of the 1964 line has been calculated as 0.316. For 1968, the slope is 0.34.

Policy decisions in 1967 were particularly inappropriate. As Chapter 5 discussed in detail, neither the CEA nor the President could muster the moral resolve or the political resources to get a tax increase in time to shift the 1967 budget line upward. Instead, when output exceeded potential GNP by 1.1 per cent, the budget deficit at full employment was estimated to be about 2 per cent.

This was a watershed year. Before 1967 it was possible to argue in favor of deficits to stimulate aggregate demand, but after that year surpluses did not appear when they were needed for countercyclical purposes. The dam had been breached and it could not be repaired. After so many arguments in favor of deficit spending, it seemed impossible to tell Congress that higher taxes and budget surpluses were now paramount. In 1967 high-employment revenues were 18.8 per cent of potential GNP, up only 0.2 per cent from 1966; expenditures, on the other hand, rose from 19.5 to 20.8 per cent, largely due to the uncontrollable spending on the Vietnam war. What was required in 1967 did not take place until 1969 when receipts rose by one percentage point of potential GNP and expenditures fell by one percentage point.

REMOVING THE BURDEN OF THE DEBT

In 1963 Robert Heilbroner and Peter Bernstein published *A Primer on Government Spending*, a book that argued as strenuously as the Council against the critics of deficit spending. In fact Heller provided the President with a concise review and suggested (K40), "If you should be asked publicly about this book, I'd be in favor of an endorsement, not unqualified, but sympathetic, both to the basic arguments and to the book as a major contribution to the dialogue on economic policy."

The Distinction Between Private and Public Debt

Contrary to the traditional fear that any debt, whether individual or government, was a sure sign of irresponsible behavior, Heilbroner and Bernstein wanted to create a fundamental difference between private and public debt. They began by characterizing consumer and business borrowing. "In the consumer 'sector' total debt rises steadily, a fact that appears less alarming when we remember that it is only an indication that consumer-owned wealth is also rising" (p. 52). The implication is that consumers are purchasing capital equipment (i.e., houses, cars, refrigerators) that will produce services over time. The increased debt is matched by the increase in capital assets, but net wealth for the consumer sector remains constant. Consumer debt is just one alternative of many possible financing decisions; another one would be to rent the capital on a pay-as-you-go basis, in which case there is no accumulation of debt or assets.

The argument is carried forward to the business sector where the example of two esteemed corporations, A.T. & T. and Consolidated Edison is used. After showing that debt increased five-fold between 1929 and 1962 for both companies, they ask rhetorically (p. 54):

> Can an individual business carry its debt forever, *never* paying them back? If its earning power remains high enough to cover the interest payments and if the bond-buying public continues to trust its future prospects, there is no reason why a corporation debt cannot be carried indefinitely. There is no prospect of A.T. & T. or Consolidated Edison repaying their debt in the foreseeable future — a fact that in no wise weakens public confidence in these well-managed companies.

What is not specified as a condition of debt-carrying capacity of these firms is that they use the proceeds of the loans to buy productive capital that will generate additional income to service the debt. If instead the firms built monuments to their founders or otherwise squandered the funds, they would not be able to pay the interest on their loans and they would, in due course, become bankrupt. Again the debt is only a burden if its earning assets do not increase to the same extent. The point at issue is the productivity of the debt. If the additional debt is not translated into extra productive capital, profits could decline even if the marginal product of capital exceeds the interest rate.

The federal government differs from individuals and corporations, according to Heilbroner and Bernstein, in its ability to expropriate private income or wealth through the power to tax. They rely on the following line of reasoning to show this difference (pp. 55–6, emphasis in original):

> Can we think about the problem of government borrowing as if the United States Government were in fact a gigantic business? The image may help us comprehend certain aspects of spending and borrowing, but we must realize how enormously more powerful the government is than any business, of no matter what size. A business — even a legal monopoly like A.T. & T. — is never *sure* of its income ... [I]t is always conceivable that any business will not be able to enjoy its income, and will therefore be unable to take care of the interest on its debt. Can this happen to a national government? We have but to think the problem through to see the difference — a difference of kind and not merely of degree — that separates governmental economic power and business economic power. A business obtains its income by selling its wares — that is by *persuading* some people to give it a part of their incomes. A government derives its income by taxing people — that is by levying a *compulsory* charge on their incomes, property, or purchases.

Hence as long as the government retains the sovereign power to tax, it can always depend on receiving the income it needs to pay its interest.

But a government need not inflict pain on its citizens by invoking this sovereign power to tax because the debt that is created by deficit spending does not involve an economic burden. The "we-owe-it-to-ourselves" view of government bonds is enunciated by Heilbroner and Bernstein at this stage (p. 58): "There would be no trouble in paying the interest. The government would tax each family $25,000 and then immediately turn around and pay each family $25,000 in interest. No one would be worse off, and the debt of gigantic size could be effortlessly serviced." However reversing the sequence of events proposed by Heilbroner and Bernstein identifies the impossibility of such a scheme. If a family is first paid the $25,000 in interest and then taxed $25,000, the after-tax rate of return is automatically zero. No one would want to hold a government bond unless the after-tax "reward" exceeded the rate of time preference to compensate for consumption postponement. The only way that government debt can compete for a place in private portfolios is to pay the same positive after-tax rate of return as the next-best alternative asset, which requires that interest receipts exceed tax liabilities. Heilbroner and Bernstein, of course, do not suggest how the government will raise these extra funds for this purpose. If public finance were really as simple as they assert one wonders whether they had any limits in mind on the government debt. In fact why bother to collect any taxes at all? The interest could be paid out of new bond issues which are eagerly sought by the public, "being as near to cash as a security can be and yet pay the holder a reward (interest)." (p. 60).

The authors fail to explain that governments that issue debt and do not create additional capital will be technically bankrupt, just as any business would be. For them, "the question of whether government spending is today a burden or a stimulus depends on whether or not the American economy is operating at something like full employment and capacity." (p. 90). To see the short-sightedness and naivety of this proposition, let us consider an experiment that follows their requirements and analyze its long-term impact.

If a government has had a balanced budget in the past, but then decides to rely on a temporary deficit to reduce unemployment, it will now have a publicly-owned debt on which it must pay interest. If the budget were to move to a *surplus* the following year, the debt could be repaid and there would be no long-run consequences to this countercyclical policy choice. This action merely represents a one-period time-shifting of government demand for goods and services to counter the opposite movement of private demand and in the process smooth out the path of employment. On the other hand if the subsequent budgets are now *balanced*, the debt will be permanent and according to equation (6.4), this requires either a higher τ or a lower g in perpetuity in order to pay the interest. The current tax payers were not the beneficiaries of the extra employment made possible by the deficit spending, but they will now have reduced public-goods availability or they will have higher taxes which eliminates some private consumption. In either case they bear the burden of the debt because $s^* < 0$ in one period is not offset by $s^* > 0$ in the subsequent period. In other words this choice represents an intergenerational time-shifting of public spending: the first generation gains at the expense of the second. In this context government debt can hardly be considered harmless or even a Pareto improvement as Heilbroner and Bernstein assert.

The burden of the debt would also be eliminated if the government increased the capital stock of the country with its deficit finance. In that case there is additional income to tax that would cover the higher interest payments. Nevertheless this argument makes the government behave like a private corporation, a position that Heilbroner and Bernstein would not support. They write (p. 63, emphasis in original):

> The government does not, by convention of accounting, issue its bonds against stated assets, as a company might. As a result, the holder of $10,000 worth of Series H Savings Bonds or of $100,000 worth of Treasury $2\,^1/_2$s does not have a lien on a PT boat or on a section of U.S. Highway 914 or of a veteran's hospital or a housing project. He might feel better if he did, but it would make no real difference. For what the bonds really promise us is that we have a claim on the Treasury of the Government of the United States for so-and-so many years of interest, and thereafter for the face value of the bond. We will get the interest paid to us, not only because the full power of the government is prepared to see to it that its obligation is honored, but because the very same national community will be both paying the taxes which pay the interest, *and* receiving those taxes back again *as* interest.

They are not concerned with the productivity of deficit spending, only with providing extra aggregate demand in the economy. Government debt may add to the demand for output through deficit spending, but it does not add to the supply of output; only real capital goods can do that. Debt does not make the economy more productive, but if it results in less capital formation it can make it less productive. If government debt that is not backed by additions to the capital stock, competes for a place in private portfolios with corporate debt, it will raise interest rates and reduce private capital formation. In the short run deficit financing can help the economy move to potential output but in the long run it will reduce the growth rate of that potential output. Governments do have some choice in this matter; they can raise tax rates now and eliminate deficits or they can raise them in the future to prevent the erosion of the economy's growth. As was shown earlier the larger is the accumulated value of b, the higher is the tax rate needed to stabilize b; thus postponement itself creates a burden.

The Evolution of the Debt Ratio and the Tax Rate

The difficulty is that Heilbroner and Bernstein treat the debt–income ratio as a historical fact instead of a welfare-influencing choice. At any point in time, b is the value of accumulated deficits irrespective of what happened to the resources that the government spent. If the government now faces a choice between raising τ or letting b increase it will find it easier to follow the second choice since the alternative has immediate political costs as we will discover shortly. If, on the other hand, there existed a strong argument in favor of an optimal value of b, with clear and undesirable welfare implications for both positive and negative departures from this value, the current trade-off between these variables would be more apparent. This can be seen with the aid of Figure 6.1.

The budget constraint of equation (6.3′) and the equilibrium tax-rate equation (6.4) represent two relationships between b and τ that are plotted in Figure 6.1. To the left of the latter constraint, there exists a budget deficit and to the right, there must be a surplus. In addition let us assume an intertemporal utility function of the simple form:

$$U = U(C_0, C_1) = U(\tau, b), \qquad (6.5)$$

where C_0 and C_1 are current and future consumption. Utility decreases with τ because it reduces current private consumption and with b since it restricts private capital formation and hence future consumption. Therefore an indifference curve is drawn as concave from below.

Starting from a balanced budget at E, utility can be increased by moving to A where U_0 is tangent to the short-run constraint. This allows for a lower tax rate, τ_0 instead of τ^*, and the debt ratio rises from b^* to b_0 because of the deficit. But this position cannot be sustained. The increase in b will now cause the budget constraint to shift outward in the next period, more on the vertical axis than on the horizontal axis. As a consequence the new choice will involve a lower level of welfare at B (i.e., $U_0 > U_1$) and this process will continue until a tax rate is chosen that lies on the $b = b_{-1}$ constraint. Alternatively, if the original choice of b^* and τ^* had been continued, this would be consistent with long-run equilibrium as $s = 0$. The tangency at A, instead of at E, implies that the public or its political representatives have a high rate of time

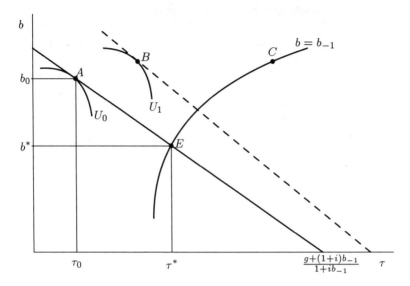

Figure 6.1   Choosing b and τ

preference which translates into a low marginal disutility of debt. This can be seen by the fact that an indifference curve drawn through E (not shown) would be steeper than the budget constraint of equation (6.3′) and that the "optimal" choice at A was made so as to reduce the tax rate and increase current consumption at the expense of a higher debt ratio and lower future consumption. Despite the lack of tangency at E, this is a better long-term choice than A which must lead ultimately to a position such as C. The crux of the problem is that the trade-off between b and $τ$ may be negative in the short run, but in the long run, tax rates and debt ratios will both have to increase as long as $s < 0$. The temptation to prefer A over E is another instance of choices that are not consistent over time, but it is perfectly plausible if the move to C can be postponed until the next generation.[3]

The Power To Tax

Heilbroner and Bernstein give governments "the sovereign power to tax," but they do not indicate an optimal tax rate, nor do they discuss how

---

[3] The analysis in Figure 6.1 is limited to a fixed value of g because it is not incorporated into the utility function of equation (6.5). If g rises it shifts the short-run budget constraint outward and would appear to make taxpayers worse off, but this is not necessarily the case.

it should be determined to help their countercyclical policies. From the discussion above it appears sensible to choose τ^* as the tax rate that will keep $s = 0$; this still allows for lower taxes during a recession and higher taxes during a boom period, as long as the average is τ^* during a business cycle. While they acknowledge the need to raise taxes during an inflationary period (p. 70), there is no mention of the need for symmetry around τ^*. Moreover they stress the legislative powers rather than the political constraints on taxation. The sixteenth amendment to the Constitution, ratified in February 1913, gave Congress almost unlimited and unfettered authority to tax incomes. However, the ability to introduce new taxes or to change old ones depends less on its constitutional powers than on its assessment of the mood of the country. Legislators know instinctively that taxes are treated as a burden by the electorate and given the shortness of the election cycle, Congressional reluctance to raise taxes while allowing debt to accumulate is the predictable outcome. That is why position A in Figure 6.1 is chosen over E at almost any time in the business cycle; the burden of the debt is difficult to quantify and far in the future. In fact Heilbroner and Bernstein convinced a generation of Americans that there was nothing to worry about. They soothed the skeptic with, "Government borrowing is demand-creating whether or not it is ticketed against asset-creating expenditure or merely against office pay. It is perhaps a curious way of arranging things, but if the process of business-demand creation is insufficient, there is no other way to avoid unemployment." (p. 64).

In 1966 when unemployment had been reduced and inflation began to accelerate, there was no countervailing argument that current aggregate demand by the private sector was excessive and that governments should eliminate or reverse their borrowing. As far as one can tell, Heilbroner and Bernstein did not write to President Johnson or to Congressman Mills to convince them that taxes should be raised and that deficits were damaging to the economy. They did not appear at Congressional hearings to argue that the macroeconomy required contractionary fiscal policy to stem inflation.[4] In fact, Heilbroner and Bernstein anticipated the inflation problem and convinced themselves that until 1962 there had been "absolutely no systematic relationship between government deficits and changes in the price level." (p. 67). Again one can see a lack of symmetry in their position: a strong Keynesian link between fiscal policy and the elimination of unemployment, but no effect of deficits on

---

[4] As late as 1974, Heilbroner did not seem to be concerned about budget deficits. In an American Economic Association session on "Major Economic Problems," he avoids any mention of the subject.

inflation. Despite Okun's popularization of the potential-output concept as a balance point in the macroeconomy and the CEA's emphasis on eliminating any output gap, policy makers and advisers seemed always to concentrate on the dangers of too little aggregate demand, never on the perils of too much demand. In the process the need for a fiscal surplus to offset previous deficits ceased being a constraint and the accumulation of debt began in earnest.

In 1963 Heilbroner and Bernstein seemed completely oblivious to the possibility that their argument was built on a foundation of quicksand. On the one hand, they eliminated any burden of the debt so that the debt ratio, b, was immaterial to the welfare of the country. On the other hand, they emphasized the sovereign power of the government to set any tax rate that it chose, eliminating any optimality condition for τ. In the process they allowed governments to escape their current budget constraint, without realizing that the intertemporal constraint became even more binding.

Comparing Required and Actual Tax Rates

In spite of the lack of any mention of optimality of tax rates in the Heilbroner–Bernstein book, it is a useful retrospective exercise to calculate the tax rate that would be needed to have a balanced budget in any one year and to compare this to the tax rate that actually prevailed. The former is labelled τ^* and is calculated according to equation (6.4) assuming that g has been optimally chosen. The numerator is total federal "high-employment" expenditures as a proportion of potential GNP, taken from deLeeuw *et al.* (1980, p. 24); in the denominator ib_{-1} is measured as the ratio of "net interest payments" from the 1980 *Economic Report of the President*, Table B-73, divided by the nominal value of potential output from deLeeuw *et al.* (Table 1). The actual tax rate, τ, is taken as the high-employment receipts by the federal government (Table 3), divided by potential output, to eliminate the cyclical aspects of tax collections. These two tax rates are shown for the calendar years 1955–79 in Chart 6.3.

Again the focus of our attention is on the years 1963–68 although the longer time period is displayed for historical perspective. If τ^* is consistently greater than τ, this would be an indication that deficits are tolerated at full employment and vice versa. There are no countercyclical implications to variations in either τ^* or τ since all magnitudes are evaluated at potential GNP. Thus changes in τ reflect the need to finance a given value of g and to pay interest on the accumulated debt, ib_{-1}. If $\tau < \tau^*$, b will rise over time since revenues are inadequate to pay for

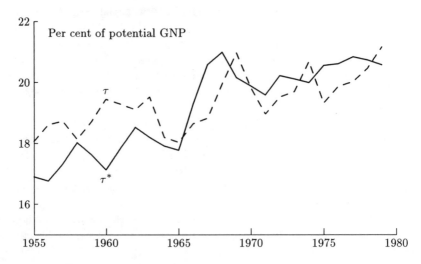

Sources: deLeeuw *et al.* (1980, Table 1 and Table 3) and *Economic Report of the President* (1980, Table B-73).

Chart 6.3   Calculations of τ^* and τ, 1955–79

government programs and to service the debt.

Perhaps surprisingly there is no indication of this fiscal stance; in fact, for 1955–79, the mean value of τ is 19.35 per cent, while for τ^* it is 19.13 per cent indicating that b should be lower at the end of the period than at the beginning.[5] From 1955, when the gross federal debt held by the public was 58.9 per cent of GNP, this ratio fell to 26.4 per cent in 1979. Nevertheless, in the crucial period of 1965–68, τ is substantially lower than τ^*. In 1967, when the output gap was clearly negative and contractionary fiscal policy should have dictated a tax rate considerably above τ^*, we find that $\tau = 18.28$ per cent, while $\tau^* = 20.58$ per cent. This gap is another indication of the asymmetrical fiscal policy that the Kennedy–Johnson Council tolerated. While the deficits of 1964–65 were required to eliminate the positive output gap, there should have been surpluses in 1966–67 that would have allowed the interest burden of the debt to remain constant from one business cycle to the next. Instead, between 1963 and 1967, ib_{-1} increased from 1.12 to 1.25 per cent. While this change may appear as miniscule and undeserving of attention, the

---

[5] It was only in the late 1970s and 1980s that τ was consistently less than τ^*. For example, in 1987 $\tau = 20.2$ per cent while $\tau^* = 23.2$ per cent. (Data are from *Survey of Current Business*, August 1988, Table 3, p. 20.)

inexorable growth of the debt burden started from small beginnings in the 1960s; by 1995, it had tripled to 3.32 per cent.

Government Capital Accumulation

An additional acceptable reason for deficit finance is that capital equipment with a long service life is being bought with the bonds that are issued to cover its cost. Then the government either leases the capital to the private sector, as it might in the case of airports or toll roads, or it taxes the extra income that is available from increased private productivity as would happen with educational expenditures. In either case the additional revenue would have to cover the interest payments on the debt and its amortization.

Data for government capital stocks are shown in Table 6.1 for the period 1963–68. While military hardware, both equipment and structures, dominate the net stock of government capital, there is no reason to exclude them if they contribute to the security and productivity of the country. It can be seen that the growth rate of the total capital stock slows down from about 2 per cent in 1964 to virtually zero in 1968 and this growth rate is substantially below that for total capital shown in Chart 2.3. On the basis of this evidence one cannot argue that government capital accumulation through deficit finance is an engine of economic growth in the late 1960s. Moreover, comparing the absolute increase in the capital stock (i.e., second last line) with the full-employment deficit (last line), also measured in millions of 1972 dollars, shows that they move in opposite directions instead of together. Again there is no evidence that the bonds issued by the government to cover the deficits of 1966–68 were at all related to capital accumulation.

What Heilbroner and Bernstein failed to realize is that the bondholder feels more confident if government assets are used to back the bond because one can then judge whether the productivity of a PT boat will be sufficient to pay the interest on the loan. In the absence of income growth derived from capital accumulation, future citizens are burdened by higher tax rates or lower government services. The "national community" that pays the taxes to service the debt is not the same that received the benefits of deficit finance and it is a false hope to rely on the taxation power of the government to pay its interest obligations. By claiming that increased transfers within the nation make everyone better off, Heilbroner and Bernstein soothed potential critics but ultimately their argument remained unconvincing.

Table 6.1   Net stock of fixed Federal Government capital, 1963–68

Year	1963	1964	1965	1966	1967	1968
	millions of 1972 dollars, end of year					
Equipment						
excluding military	16,487	17,092	18,209	19,534	20,025	20,193
military	80,016	81,372	81,393	82,085	81,562	81,223
Structures						
industrial buildings	15,750	15,336	14,862	14,442	14,031	13,867
educational buildings	461	484	491	494	510	513
hospital buildings	1,977	2,077	2,199	2,324	2,391	2,412
other buildings	5,182	6,091	7,057	7,784	8,107	8,250
highways & streets	3,151	3,343	3,515	3,783	4,028	4,239
military facilities	42,956	42,896	42,669	42,236	41,711	41,286
conservation and						
development struct	33,903	35,101	36,393	37,810	38,862	39,626
other	1,364	1,404	1,434	1,456	1,481	1,472
Privately-operated						
capital, all industries	14,068	14,257	14,316	14,664	14,668	14,435
Total	215,315	219,453	222,538	226,612	227,376	227,516
Percentage change		1.92	1.41	1.83	0.34	0.06
Absolute increase		4,138	3,085	4,074	764	140
Addendum:						
full-employment deficit	−9,498	−550	−538	8,468	20,248	13,685

Sources: US Department of Commerce (1982, pp. 366–75, 384), deLeeuw *et al.* (1980, Table 3), and US Department of Commerce (1977, Table 7.1).

The Crowding-out Counterargument

In the same year that the Heilbroner–Bernstein book was published, the Joint Economic Committee held hearings on the proposed tax cut and issued the 1963 *Joint Economic Report*. Much of that material was summarized and quoted in Chapter 3. Of interest here is the fact that the "Minority Views" made predictions that, in retrospect, could be interpreted as conforming with the idea of fiscal deficits "crowding out" private demand, expressly because of the burden of the debt.

The Republicans on the Committee were concerned about the long-term effects of a prolonged budget deficit. They predicted (p. 82):

[I]f the deficit is largely financed out of savings, with the new Government securities sold to individuals and nonbanking institutions, such as insurance companies, the effect would be an increase in interest rates above what they would have been without the Federal deficit ... Since a rapid rate of economic growth requires a high level of private investment, growth is slowed when high interest rates deter investment and when savings are drawn off to finance Federal deficits rather than investment.

In terms of an *IS–LM* model, the rightward shift of the *IS* curve caused by the deficit spending will raise interest rates and reduce investment to an extent determined by the slope of the *LM* curve. In the long run the reduction in private investment which is not replaced by government capital formation will reduce future economic growth.

The minority on the Joint Economic Committee was also concerned about the possible sale of the new bonds to the Federal Reserve and its inflationary consequences. They worried that "Not one administration spokesman before the committee has given any evidence that the financing of deficits will not result in increases in money supply more rapid than the increases in gross national product." (p. 83). This reduced velocity of money implies that not only is the *IS* curve shifting upwards, but that the *LM* curve is also shifting to the right, making the tax cut more expansionary than would have been the case without monetary accommodation.

Theodore Yntema, who testified at the hearings and who is quoted in the minority report, anticipated the need for budgetary symmetry that is at the heart of the argument made in this chapter. He urged, "not being satisfied merely to balance the budget at high employment but to seek a surplus, which will retire public debt and in so doing add to the funds available for private investment." (p. 82).

CONCLUSION

Walter Heller's proposal to generate deliberate budget deficits during a recession was an essential component of a successful countercyclical fiscal policy. If this had been accompanied by a symmetrical requirement for a surplus during a boom period, the long-term gains to macroeconomic stability would have been substantial, at least in my view. Instead he and popularizers such as Heilbroner and Bernstein chose to concentrate on the short-run relationship between the budget and total aggregate demand while forgetting the long-run relationship between the federal debt and economic growth. They ridiculed their more "old-fashioned" opponents, who were concerned about this burden of the debt. We saw earlier that the Council of Economic Advisers had a bias in favor of stimulative action; they could hardly convince themselves in 1966–67 that restrictive action was called for. This bias is also expressed in the threat of fiscal drag and the propaganda that the debt merely represented an internal and inconsequential transfer payment between taxpayers and interest recipients. In the process they lowered the quality of budgetary debates at a time when useful improvements could have been made in stabilization policy.

This was another missed opportunity. If the budget had been balanced over the entire business cycle of the late 1960s, it would have made it less likely that the immense and pointless deficits of the 1970s and 1980s would have been tolerated. In turn the lower servicing costs of the debt would have made it possible to have more decisive fiscal intervention in the recessions of 1982 and 1990. Instead the tax rate needed to balance the budget became higher and higher which made it politically less and less possible to implement.

7

Taxes and Voter Welfare

The tax rate on personal and corporate income was the preferred instrument of the Kennedy–Johnson Council of Economic Advisers to adjust aggregate demand to potential output. However, taxes play at least two other roles in an economy: they help to determine the budget balance and they influence directly the welfare of those who are taxed. Chapter 6 dealt with the budgetary effects of taxes; this chapter will concentrate on the role of taxes in the determination of voter welfare. In a democratic process, predicting whether tax rates that are "optimal" are in fact legislated is crucial in a policy context. The gist of the argument here is that there is virtually no correspondence between macroeconomic optimality and political feasibility because of the difficulty in linking voter preferences and legislative outcomes. By concentrating on aggregates or on the "representative agent," optimal choices derived from macroeconomic theory involve economy-wide goals such as full employment, consistent with equilibrium in the labor market. Nevertheless the concept of equilibrium is of no personal interest to the millions of people who either have jobs or who are not looking for one. Therefore politicians have very little reason to understand the notion of optimility; to them the profile of the electorate is crucial. If they do little else but count votes and follow the dictates of the "median voter," the needs of the representative agent will have to be sacrificed. In this chapter an attempt is made to understand why the representative agent and the median voter do not coincide.

The 1964 tax cut was primarily a response to a macroeconomic problem; the Council of Economic Advisers did not concern itself too much with the microeconomic considerations of taxes as distortions or welfare indicators. Although reforming the tax code to make it fairer was of almost equal importance as tax reduction in the preliminary discussions, the Council must have realized that a tax system that was perceived as "fair" by a majority of citizens was virtually impossible to design. Their experience in 1961–62 with the reform of business taxes, as chronicled by Stein (1996a, pp. 390–91), which resulted in the passage of the revenue-losing part of the proposal but not the revenue-raising part, gave them early warning of effective opposition based on self-interest of powerful groups in the economy.

TAXES AND INDIVIDUAL WORKER WELFARE

Although taxes are pervasive in a modern economy, a general-equilibrium approach is avoided here by concentrating on income taxes and their role in labor-supply decisions. Corporate taxes and their effects on investment are much more complicated; they played a role in the macro-economic predictions on aggregate demand and cannot be forgotten, but looking only at the effect of taxes on wage income does involve about 70 million workers and their families in 1963–68.

Taxes and Labor Supply

A person consumes both goods and leisure and a typical utility function takes the form:

$$U(L, C) = U(T - H, C), \tag{7.1}$$

where L is leisure available after the person works H hours out of a total of T and C represents the consumption of a basket of goods and services. The person maximizes this utility function subject to the budget constraint:

$$C = W(1 - \tau)H + Z(1 - \tau), \tag{7.2}$$

where W is the nominal and real wage rate per hour of work with the price level constrained to unity, τ is the tax rate so that $W(1 - \tau)$ is the after-tax purchasing power of one hour of work. Also Z represents nonwage income which is taxed at the rate τ. Substituting (7.2) into (7.1), differentiating with respect to H, the variable under the control of the individual, setting the result equal to zero, provides us with the first-order condition:

$$W(1 - \tau) = \frac{U_1}{U_2}\Big[H, Z(1 - \tau)\Big], \tag{7.3}$$

where U_1 is the marginal utility of leisure or the marginal disutility of work and U_2 is the marginal utility of goods consumption; both are positive but depend on values of L and C, which in turn are determined by H and $Z(1 - \tau)$. Since $\ln W(1 - \tau)$ can be approximated by $w - \tau$

and $\ln Z(1 - \tau)$ by $z - \tau$, with w and z as the natural-log counterparts of the upper-case letters, equation (7.3) can be converted to:

$$w - \tau = \frac{1}{e_1}h + e_2(z - \tau),$$

where $1/e_1$ is the elasticity of U_1/U_2 with respect to hours worked and e_2 is the elasticity of U_1/U_2 with respect to after-tax, nonwage income. The former is likely to be positive; as hours of work rise, the marginal utility of leisure increases and the marginal utility of goods consumption falls. On the other hand e_2 may be positive or negative. If both C and L are normal goods, an increase in nonwage income will lead to more of both being consumed which would reduce U_1 and U_2. If the two marginal utilities fall in the same proportion $e_2 = 0$; if not the sign of e_2 is indeterminate. By re-arranging terms, the first-order condition becomes a labor-supply curve for each individual:

$$h = e_1(w - \tau) - e_1 e_2(z - \tau), \qquad (7.4)$$

which indicates that hours of work will increase with the after-tax real wage but will decline if other resources increase, as long as $e_2 > 0$.

The relationship between h and τ from equation (7.4) is plotted in Figure 7.1. It is negatively sloped on the assumption that $e_2 < 1$. The purpose of this diagram is to show the effect of tax rates on the individual's welfare. At τ_0, this person's consumer surplus is the triangle above τ_0 inside the supply curve. It is immediately obvious that lowering the tax rate increases welfare and that the individually optimal tax rate is zero. Moreover any positive tax is distortionary; it increases the marginal utility of leisure and causes individuals to supply fewer hours of work. Alternatively viewed, the tax drives a wedge between the marginal product of an hour's work and the marginal disutility of that hour for the worker; reducing the tax makes that wedge smaller and increases the hours of work exchanged in the labor market.

The distortionary element of the tax is eliminated if the reservation-wage model is considered to be more appropriate. Based on evidence from the Current Population Survey and other sources, it is argued (Prachowny, 1997, Chapter 1) that individuals have very little choice about the hours that they work and that they make an all-or-nothing decision based on fixed $\bar{H}$ hours that they are offered. The reservation wage is found as the point of indifference between working $\bar{H}$ hours and not working at all, according to the following equal-utility constraint:

$$U\left[T - \bar{H}, W_r\bar{H} + Z(1 - \tau)\right] = U\left[T, Z(1 - \tau)\right]. \qquad (7.5)$$

The reservation wage, W_r, is the variable that solves the constraint in equation (7.5). If the actual wage exceeds W_r, the person will want to

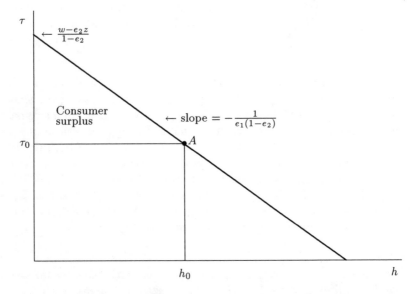

Figure 7.1   Taxes and welfare

work, but not otherwise. The reservation wage will depend on a number of factors found by differentiating equation (7.5) and solving for dW_r in terms of $d\bar{H}$ and dZ: (1) an increase in fixed hours will lead to a higher reservation wage and (2) an increase in nonwage income will lead to a higher reservation wage as long as there is declining marginal utility of goods consumption.

The individual labor-supply decision conforms to the following requirements:

$$H = \begin{cases} \bar{H}, & \text{if } W > W_r, \\ 0, & \text{if } W < W_r, \\ \text{either } \bar{H}\text{ or } 0, & \text{if } W = W_r. \end{cases} \qquad (7.6)$$

In Figure 7.1 the supply curve would become vertical at $h = \bar{h}$ for those who have made a positive supply decision and for them the distortionary effect of the tax is removed; for the other group, $h = -\infty$ which cannot be plotted in Figure 7.1. Moreover the consumer surplus at any tax rate becomes undefined and it is more useful to concentrate on the relationship between tax rates and economic rents, since the tax does not cause one to alter the labor-market decision. Raising the tax rate reduces the rents available from working fixed hours as less of the earned income will support lower goods consumption. In a unified and otherwise homogeneous labor market, everyone receives the same real wage but individuals will differ with respect to their reservation wages. The difference between actual and reservation wages represents economic rents for each employed person.

For the economy as a whole, a higher tax rate lowers the after-tax real wage, $W(1-\tau)$, and creates three groups: (1) those whose after-tax wage remains above their reservation wage, (2) those whose after-tax wage now falls below their reservation wage and (3) those whose after-tax wage was previously below their reservation wage. The first and the third groups will not alter their decisions about labor-force participation and for them the tax increase is not distortionary. The second group will now withdraw from the labor force; hence the tax distorts their decisions in the labor market. On the other hand only the third group does not suffer a loss of welfare since they earn no wages on which to pay taxes.

If the tax on nonwage income is also increased, some individuals will have the inequality between reservation wages and after-tax real wages change to the opposite inequality and their labor-market decisions are also distorted by the tax; moreover some in the third group whose welfare was previously unaffected, will now have lower utility. Overall, income taxes are distortionary for only a small group of individuals who change their participation decision, but the welfare effects of higher taxes are widespread.

The Need to Finance Public Goods

To this point the discussion has not provided a motive for raising taxes in the first place, which would presumably be to finance the provision of public goods. Public goods can replace leisure in the utility function, which is now fixed at either $T - \bar{H}$ or T hours. The standard technique to determine optimality in this environment is to focus on the utility of person 1, holding the utility of all other individuals constant. Thus:

$$\max U_1(C_1, G),$$

subject to

$$U_i(C_i, G) = \bar{U}_i, \quad i \neq 1 \quad \text{and} \quad C_1 + \sum_{i=2}^{n} C_i + q(G) = Z'_1 + \sum_{i=2}^{n} Z'_i,$$

where $q(G)$ represents the cost function of the provision of the public good and $Z' = Z + W\bar{H}$. The "Samuelson condition" that must be satisfied is given by:

$$\frac{U_{C_1}}{U_G} + \sum_{i=2}^{n} \frac{U_{C_i}}{U_G} - \frac{dq}{dG}, \tag{7.7}$$

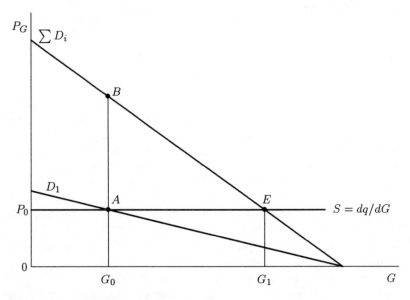

Figure 7.2   Public-goods determination

or the sum of the marginal rates of substitution must equal the marginal cost of the public good. If the former exceeds the latter, this is a signal to increase the amount of the public good and vice versa.

Most of the public-goods literature concentrates on the market failure and free-rider problem that arise in this area. Since voluntary contributions are unlikely to pay for the Pareto-efficient amount of G, the state imposes taxes to reach this equilibrium. The difference between private demand for public goods and the social optimum is shown in Figure 7.2, where D_1 represents the demand for public goods by the first individual based on the fact that U_{C_1}/U_G in equation (7.7) is likely to fall as the quantity G increases. The "total" demand curve, $\sum D_i$, is derived by summing individual demand curves *vertically* to conform to the Samuelson condition. If, for simplicity, public goods are produced at constant cost, the supply curve is horizontal and the price will be P_0 at any level. Individuals would choose the quantity G_0 voluntarily, but there is a positive gap between the social valuation of public goods at B and their private valuation at A. The total cost of G_0 is the rectangle $P_0 A G_0 0$ and if all individuals were the same, each person would pay $1/n$ of that amount. One of the few ways to reach E, which provides the socially optimal G_1, is to force individuals to pay taxes but since people now substitute tax-financed G for privately provided public goods, tax revenue must equal $P_0 EG_1 0$, not just $AEG_1 G_0$. If these taxes are based on labor income and if individuals are unable to adjust their hours of work, the distortionary effect is small and only affects those workers at the extensive margin of employment.

UNEMPLOYMENT AS A PUBLIC GOOD

The primary reason for the Kennedy–Johnson tax cut in 1964 was to deal with involuntary unemployment; by increasing aggregate demand to potential GNP, the unemployment rate would be cut to 4 per cent. Being unemployed imposes private costs on those who are unemployed but the public-goods aspect of this intervention is more difficult to identify. First we can summarize the welfare effects of unemployment and then move on to the spillover effects that Okun (1962; 1970) identified, but failed to exploit in defense of countercyclical fiscal policy.

Unemployment and Welfare

The difference between welfare for an employed person and for an involuntarily unemployed person must be positive if the term "involuntary" is to have any meaning. The comparison is between utility at $H = 0$ and utility at $H = \bar{H}$; thus the reservation-wage model of labor-force participation is appropriate here and according to equation (7.5):

$$U(T - \bar{H}, W\bar{H} + Z) > U(T, Z'), \qquad (7.8)$$

where Z' includes unemployment insurance payments in addition to other nonwage income. That is, the loss of consumption goods when a person is unemployed is not compensated by the gain in leisure. In turn this implies that the loss of wage income, $W\bar{H}$, is greater than the unemployment insurance payments, $Z' - Z$.

This loss of welfare is not a justification for government intervention, since insurance markets can cope with situations that involve both "good states" and "bad states" as long as their probability is known. Each participant in the insurance program pays a premium in the good state and receives a payment in the bad state. The "fair" premium for full insurance is based on the ratio of probabilities of the two events. However, any unemployment insurance scheme that attempted to keep utility at $H = 0$ the same as at $H = \bar{H}$ would suffer from moral hazard as everyone would have an incentive to be unemployed. For that reason alone unemployment-insurance programs have "replacement ratios" that are less than one, or $W\bar{H} > Z' - Z$. Nevertheless this leaves those who are truly involuntarily unemployed to bear the burden of insufficient aggregate demand, while those who remain employed are unaffected.

Okun's Spillover Effects

If business cycles cause unemployment to vary, the impetus to use countercyclical policies should be based on an equity argument that it would be unfair for a small group of individuals to carry the burden of these cycles. But such an equity argument requires majority support. Because unemployment is concentrated in a small minority, it is difficult to see how the majority would support programs to relieve this burden. Nevertheless Arthur Okun, in the celebrated presentation of his Law, pointed out that there are efficiency gains as well from government intervention in business cycles. He wrote:

> If programs to lower unemployment from $5\frac{1}{2}$ to 4 percent of the labor force are viewed as attempts to raise the economy's grade from $94\frac{1}{2}$ to 96, the case for them may not seem compelling. Focus on the [output] gap helps to remind policymakers of the large reward [in terms of extra output] associated with such an improvmement. (1962; 1970, p. 314)

> Clearly, the simple addition of 1 percent of a given labor force to the ranks of the employed would increase employment by only slightly more than 1 percent ... If the work-week and productivity were unchanged, the increment to output would be only that 1+ percent. [This implies a constant marginal product of labor, which is not consistent with most production functions.] The 3 percent result implies that considerable output gains in a period of rising utilization rates stem from some or all of the following: induced increases in the size of the labor force; longer average weekly hours; and greater productivity. (p. 319)

> [A] 1 percentage point reduction in the unemployment rate ... will also be accompanied by an increase of nearly one half of 1 percent in hours per man, or an addition of about 0.2 of an hour per workweek. With an allowance for induced gains in the labor force [of 1.3 per cent] ... manhour productivity must rise by 1.4 percent. (p. 320)

These productivity improvements represent spillover effects of reducing unemployment. Not only do the unemployed get jobs and higher utility, but everyone else can benefit by being more productive without using more capital or putting in longer hours. This feature of the US labor market was discussed previously in Chapter 2, in connection with an estimated labor-demand curve. Deviations from the estimated line, shown in Chart 2.4, tended to be cyclical, with points below the line during recessions. This suggests re-estimating equation (2.6) as:

$$n = \gamma_0 + \gamma_1 k - \gamma_2 w + \gamma_3 (u - u_e), \tag{7.9}$$

where n, k, w are natural logs of employment, the capital stock and the real weekly wage. (See p. 37 for data sources.) Added here is the difference between the unemployment rate (LHUR in CITIBASE) and Gordon's (1993) natural rate of unemployment. If the coefficient γ_3 were equal to -0.01, this equation might be re-interpreted as a labor-supply curve since $n^s = n + 0.01u$. However, according to Okun's argument (1968; 1970, p. 321), lower unemployment makes all employees more productive by reducing average fixed costs of supervision and management, or by influencing other factors that overpower the normal declining marginal product of labor. This position was amplified by Diamond (J4), who pointed to the role of underemployed workers and of underutilized capital during a recession as well as to the "greater cyclic sensitivity of high productivity industries."

When estimated for the same time period, 1948–92, the new results were as follows: $\gamma_0 = 8.404$ instead of the previous value of 8.395, $\gamma_1 = 0.651$ instead of 0.637, $\gamma_2 = 0.452$ instead of 0.429 and $\gamma_3 = -0.0075$, which was not significantly different from -0.01. The prediction error for 1963, for example, falls from -0.0103 to -0.0052 and although residuals are still serially correlated, they are not as sensitive to cyclical factors. When re-written as a productivity-adjusted wage rate, the demand curve becomes:

$$w - 1.441k = 18.605 - 0.0166(u - u_e) - 2.214n. \qquad (7.10)$$

The implication is that as long as $u > u_e$ real wages could have been higher by about 1.66 per cent for every one percent reduction in the unemployment rate, which is very close to Okun's residual estimate of 1.4 per cent. In 1963 this would have entailed an increase in the real weekly wage from \$278.19 to \$282.83. That is, every *existing* worker would have had about \$5 a week more to spend if the unemployment rate had been 1 per cent lower. Alternatively a reduction in the unemployment rate by 1 per cent substitutes for 1.15 per cent of capital in maintaining the productivity of labor. By the same token, excess demand in the labor market (i.e., $u < u_e$) requires that wages be lower to accommodate further reductions in u. It is true, of course, that the wage rate and the capital stock did not adjust or it would have been impossible for $u - u_e$ to have an independent influence on the demand for labor. Nevertheless this improvement in productivity is available to some groups in the economy and they are the beneficiaries of the spillover effects of any attempt by the government to increase aggregate demand in a recession.

Although the quote from Okun makes clear that he understood the large benefits from applying his Law, it is surprising that the Council of Economic Advisers did not rely on this public-goods aspect of Okun's argument in selling their tax cut to Congress, union leaders and business groups. With the publication of Samuelson's celebrated article in 1954, by the early 1960s, the profession was fully aware of the spillover characteristics of public goods. Nevertheless the connection between widely-shared productivity increases from lower unemployment and optimal government intervention in the macroeconomy escaped the notice of the CEA who relied on other and weaker arguments to build a majority in favor of the tax cut.

Perhaps the difficulty was identifying the beneficiaries of the improved productivity. Since wages did not adjust to these productivity gains, labor unions would not have found this to be a compelling argument in favor of the tax cut. If profits of corporations increased, the business lobby would have given the tax cut a warmer welcome but it would have been difficult to establish a convincing empirical link between profits and unemployment rates. Finally, although it was possible that running the macroeconomy at a lower unemployment rate could have led to smaller capital-stock requirements while maintaining productivity, it would have been difficult if not impossible to link this with lower saving and higher consumption possibilities. Nevertheless it remains puzzling that Okun who was so influential in making potential output the lynchpin of the tax-cut proposal was unwilling or unable to convince the Council that it should rely on unemployment as a public "bad" to make the tax cut more appealing to the public.

The most comprehensive statement of the benefits of the tax cut made by the Council of Economic Advisers can be found in the 1963 *Economic Report of the President* but it contains nothing that could be construed as a belief in spillover effects. Although the tax cut promises to "strengthen incentives and expectations" (p. 45), the only way that labor productivity would increase is through larger investment expenditures. This would have been the opportunity for the Council to state that individual workers are unable to reduce unemployment in the economy as a whole and they cannot benefit from the operation of Okun's Law, but the government through expansionary fiscal policy can make most people better off by increasing everyone's productivity.

The irony is that if the Council was concerned with making the tax cut a Pareto improvement over the status quo ante, they did not have to rely on Okun's spillover effects to make their case. Since a tax cut increases almost everyone's welfare, it can stand on its own and does not require any reference to stimulation of aggregate demand or lowering of unemployment rates or the optimal provision of public goods. In 1963–64, if there had been a Gallup poll that asked the specific question: "Do you want *your* taxes reduced this year?" anyone who gave a negative answer would be suspected of irrationality or misunderstanding the question. But this approach to tax changes that relies only on voter appeal is myopically asymmetrical. Under different circumstances, such as in 1966–68, there may be well-founded macroeconomic reasons that require a tax increase but such a move will not appear to be a Pareto improvement when the vast majority experience a decline in their after-tax income. For these situations the spillover effects must be invoked to get the right response.

According to equation (7.10), eliminating a positive unemployment gap (i.e., $u > u_e$) would allow w to be higher for any given level of employment, but Okun did not spell out what would happen to productivity if the labor market moved to an unemployment rate below 4 per cent. He did warn of the inflation that might arise and indicated the need to find a balance point: "The full employment goal must be understood as striving for maximum production without inflationary pressure; or more precisely, as aiming for a point of balance between more output and greater [price?] stability, with appropriate regard for the social valuation of these two objectives." (1968; 1970, p. 314). In terms of spillover effects, when the economy is operating above potential GNP, most everyone experiences undesirable side-effects through higher unexpected inflation that cannot be incorporated into contracts and causes real wages to fall. Now each working individual, looking at the after-tax real wage, $W(1 - \tau)$, as one's welfare indicator, has to be convinced that an increase in τ is "better" than a decrease in W.

Tax Rates During a Business Cycle

It is critically important for the design of successful countercyclical fiscal policy that relies on variations in the tax rate to make voters and their representatives in Congress accept the need to have higher tax rates in a boom period. Since individualistic welfare is best served by low tax rates, regardless of the stage of the business cycle, the spillover effects discussed above must be incorporated into voter preferences.

What follows is a suggested analytical framework that could have appeared as a public statement by the Council in the early 1960s and would have produced the desired result: an electorate that favored procyclical tax rates. It relies on tools that were available in the 1960s: Henderson and Quandt (1958, pp. 23–4) for labor supply models and Perry (1966) for the Phillips curve. It also incorporates Okun's Law. It concentrates on the welfare calculations made by a worker who votes one's self-interest. Other individuals, with different characteristics (e.g.,

nonwage income or variable overtime hours) could be included at the
cost of a more complicated discussion. The worker has, by definition,
found a job that pays in excess of the reservation wage and requires $\bar{H}$
hours; hence from equation (7.5) leisure is constant and utility depends
only on the after-tax real wage, $W(1-\tau)$ or in natural logs, $w-\tau$. Hence
changes in utility are given by:

$$dU = U_2(dw - d\tau), \qquad (7.11)$$

where U_2 is the marginal utility of goods consumption. There are no
distortionary labor-supply effects here as long as the person does not
withdraw from the labor force.

Cyclically activated tax policy would require symmetry: (1) τ should
be lowered during a period when $u > u_e$ and (2) τ needs to be raised
when $u < u_e$. In the first circumstance it is easy to see that $dw > 0$
from the productivity improvement and $d\tau < 0$ from the policy change
will raise utility in equation (7.11). The only negative effect comes from
the wage reduction through the Phillips curve, but the Council could
have allayed fears by pointing to the relatively flat slope of the short-
run relationship between u and W. In such cases voters would certainly
want a tax reduction, even though they would not be concerned about
its macroeconomic effects on aggregate demand and on total output.

It is much less obvious that utility will increase when taxes are raised
in a boom period; the needed relationship is that $dw > d\tau$. It would
be vital for the voter to understand that an *increase* in the tax rate,
although having a negative direct effect on a worker's welfare, would
have beneficial indirect effects on the real wage through a combination
of lower inflation and greater productivity gains. Although Okun was
silent on the productivity of labor when the unemployment rate was
below 4 per cent, allocational inefficiencies and overwork during a period
of tight labor markets could lead to improvements in the real wage if
unemployment were deliberately raised back to 4 per cent. Needless to
say, it would have taken enormous political courage to advocate a policy
that created more unemployment just because there is excess demand
in the labor market. In other words it was acceptable to fight inflation,
but it was also an unspoken convention that prevented advocating higher
unemployment to achieve this result. Although this analysis can be made
more complex and more accurate with additional features, the Council
of Economic Advisers could have used its educational role here with
lasting effects on the more prudent conduct of fiscal policy. This, as we
now know, was never attempted.

Even more critical to the issue of the tax increase in 1966–68 is the
observation that the median-voter model of predicting legislative outcomes was almost totally irrelevant. As far as one can tell, there were

only a few specific individuals and groups who were locked in combat over the need to legislate tax increases. According to Ackley's recollections in Hargrove and Morley (1984, pp. 247–59), promoting the case for the increase were members of the Council, the Treasury, the Federal Reserve, and the Bureau of the Budget; against the tax increase — at some time or other — were President Johnson, Congressman Mills, *The New York Times*, *The Washington Post* and opponents of the Vietnam war.[1] In that environment, it would be difficult if not impossible to predict which side will win.

PREDICTING LEGISLATIVE OUTCOMES

In retrospect we now know that it was easier to muster the votes in Congress for a tax cut in 1964 than for a tax increase in 1966. Voters always have strong personal incentives for wanting lower taxes; they do not recognize or understand the spillover effects discussed in the previous section or the burden of the debt presented in the last chapter. Even President Johnson was aware of this lack of electoral appeal of higher taxes when he wrote (1971, p. 440), "It is not too difficult to convince someone that he will be better off with more take-home pay. But try to convince him that he will be better off tomorrow by losing part of his income today." Nevertheless participatory democracy is much more limited in this application. Most individuals do not choose to involve themselves in legislative battles over taxes or are prevented from doing so because of the high costs of participation. As a consequence one needs to be highly skeptical of political claims that certain tax-policy initiatives are "good for the American people." Manley (1970, pp. 356–7) describes the process in which tax legislation moves through the crucial House Ways and Means Committee: "Interest groups and lobbyists are, of course, intimately involved in the tax-making process from start to finish." He then quotes an anonymous Treasury Department official:

> We call in people who will be affected, get their views, sometimes modify or drop proposed ideas. We try to get their opinion on what we think might be a good idea. Representatives of industry and other people who are affected by what we consider are consulted — sometimes we call them in, sometimes they get wind of it and contact us. It's quite informal.

The haphazard procedure described here has little in common with the median-voter model, as can now be shown. In the wake of some tax

[1] For more details, see Stein (1996a, pp. 524–31; 1988, pp. 113–22), and Manley (1970, Chapter 4).

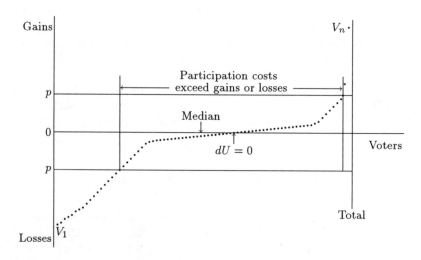

Figure 7.3   Voter profiles

proposal, individuals will calculate its effect on their income, wealth and ultimately their welfare. These persons are shown in Figure 7.3 as the array $V_1 \ldots V_n$. To arrive at the median voter, they are arranged from those with the largest loss on the left to the person with the largest gain on the right. This voter profile can take any number of shapes but it must be monotonic. Nevertheless it is not unreasonable to suppose that most individuals will experience only small gains or losses while a minority, because of their special characteristics, will have large changes in their welfare.

As the voter profile is drawn, the median voter suffers a loss and would vote against this proposal as would everyone else to the left of this voter. Moreover since there are still some losers to the right of the median voter, this tax change would be resolutely defeated in a fully participatory democracy. Furthermore an economist would recommend against this proposal, based either on the stringent Pareto-optimality condition or on the fact that losers could not be compensated by the gainers, since the mean value of the welfare change in this hypothetical example has been rigged to be negative. From this accumulated evidence one would be tempted to predict that this proposal will not be adopted, but one must resist that temptation until we investigate how politicians decide on the outcome.

Once we turn to the political process the outcome becomes highly unpredictable. First we have to consider participation costs which are shown by the vertical distance to p, in both directions from zero. They are assumed to be fixed costs and applicable to all potential participants, both losers and gainers. They involve information costs, costs of communicating with legislators and costs of lobbying. These costs are not trivial. In a legislative process that involves thousands of tax-related bills, it is virtually impossible for a private individual to remain informed about the welfare effects of each bill. In the 1960s it was possible to write (or preferably wire) one's Congressman at little expense, but the effect was probably minimal and a face-to-face meeting was likely to be more effective as well as more expensive. The choice would depend on what was at stake because voters want the welfare gain to exceed the cost of achieving it. For those with high stakes, a well-organized lobby group would get the attention that was needed. Lobbys are an institution that arises from the fixed costs of political participation and their ability to exploit economies of scale. The value added from a lobby comes from its power to convince politicians that it represents a larger group than actually pays for its services. Birnbaum (1992) provides many examples.

Those who find that the participation costs exceed the gains or losses from the proposal would voluntarily disfranchise themselves from participation in the outcome. In Figure 7.3 this eliminates about two-thirds of the potential voters but, of course, the number of exclusions is very sensitive to the size of p and the shape of the voter profile. In this case about the same number of gainers have been eliminated as losers, given the symmetrical shape of the voter-profile between the two horizontal lines marked p; the outcome from the remaining participants is that the proposal is still rejected. More generally it is now possible that a majority of the population opposes a particular measure but they also resign themselves to the fact that it will be adopted because their opposition is not "strong" enough. For example, a Gallup poll reported in *The New York Times* of 24 January 1968 found that 80 per cent of those interviewed opposed the tax surcharge that was being debated in Congress and in the press at that time, but 94 per cent thought that it would pass.

So far the value of p has been assumed to be exogenously determined but that need not be the case. Each side has an incentive to impose higher costs to eliminate their opponents. As long as the largest gains are different from the largest losses in absolute terms, one side will have an incentive to raise the stakes and increase p for both sides. As drawn in Figure 7.3, the vertical distance to V_n from the horizontal axis is larger than the distance to V_1 and the former group will want to increase the costs of political participation high enough to eliminate the latter group, which still leaves V_n with a net gain from its lobbying activity. Through a war of attrition one person or a group of like persons is left to decide the issue and the measure will pass.

Although this particular example has been contrived to produce a specific result, it is generally true that median voter models are unreliable in predicting legislative outcomes and economists should not assume that the perception of welfare improvements will automatically lead the political process to adopt those changes. The struggle over the tax surcharge proposed by President Johnson in 1967 serves as a tragic reminder of the irrelevant macroeconomic advice offered by his Council of Economic Advisers in the face of strong political resistance.

THE POLITICAL STRUGGLE OVER THE SURCHARGE

From the time that GNP caught up with potential output in mid-1965, as shown in Chart 5.1, it took almost exactly three years to get the legislation for a tax increase on President Johnson's desk and the outcome was in doubt the whole time. Lags in fiscal policy were well understood at this time and were enumerated by Ando and Brown (1963; 1970), but the political struggle to increase taxes between 1966 and 1968 must have set a record for futility and self-deception. This is not a place to write a potted history of this episode; instead the emphasis here will be on the factors that caused a dispute in the first place.[2]

The lack of consensus on tax issues dogged macroeconomic policy throughout this period and the inability to implement timely contractionary measures when the output gap was negative must call in question the advisability of the 1964 tax cut to eliminate a positive output gap. Either stabilization policy has symmetry or it must be abandoned. Macroeconomists, accustomed to thinking about the "representative agent" or in terms of aggregates, are ill equipped to cope with the fact that there may be heated disagreements among potential voters about the benefits of tax increases. Consider the assertion by Ando and Brown (1963; 1970, p. 359): "The minimum lag in the legislative enactment of a recommended tax or transfer payment program is less than a month, provided that the change in the law is one requiring simple action, such as modification in rates or exemptions." There is no understanding here that

---

[2] Participants in these events typically did not provide documentation; as a substitute one has to rely on press reports. Despite its editorial bias in this case, *The New York Times* has a well-deserved reputation as "the newspaper of record" and it provides a detailed annual index. For the headlines of the day-to-day events surrounding the surcharge, see *The New York Times Index* for 1965, pp. 933–5; 1966, pp. 1117–23; 1967, pp. 1138–44; and 1968, pp. 1386–93. For the opposite bias, see Johnson (1971, Chapter 19).

tax increases are more difficult to enact than tax reductions, that looming elections will put on hold a proposal that will cost the incumbents any votes, that committee chairmen can make tax bills into hostages for strictly personal reasons, or that lobbies can have unpredictable effects on Congressional votes.

The 1968 tax surcharge is a classic case of confrontational politics on an issue that should have been noncontroversial from a macroeconomic perspective. Even then the opposing views are difficult to summarize and an *ex-ante* prediction is impossible to make for a number of reasons: (1) macroeconomic conditions changed during the period in which the surcharge was being debated; (2) positions of the antagonists changed over time; (3) conflicting motives; and (4) conflicting actions. It is worth considering each of these points in an attempt to understand the dynamic process at work.

Changing Conditions

By the end of 1965 it must have been clearly evident that the recovery sparked by the 1964 tax cut had been too strong when combined with additional Vietnam and Great Society spending. During 1966, inflationary pressures continued to mount and the output gap was now negative. This is shown in Chart 7.1. However, by early 1967, not only did the inflation rate drop to some extent, but also the CEA introduced its new and higher level of potential GNP, which created a positive gap during this time. This evidence suggested that a tax increase may have been inappropriate during 1967. Even Chairman of the Council, Gardner Ackley, said in April 1967 that the Administration would not press for immediate Congressional action on President Johnson's tax surcharge proposal because of economic uncertainties. But the downturn was temporary and by 1968 inflation began its upward trend once more. The inordinate time spent on recognizing that a tax increase was needed and on mounting a convincing argument to Congress meant that counterarguments to the surcharge were plausible and that the legislation was far from urgent until 1968. As was pointed out in Chapter 5, if the Council had kept its focus on the old version of the output gap and avoided fine-tuning the macroeconomy, it would not have needed to hesitate in its advocacy of a tax increase throughout 1967. When Ackley suggested in December 1966 that the tax increase be "put on the shelf" (B31), the cumulative pressure on Johnson, Mills and other opponents of fiscal restraint was irretrievably lost.

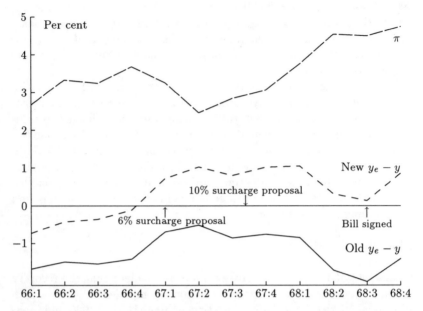

Source: Same as for data in Chapters 4 and 5.

Chart 7.1   Output gaps, inflation and chronology of events, 1966:1 to 1968:4

Changing Positions

In December 1965, Gardner Ackley wrote a memorandum (B24, reproduced in the Appendix) to the President outlining the inflationary dangers ahead and recommending a tax increase. In January 1966, Johnson told a news conference that he was convinced that higher taxes would be better than accepting inflation, but by April he did not want to pursue this change in macroeconomic policy because it would contradict his public assertions that the Vietnam war did not create unpopular domestic repercussions. Also he realized that it would have been a troublesome policy plank in the November 1966 mid-term elections. Thus the Johnson Administration was officially against a tax increase until 1967 and relied on voluntary wage and price controls to fight inflation. Even within the administration differences surfaced; Ackley indicated on 17 May 1966 that a tax rise may soon be desirable, but a week later the President said that while he was watching developments he saw no need for a tax increase at that time. Throughout the rest of 1966 there was delay in making a decision, mostly dictated by the November elections.

In January 1967, Johnson finally asked for a 6 per cent surcharge on personal and corporate income for two years, not to reduce aggregate demand in the economy, but to finance the additional needs of the Vietnam war and domestic programs. Then, in August 1967, the proposed surcharge was raised to 10 per cent, largely because of a mounting deficit that had not been previously anticipated.

The most influential newspaper, *The New York Times*, in the meantime moved in the opposite direction to the Administration in its editorial policy toward taxes. On 1 July 1966 it "scored" the administration for its failure to raise taxes and curb inflation. But on 18 September 1967 the editors argued that current economic facts did not sufficiently support the administration's proposed surcharge. On 28 January 1968 an editorial stated: "A tax was clearly called for in 1966; but it was not enacted and the economy has already suffered the imbalances and strains that the Administration is now forecasting for the future." It called for "an acceleration of the cuts in nonessential nonpoverty Federal spending." *The Times* continued its opposition until March 1968 when it became convinced that the surcharge was needed to preserve the international monetary system and to stem the capital outflows that followed in the wake of the British devaluation. One interpretation of its opposition to tax increases in 1967 was that it was not only connected to macroeconomic performance but also to the paper's anti-Vietnam war position; denying the President more funding would force him to scale back or even abandon the war effort.

At the same time Wilbur Mills, the Arkansas Democrat who was Chairman of the House Ways and Means Committee and who would have to approve the tax increase if it was to clear the House of Representatives, initially favored the 6 per cent surcharge in June 1967, but later in that year and throughout the early part of 1968 was adamant in his refusal to let the Committee vote on the 10 per cent surcharge unless Federal government expenditures were lowered as well. He finally relented when international factors became more important and when the President indicated his grudging willingness to compromise on the spending limits.

The business community was generally in favor of higher taxes, perhaps because they understood that the inflationary consequences of inaction were worse for their profits than the surcharge. On the other hand a Harris poll reported in *The New York Times* of 17 October 1967 found that 78 per cent of the respondents opposed the tax increase and 15 per cent favored it; but by a ratio of two to one there was support for the general idea that taxes and other federal policies could help stabilize the economy. A more selective poll taken by the American Statistical Association in December 1967 found that two-thirds of the economists surveyed favored the tax surcharge. Three months earlier Ackley had "suggested" to Joseph Pechman that he organize a letter-writing campaign to Wilbur Mills in favor of the tax bill. He was able to report to the President (B42 and B47) that 260 academic economists — "the cream of the economics profession" — had signed a supportive statement.

From late 1967 to early 1968, there was a six-month impasse when positions hardened and participants in the debate kept making the same arguments over and over again. While the macroeconomy deteriorated there was a test of wills between President Johnson and Representative Mills that no economic model could predict and no game theorist could solve.[3] If the President's main concern was closing the output gap, then a reduction in federal expenditures would have had roughly the same effect as a tax increase and it should not have been beyond his powers to find a compromise package that would have satisfied the Ways and Means Committee. But the President's chief aim was not macroeconomic stability; uppermost in his mind were the Great Society programs and the prosecution of the Vietnam war, both of which had voracious appetites for funding (J66). The fundamental disagreement between Johnson and Mills was the size and scope of government to which the macroeconomy was held hostage. In a memo to the President (J69), Barefoot Sanders reported a conversation with Mills in which the Congressman demanded that the Administration make a choice between guns and butter. Sanders advised the President: "You may wish to consider having Mills for a visit. My own view is that it would be a mistake to make a public choice between 'guns and butter' ... We have just got to have it both ways and Mills has to be convinced of this." Gardner Ackley and later Arthur Okun, as the chief macroeconomic policy advisers, could not possibly make their views prevail in that environment. In a war between titans, the skill of the spear-carriers is irrelevant to the outcome.

In the end, Johnson had to accept a $6 billion cut in federal spending for fiscal year 1969 in order to get the 10 per cent surcharge for the relatively short period of 1 April 1968 to 30 June 1969. Even before the bill was signed, the view that the spending cuts were likely to be more effective than the surcharge in reducing aggregate demand became widespread. A survey conducted at the University of Michigan found that consumers had already discounted the coming tax rise. The President announced that "our democracy passed a critical test," but

---

[3] In their chapter on brinkmanship, Dixit and Nalebuff (1991, Chapter 8) present a number of examples including the Cuban missile crisis but the Johnson–Mills standoff must have been too complicated for them to analyze.

his re-election hopes were dashed and the macroeconomy's performance
had become an avoidable disaster. Only Undersecretary of Commerce
Howard J. Samuels in a speech on 2 May 1968 had the courage to admit
publicly that, in the light of recent developments, the 1964 tax cut had
been a mistake.

Conflicting Motives

The disagreements about macroeconomic performance, discussed above,
were minor skirmishes compared to the conflict on political and military issues. Opponents of the Vietnam war saw this debate as an opportunity to embarrass the administration. In January 1968, Professor
William Nordhaus of Yale University led 320 other economists in urging Congress to reject the surcharge to bar further intensification of the
war. They said, "Academics and scholars [who support the surcharge
for macroeconomic reasons] must realize that such technical support
in fact assists the Government in the pursuit of harmful goals." (*The
New York Times*, 14 January 1968, p. 7). Even more adamant were a
group of 448 writers and editors who announced that they would not pay
the surcharge because of their moral opposition to the war. In March
1968, Senator Eugene McCarthy's unexpectedly narrow defeat by the
incumbent President in the New Hampshire primary was viewed as a
repudiation of the Vietnam war, but McCarthy also thought that his
opposition to the surcharge aided his cause. On the other hand James
Reston, a columnist for *The New York Times*, wrote on 16 February
1968 that in the light of sacrifices made by US troops in Vietnam there
was a moral case that could be made for the surcharge. Moreover a
number of rabbis said that support for the surcharge would be stronger
if it were earmarked for anti-poverty programs.

Mills's opposition to the surcharge was based on his desire to see lower
government expenditures and the elimination of the budget deficit.[4] Although the absence of higher taxes in 1966–67 made the budget deficit
worse, he had a pre-Reaganite strategy of starving the Administration
for funds. There is no indication that Mills believed that the economy
was heading toward a recession that would have made a tax increase
undesirable. He was, throughout his tenure on the Ways and Mean
Committee, more concerned about the microeconomic effects of taxes
on individuals or groups and on their voting behavior. For example, in
June 1968 the Chairman postponed a vote on the tax surcharge to help
his New York colleagues survive the state primary election. In October

---

[4] See *The New York Times*, 15 October 1967, p. 45 and 1 March 1998, p. 1.

1967, President Johnson said that, "people don't picket for higher taxes" and in May 1968 he called upon Congressmen to "stand up like men" and pass the tax bill in an election year, but Mills believed that cutting expenditures and raising taxes would be more vote-effective than the latter action alone and his view finally prevailed. Most critical to an understanding of his opposition to the tax surcharge is that Mills felt betrayed by the Kennedy–Johnson Administration. In August 1963, as part of a compromise that included the original tax cut, Mills had received assurances from Kennedy that expenditures would be cut as well. In a personal letter to Mills, Kennedy wrote (K54), "tax reduction must also, therefore, be accompanied by the exercise of an even-tighter rein on Federal expenditures, limiting outlays to only those expenditures which meet strict criteria of national need." By 1967, Mills was adamant that President Johnson would have to honor that pledge.

In time, international developments and balance-of-payments crises became additional arguments for the tax increase. *The New York Times*, in its editorial on 15 March 1968, explained that its long-standing opposition to the tax surcharge was now overwhelmed by the need to preserve the international monetary system. The potential conflict between internal and external balance was well understood by the late 1960s after Meade (1951, Part III) and Mundell (1962, 1963) had published their work, but here was a situation where tighter fiscal policy was needed both to eliminate a negative output gap and to reduce a trade deficit. By 1968 the latter had become more worrisome than the former and became the rallying point for proponents of the tax increase.

Since the tax increase meant different things to different people, it is not surprising that a median voter is virtually impossible to identify. Even if the majority of the public understood that a tax increase was better for their individual welfare than further inflationary pressures — and it is not at all clear that this was the case — one's opposition to the Vietnam war or one's dependence on Great Society spending would cause many of them to campaign actively against the tax surcharge. The crucial fact is that the forces leading to the final passage of the tax bill in June 1968 were impossible to predict in December 1965, when Ackley first recommended a tax increase.

Conflicting Actions

Barely three months after President Johnson asked for the initial tax surcharge, he also proposed the immediate restoration of the 7 per cent investment tax credit and accelerated depreciation on capital goods. It did not take long for the President's opponents to point out the contradictory nature of his macroeconomic policies and Murray J. Rossant, a columnist in *The New York Times*, noted that the restoration decision pointed up the "new economics' inability to forecast business developments." (15 March 1967, p. 65). It is interesting to note that the legislative process for the tax credit was completed in three months.

In January 1968, the Administration recommended a rebate of federal taxes on exports and an equivalent new tax on imports without considering the impact of these measures on stimulating aggregate demand for US goods and services even more. Congressman Mills agreed with the proposal on basically chauvinistic grounds.

The point is that macroeconomic requirements are never at the head of the list when governments make budgetary or tax decisions. There are always interest groups with strong lobbying activities that can get special consideration and in this case business groups traded their support for the surcharge against tax breaks on investment or exports. In the end Heller and the other initiators of the "new economics" were much too optimistic about their ability to mold the budgetary process for the sole purpose of eliminating output gaps.

CONCLUSION

Voters have a complicated welfare evaluation of taxes and are most likely to prefer lower taxes in all circumstances, which makes cyclical adjustment of tax rates especially inappropriate as a stabilization instrument. Not only are there long lags between the time that a change in aggregate demand is needed and the time that new tax rates are implemented, the political process frequently makes the outcome uncertain or much different from what was intended. The fiasco surrounding the tax surcharge in 1968 exposes all the political elements that conspire to make such an exercise akin to Russian roulette.

During this period a number of individuals and groups suggested that the President should have stand-by authority to change tax rates within prespecified boundaries, thus avoiding both the long lags and the political log-rolling that was so evident both in 1963–64 when taxes were lowered and in 1966–68 when they had to be raised. Kennedy himself made such a suggestion in January 1962, well before the Heller-inspired tax cut was proposed. On 1 June 1967, *The New York Times*, despite its opposition to the Johnson Administration tax increase, editorialized about the virtues of "flexible" tax policy to regulate the economy. They wrote, "The best way to insure rapid flexibility is by providing the President with temporary and discretionary authority to raise or lower corporate and individual income-tax rates. Without this weapon, timing of tax changes will always be subject to the whim of Congress. An Administration can always hesitate over potentially unpopular decisions, explaining that it does not know what Congress will do." Such proposals have never been taken very seriously; Okun thought that it was like "wishing for Santa Claus." (B49). Not only is Congress unwilling to abdicate its role in tax legislation, but there is no automatic presumption that the President would make optimal decisions if Congressional opposition were absent. Ackley had warned the President (J44, emphasis in original), "if you had such powers, the responsibility would rest clearly on your shoulders. There would be increasing pressures directly focused on you to make use of it — or not to. You'd be damned *whether you did or didn't.*" President Johnson's performance in 1966–68 is far from reassuring on this account. Also the vacillating advice of his CEA and Treasury officials does not inspire the kind of confidence one needs to give the executive branch such enormous powers. There are good reasons for the checks and balances in the current system and macroeconomic requirements are not sufficient to abandon them. The simple truth is that taxes should be set at rates that will ensure a balanced budget over an average business cycle and left alone thereafter. When politicians and their advisers cannot resist the temptation to pursue short-sighted fine-tuning, it is time to remember the old dictum that "the only good tax is an old tax."

DATA APPENDIX

To estimate equation (7.9) requires the data shown in the appendix to Chapter 2 plus the unemployment gap listed below.

$$u - u_e - 1948\text{--}95$$

−1.250 1.050 0.208 −1.717 −2.075 −2.175 0.492 −0.733 −0.975 −0.800 1.842 0.350 0.342
1.492 0.267 0.242 −0.342 −1.092 −1.808 −1.758 −2.042 −2.108 −0.617 0.150 −0.200
−0.942 −0.258 2.475 1.800 1.050 0.167 −0.005 1.275 1.617 3.708 3.600 1.508 1.192
1.000 0.175 −0.508 −0.742 −0.383 0.850 1.492 0.908 0.009 −0.408

8

Lessons To Be Learned

This last chapter dwells on the lessons that could be learned from the episode in stabilization-policy implementation which started with the planning for *The Revenue Act of 1964* and ended with the passage of *The Revenue and Expenditure Control Act of 1968*. It is almost too late for such an exercise. This book could and should have been written many years ago by one of the participants, preferably Walter Heller, Gardner Ackley or Arthur Okun, who were the successive Chairmen of the Council of Economic Advisers and in that position would have had the detailed knowledge of events and arguments that cannot be reconstructed at this stage. Their recollections in the oral-history project (Hargrove and Morley, 1984) do not substitute for a detailed *ex-post* evaluation of the benefits and costs of the stabilization-policy decisions in this period. The reason that the authors of this project did not ask any probing questions is that Heller, Ackley and Okun would not have participated in what they would have characterized as a witch-hunt. Even the administrative history project undertaken in 1968 (J92), which was meant to be kept secret for 20 years, does not contain the kind of self-evaluation that was needed for a critical assessment of the countercyclical fiscal policy that was attempted by the Kennedy and Johnson Administrations.

At the current time, activist fiscal policy has become so discredited that it is virtually irrelevant to suggest that there are lessons to be learned from events that transpired almost thirty years earlier. But history has a way of repeating itself if people forget what went wrong the last time that someone promoted a "new and innovative" policy that governments should pursue. It is this fear that some economist will attract serious attention by advocating once again a countercyclical policy based on changes in tax rates on individual and corporate income that creates some urgency to the task at hand. What follows is a list of

suggested improvements in the application or implementation of stabilization policies. They are gleaned from the critical assessment of the
actions taken or not taken by the Council of Economic Advisers between
1962 and 1968. Both positive and negative lessons make up this list.

RIGHT TARGET

The concept of potential GNP was a superb innovation in macroeconomic theory even if its implementation and measurement left a lot to
be desired. Okun's great insight was to balance the previous emphasis
on aggregate demand with an easy-to-comprehend supply side of the
macroeconomy: how much output could be produced if 96 per cent of
the labor force were employed? This also simplified policy decisions to
a large extent, as the Council of Economic Advisers pointed to the $30
billion output gap to justify the tax cut they were proposing during
1962–63 when economic growth was already relatively high. Previous
emphasis on dating business cycles, pioneered by Wesley Mitchell at the
National Bureau of Economic Research, required a great deal of information about the amplitude and timing of cycles and how indicators of
business conditions should be interpreted. Instead Okun's production-
function approach brought to the forefront the idea that a macroeconomy made supply decisions as well as demand decisions. Firms derived
a demand for workers based on their anticipations of sales; they also
had to determine the hours that they worked, the capacity utilization
of their existing capital, the replacement of worn-out equipment and investment in new capital. These magnitudes also varied during a business
cycle and could easily be confused with demand conditions. However,
Okun convinced the Council of Economic Advisers and the rest of the
profession that it was useful to think of equilibrium or sustainable values
for factor inputs and their productivity in order to generate a value for
potential GNP.

   If governments were still interested in stabilization policy, Okun's concept would continue to be useful today. A positive output gap should
lead to expansionary policy decisions, but a negative gap should also
call forth contractionary moves. Lack of symmetry in the application of
both of these rules, rather than the rules themselves, tolled the death
knell of activist fiscal policy. Although Fellner (1982) has criticized the
concept of potential output as a policy target because it substituted for
an inflation target, there is no reason to believe that they are incom-
patible objectives. If properly chosen, potential output is the dividing
line between rising and falling inflation. From that perspective, fiscal

policy could be geared to matching potential output through short-run changes in aggregate demand and the monetary authorities could fix on a Friedman-style monetary growth rule to achieve whatever inflation rate was considered desirable in the long run. The danger from such an allocation of responsibilities comes from an upward bias in measuring potential output, as happened in 1965 and again in 1967. By that time the Council of Economic Advisers became too optimistic about long-term trends in the US economy and revised the previous growth of potential GNP from 3.5 to 3.75 per cent and again to 4 per cent per annum. This meant that aggregate demand was being pushed too far through expansionary fiscal policy and inflation accelerated in the absence of tighter monetary policy. The lesson is for the Council to be conservative in the estimation of potential GNP or its trend and to listen to competing views about this vital macroeconomic indicator. It is important to avoid translating potential output into maximum output.

The ultimate aim of the Kennedy Council of Economic Advisers was to reduce the unemployment rate to 4 per cent. Looking back at this period, Solow and Tobin (1988, p. 9) recollect:

> We economists looked at unemployment statistics not just as measures of the personal deprivation and hardships of the millions unemployed, but also as barometers of the overall economic weather. Compared to the prosperity accompanying a 4 percent unemployment rate, a 7 percent rate signified bad news in many dimensions: among them production, incomes, profits, capital investment, capacity utilization, and government budgets.

If the target unemployment rate in the labor market had all these beneficial effects, it might have made more sense to deal directly with the unemployment gap rather than indirectly with the output gap. Somehow the advantage of a clearly specified goal that was easily measured was lost in the Council's deliberations and decisions.

If 7 per cent unemployment was bad news, how did the Council react when the unemployment rate fell below 4 per cent? Again the lack of symmetry made the previous goal unacceptable when policies had to be initiated that would raise the unemployment rate. It was easier to argue that inflation was the consequence of ill-mannered businesses and unions than to admit that excess demand had appeared in the labor market in 1965 or 1966. Moreover the Kennedy–Johnson Council convinced themselves that 4 per cent unemployment was only an interim goal and that there were no serious structural problems in the labor market that would preclude a falling equilibrium unemployment rate. Although natural rates remain elusive in their estimation or measurement, hindsight suggests that this rate was rising rather than falling during the 1960s and 1970s. By aiming for 4 per cent and even lower, instead of 5–6 per cent, such policies would generate continuing excess demand in the labor market with rising wages and inflation. In deciding on macroeconomic goals, there is a need to avoid wishful arguments and to concentrate on hardboiled analysis.

WRONG INSTRUMENT

If governments are to move total aggregate demand to equal potential output, the tax rate is the clumsiest and least reliable instrument that can be used for this purpose. It would be more sensible to depend on variations in direct government demand for goods and services than to manipulate private disposable income to achieve the same result. There are two reasons why taxes on income are the wrong instrument: (1) the connection between taxes and aggregate demand is not strong or contemporaneous and (2) tax changes have too much political baggage attached to them.

Modern consumption theory relies on expectations of life-time resources as the budget constraint instead of currently observed disposable income. Thus it is possible that an announcement of a permanent tax increase that is not actually implemented will have a larger immediate effect on consumption expenditures than an explicitly temporary tax increase that does go into effect. As Romer (1996, p. 251, emphasis in original) noted:

> There is a close relationship between disposable income and consumption spending. Yet to some extent this relationship arises not because current disposable income determines current spending, but because current income is strongly correlated with *permanent* income — that is, it is highly correlated with households' expectations of their disposable incomes in the future. If policymakers attempt to reduce consumption through a tax increase that is known to be temporary, the relationship between current income and expected future income, and hence the relationship between current income and spending, will change. Again this is not just a theoretical possibility. The United States enacted a temporary surcharge in 1968 and the impact on consumption was considerably smaller than would be expected on the basis of the statistical relationship between disposable income and spending.

Since stabilization that relies on tax changes will require such changes rather frequently as an economy moves through a business cycle, they will be viewed by households as temporary and lose their effect on aggregate demand. In a speech on 17 April 1967, Gardner Ackley warned, "we must accustom ourselves to the idea of frequent adjustment of tax rates." (*The New York Times*, 18 April 1967, p. 20). From that perspective, adjustments to direct government demand for goods and services will have much more predictable and immediate effects on total demand. There has been much discussion in the past (e.g., Teigen, 1970) of having a list of public-works projects that could be accelerated during recessions or slowed down during a boom period. But even here, it is possible to imagine how political intrigue can interfere with macroeconomic requirements.

One must also have concerns about the political difficulties of realizing "optimal" tax rates whether for macroeconomic purposes or for reasons of efficiency and equity. Within two years of *The Tax Reform Act of 1986* which concentrated on the latter issues, McLure (1988, p. 303) found that "attempting to implement a conceptually correct income tax ... is impracticable." Later Auerbach and Slemrod (1997, p. 628) concluded that "Advocates ... will ... be frustrated that a retrospective analysis of the most comprehensive attempt in history to achieve this goal offers little hard evidence of the fruits of this effort." Neither of these studies asks why economic analysis of tax reform did not prevail in the political process. The reason is that everyone's idea of optimality is different, depending mainly on their endowments and tastes and these differences are impossible to reconcile in a system of representative government.

If I were asked to design an optimal tax system based on my own preferences, two features would be paramount: (1) that my taxes be as low as possible so that I can enjoy as much in the way of private goods as my resources will allow and (2) that everyone else's taxes be as high as possible to allow me to have as much in the way of public goods as I want. Of course all voters have the same conflicting aims, which makes it impossible to achieve a Pareto improvement as any tax reform that is implemented will have some losers. For example, widening the tax base and lowering the tax rate may improve efficiency of the tax system, but some groups will be potential losers in such legislation. Those who have political power, especially through effective lobbying, will continue to receive tax-exempt status and those without political power will have to pay higher taxes to compensate for the exemption. It is useless to pretend that the gainers from tax reform could compensate the losers and still have something left over because compensation schemes such as these are never implemented and all participants are aware of this fact.

Hence any proposal to change taxes leads to conflict in the political arena and such conflicts pay no attention to macroeconomic or microeconomic optimality. One lesson from the 1960s experience is that it is probably easier to get politicians to approve tax reductions during a period when actual output is below potential output than to obtain tax increases when the output gap is negative. From a long-term perspective, governments should either respond symmetrically or not at all. In that framework it is best to leave tax rates at levels that will balance the budget on average during the business cycle and not to tempt fate with fine-tuning.

LESS AMBITION, MORE CAUTION

Somehow an antidote must be found for the extravagent claims and promises that economists make once they become policy advisers. Three previously quoted statements by former Chairmen of the CEA need a closer examination to make this point. In his book (1967, p. 61) Heller wrote, "Standards of economic performance must be recast from time to time. Recasting them in more ambitious terms was an indispensable prelude to the shaping of economic policies for the 1960s which would be suitable to the tremendous output capabilities of the U.S. economy." What is the basis of the imperative "must be recast?" After defeating Richard Nixon by the narrowest of margins, what was President Kennedy's political mandate to move to a much more aggressive role in stabilization policy? What was the economic evidence that required "more ambitious" policies, especially when one considers that this was written in 1966–67, not in 1961–63 before the experiment was undertaken? My assertion is that activist fiscal policy has been abandoned in large measure because previous promises about its beneficial effects, such as those made by Heller, could not be achieved. Hence, less ambition will lead to fewer disappointments.

In *The Economic Report of the President* for 1968 Gardner Ackley as Chairman of the Council stated (p. 86):

> [T]he economic effects of a tax increase are the mirror image of the expansionary effects accomplished by tax reduction. But a tax cut enacted when there are ample idle resources, as in 1964, has its main expansionary effect on output, with only a minor impact on prices. Under present circumstances, however, with rapidly expanding demands and essentially full employment, the main restraining impact of the tax increase will be on prices, and only secondarily on output.

This is essentially a statement that the macroeconomy does not face any uncomfortable trade-offs. There are no sacrifices needed to reach the goal for which the tax change is intended. In 1963–64 unemployment could be reduced to 4 per cent without any inflationary effects and in 1966–68 inflation could be reduced to its previous level without creating any additional unemployment. No empirical evidence is supplied to support such a hypothesis. By 1968 there were several pieces of evidence that should have led to the rejection of such absurd notions. First, work on the Phillips curve had progressed to the point where it was considered to be established and incontrovertible. Its main conclusion was: inflation increased as unemployment decreased. Both the 1962 and 1963 *Economic Reports of the President* acknowledged this fact: "In less extreme circumstances, aggregate demand may press hard upon, but not exceed the economy's productive capacity. Increases in prices and wages may occur nevertheless" (1962, p. 45) and "Although wage pressures undoubtedly would be somewhat stronger at lower levels of unemployment, unit labor costs need not be higher because a considerable improvement in productivity would be the direct consequence of return to higher rates of capacity utilization." (1963, p. 85). Second, Ackley (1966, p. 69) made the case for wage-price guidelines by stressing the fact that inflation accelerated well before full employment was reached. Third, the recently experienced recession in early 1967 reduced both the inflation rate and output simultaneously: in 1966:4, inflation was 3.68 per cent and the output gap was −1.40 per cent; in 1967:2 inflation had fallen to 2.46 per cent, but the output gap had also been reduced to −0.51 per cent.

This inconsistency in Council statements about economic relationships can be ascribed to political requirements overwhelming economic reasoning. In its *Reports* the Council felt that it could only provide "good news" and not "bad tidings." If the evidence had shown that a tax increase would leave the inflation rate unchanged but reduce output and employment, there is not the remotest chance that the Council would have publicized that information.

Instead of arguing for greater autonomy for — or candor from — the Council, it is better to recognize its explicit political role and to rely on other elements of the profession to provide critical evaluations of government policies. The recent article by Auerbach and Slemrod (1997) is a move in the right direction; by the same token, the American Economic Association would find it uncomfortable to be the "official opposition" by providing one or more of its journals for this purpose. Ultimately we need to make *ex-post* policy research more respectable among macroeconomists once more; the resulting output will find a suitable venue. Another possibility is to allow dissenting opinions in the *Reports* submitted by the Council to the President. This actually happened in 1953, when John D. Clark wrote: "Many fluctuations will develop within our free, erratic economy during the next 3 years, but I am unable to see changes in business conditions which would bring about a recessionary trend threatening enough to require new counterdeflationary action by Government." (*ERP*, 1953, p. 102).

Even a thoroughly modern Chairman of the Council, Joseph Stiglitz (1997, p. 113), was moved to ponder: "The question is whether government is simply an arena for bargaining by special interests, or whether government can rise above that to represent the will of all." The answer to this rhetorical question is that the Council's contribution is, at best, to be an arbiter between competing special interests. Stiglitz concluded (p. 113), "the Council of Economic Advisers plays a vital part in looking out for that little-represented special interest known as the national interest." For an eminent public-finance economist to suggest that a government could "represent the will of all" is breathtaking in both its scope and its implications.

Having raised the issue, how would Stiglitz characterize special interests and how would he prevent them from having access to governments? How would he run monetary policy when lenders want high interest rates and borrowers want low interest rates? How would he decide exchange-rate policy when importers want the value of the dollar to rise and exporters want its value to fall? How would he solve the Social Security impasse when the old want to maintain current benefits and the young want lower premiums? Who represents the national will when people with jobs want high wages, but the unemployed want low wages? These are just some of the issues in which government policies will always create some losers and some winners with both groups forming lobbies to protect or promote their interests. In the real world it is senseless to assume that the representative agent is neither a borrower nor a lender, is both an exporter and an importer, is neither young nor old and is only randomly unemployed. Instead economic agents have different endowments of physical and human capital and of other attributes, the value of which is favorably or adversely affected by governmental intervention. The result is conflict and tension wherever collective action is contemplated. With fixed and opposed attitudes on noneconomic issues such as abortion, smoking and gun control among the voting public, we cannot even begin to predict how economic conflicts will be resolved. As a profession we must recognize that we have made no useful advances in our analysis or understanding of special interests since the Stolper–Samuelson theorem was published in 1941 and Olson's *The Logic of Collective Action* in 1971.

In a more recent article that appears to contradict his earlier presentation, Stiglitz (1998) probably agrees with this assessment and acknowledges the decisive role of special interests in government policies. He provides four reasons for the failure of Pareto improvements: (1) the inability of governments to make commitments, (2) coalition formation and bargaining, (3) destructive competition and (4) uncertainty about the consequences of change. Nevertheless there is still the naive belief that special interests can be overwhelmed by an appeal to obvious efficiency gains. In discussing Superfund, a policy aimed at dealing with toxic waste, he asserts (p. 12), "Surely there must be an alternative which can benefit the environment, provide strong incentives not to pollute in the future, and have economic benefits today, with only the lawyers being worse off." Why lawyers, of all groups that could be enumerated in this context, would meekly surrender in the face of such overwhelming logic is not explained. He concludes (p. 21):

> While special interests do often dominate over the general interests and while seeming near-Pareto improvements are often resisted, these failures do not undo the great achievements of the public sector, from mass education to a cleaner environment. These failures should focus our attention on re-examining both how and what the government should do.

He recommends greater transparency, participation and democracy in government, but none of this will happen. As long as individuals differ in their endowments, tastes and their ability to protect them, we will have a complicated network of overlapping special-interest goups which will render public-choice decisions essentially unpredictable. No amount of wishful theorizing will make it otherwise.

MORE CONSISTENCY

One of the evolving functions of *The Economic Report of the President* is to record the Council's economic analysis of the problems faced by the government in power and to provide their economic rationale for any initiatives or remedies that are being considered. In the 1960s this was not a well-developed feature of the *Reports*. Although output, inflation and unemployment were all determined within an overall macroeconomic framework, the Council tended to compartmentalize these important variables. In the beginning the link between taxes and aggregate demand depended on the multiplier–accelerator model. Later inflation was to be fought with guideposts based on a model of noncompetitive behavior in strategic markets. Finally the tax surcharge would only affect inflation because the Council assumed a supply curve for the whole economy that was vertical in the region in which the policy change was to be implemented. It is perhaps not surprising, given this methodology, that macroeconomic policy decisions at that time now appear to be so inconsistent.

   The challenge facing the Council is to incorporate the various shocks to the system into a unified macroeconomic model that will predict the effects of these shocks on all the important macroeconomic variables. This task is made all the more difficult by conflicting views on interventionism and the models that support these positions. Whatever one's view on this issue, it must be recognized that the federal government continues to make major decisions on taxes and expenditures that have macroeconomic effects through aggregate demand for goods and services; whether they are intended or not is almost irrelevant. In that environment the Council still needs to enunciate its view of fiscal-policy effects on output, inflation, interest rates, unemployment and sustainable debt-to-GDP ratios.

At the same time the Council should resist the temptation to design models that fit only the circumstances of the day. It was the inability to anticipate excess demand in the labor market that contributed to the expansionary bias in fiscal policy in the 1960s. By 1965, when the output gap had become negative, the Council should have used their existing model — as flawed as it was — to persuade themselves that contractionary policy was required; instead they resorted to voluntary wage and price guidelines and in 1967 to an upward revision in potential GNP. Both of these manoeuvers allowed the Council to concentrate on further reductions in the unemployment rate and blame the unsatisfactory inflationary performance on other factors.

IS THE CEA WORTH SAVING?

The prestige of the Council of Economic Advisers has fallen considerably since its heyday of the 1960s and the giants of the economics profession are no longer beguiled by the prospect of serving as members. In this light should the Council continue in its present form and with its current function or should it be abolished? Since it is a relatively inexpensive agency and since the President is entitled to the best economic advice that is available, one is tempted to save the CEA and to try to improve its performance by learning the lessons from past mistakes. Schultze (1996, p. 31, emphasis in original) has offered the following suggestion: "Instead of offering advice that seeks to balance economic insights, institutional views, political costs and other considerations, CEA members should see themselves as *partisan advocates of the efficient solution.*" Unfortunately as the story of the Kennedy–Johnson tax cut unfolded in this book, it became obvious that Heller, Ackley, Okun and other CEA members were convinced that they adhered to these principles and they took pride in advocating "the new economics" as an efficiency gain. To Heller, there was no inconsistency between being a partisan advocate of economic efficiency and a partisan Democrat (K15). To Ackley, suppressing embarrassing information (B24) achieved some greater good. To Okun, twisting the ears of businessmen to dissuade them from price increases (B54) was a Pareto improvement. Who was there in 1962 to warn them that their noble experiment was to lead directly to the demise of stabilization policy a few years later? Nothing in the record shows that these three chairmen had any doubts about their intentions or their actions. In the end, even if one disagrees with Norton's verdict (1977, p. 213) that "little blame was seriously put on the shoulders of CEA," it is probably not worth the effort to repeal the section of *The Employment Act of 1946* that established the Council and it would be vindictive to scale back its appropriations, but it is time to recognize its inescapable and irredeemable political role and to pay much less attention to its economic statements and evaluations.

I am reminded of the jester Rigoletto, in Verdi's opera of the same name, whose function it was to entertain the Duke of Mantua, a role that he presumed gave him power at the court beyond his humble station in life. Instead his daughter is seduced by the Duke, he is ridiculed by his enemies, he hires an assassin to kill the Duke, his daughter willingly replaces the Duke as the victim and the opera ends tragically with Rigoletto crying out the words: *"Ah, la maledizione!"* A similar curse involving the illusion of grand achievements has befallen the Council of Economic Advisers, when in fact their role is to amuse and indulge the President. As an example of this servile function, in March 1964, Heller wrote to the Secretaries of the Treasury, Commerce and Labor (J12):

> The President today asked me to pull together for him 3 times a week, from various agencies, what might be termed 'Economic (Good) News Notes.' ... The President has in mind not so much the routine flow of current-development-and-outlook data, but the pointing up of favorable developments, particularly newsworthy findings, and significant inferences that can be drawn from the flow of information available to the [Department]. This will call for skilled Departmental screening for significance and news value. We at CEA will distill various agencies' reports into a one-page summary of items for the President each Monday, Wednesday, and Friday.

After that it is difficult to take seriously Okun's recommendation that the Council must "be nonpolitical enough to give the President the straight unadulterated truth about the economy and economic policy, even when he won't enjoy hearing it." (J96). No one on the Council had the moral courage of the minor but heroic character in the opera, Count Monterone, who openly challenged the Duke after his daughter was seduced and paid for it with his life.

A FINAL THOUGHT

Economists think of themselves as benign imperialists because the rules that govern economic behavior can be applied in many other areas of human endeavor. Modern political economy involves economists urging governments to achieve economic efficiency on the basis that if the electorate attributes improvements in its welfare to policy changes, it will reward the incumbents who initiated them. Our great contribution is to make political action more rational and beneficial. What we, as a profession, have failed to see — until Stiglitz brought it to our attention — is that there are virtually no Pareto improvements to be found in government intervention; there are always some winners and some losers. Charles Schultze, who presided over the Council during the woeful years of the Carter Administration, is fully aware of this limitation. He writes (1996, p. 31):

> Few policy moves are Pareto superior; even actions with aggregate benefits substantially in excess of costs almost always hurt someone. Direct compensation to the injured is usually impossible, because of the difficulty of identifying or indemnifying specific winners and losers. If each decision is viewed in isolation, the logic of our profession gives economists no warrant to choose the efficient and uncompensable solution, with its widely distributed packets of small benefits and its large losses for a limited number of people.

As much as I agree with his assessment, I also wish he could have resisted the temptation to salvage the role of the economist turned policy adviser: "However, by viewing each decision as one step in an endlessly repeated process, I believe that economic advisers can justify consistently opting for the efficient solution in policy debates, in the belief that choosing the efficient approaches will in the long run advance the national welfare."

There are still too many economists who continue to believe that good economics makes for better politics. In the early years of academic economists as policy advisers — John Maynard Keynes was probably the first prominent example — economics may have held the upper hand. Since then that power has been eroded as economic policies must now achieve popularity, not efficiency. The scientific and practical progress made in opinion polling has had a much more pronounced effect on policy decisions than all the economic models of Pareto efficiency put together. Even in the Kennedy–Johnson era the advice rendered by the CEA was deeply colored by political imperatives, as the record now clearly shows, but this should not really come as a surprise to anyone who truly understands the dictum: "No one is immune to incentives."

Because they control the purse strings of the burgeoning public sector, politicians and bureaucrats set the rules by which the game will be played and economists, who have lots of ideas but precious little power, must accept these rules if they are to be policy advisers. The political arena is expressly designed as a place for adversarial confrontation. In order to win, each side needs economic experts, not as advisers, but as propagandists. Given the enormous stakes involved in these battles, the productivity of policy advisers is much more likely to be measured in terms of their ability to "sell" a program to the electorate than on their economic analysis of its benefits and costs. In the fullness of time this incentive system will lead economists to tell their political masters only what they *want* to hear instead of what they *need* to know and I, for one, cannot suggest a way of reversing this disturbing trend.

Appendix: Documents

Some of the documents which are important to this study are in hard-to-find primary sources; they are reproduced or summarized here. Long verbatim quotes are delimited by double horizontal lines.

CEA SUBMISSION TO JEC ON TAX EFFECTS

At the hearings before the Joint Economic Committee on 28 January 1963, the Chairman of the Council of Economic Advisers, Walter Heller, presented testimony on *The Economic Report of the President* and outlined the predicted effects on the tax cut. As part of a prepared statement, he submitted a "three-page appendix" which is reproduced verbatim from the *Hearings Before the Joint Economic Committee*, pp. 12–13. The text refers to colored bars in Chart 1, but its reproduction in the *Hearings* is only in black and white. The original chart could not be located.

EXPLANATION OF CHARTS OF EFFECTS OF TAX REDUCTION

The President's program would make tax reductions effective in stages between July 1963 and January 1965. But to simplify matters, the charts assume that all reductions would become effective at once.

In chart I [*sic*], the first bar on the left shows the two sources of higher consumer incomes: An estimated $8 billion from individual tax reduction, and an estimated one-half billion dollars of added dividends after taxes based on these dividends. (The additional dividends would undoubtedly begin to be paid only somewhat more slowly; but to simplify the chart, we assume them paid at once.) The second bar shows this as an increment of $8.5 billion in disposable income. The third bar shows this added income divided between added saving — about one-half billion dollars — and added consumption — about $8 billion. This added consumption would be repeated each period so long as the tax reduction was in effect. In turn, the added consumer buying would generate increased production of consumer goods, in the amount of $8 billion per period. This, of course, is an addition to GNP.

Chart II [*sic*] shows what typically happens to every added dollar of GNP — how it is divided among added taxes, added corporate retained earnings, and added disposable income. In turn the added disposable income is divided between consumption and personal saving. On the average in a period of expansion each added dollar of GNP typically generates another 50 cents of extra consumer spending.

Returning now to chart I [*sic*], the successive columns shaded in red show the growth of consumer spending over successive periods of time after the tax reduction goes into effect.

In the first period, consumer spending and GNP have grown by only the initial $8 billion. In the second time period, consumer spending and output of consumer goods is higher not only by $8 billion resulting directly from tax reduction, but also by $4 billion resulting from the previous period's increment of consumer spending. This $4 billion of respending in turn generates new disposable incomes, and, after a further lag, some $2 billion more of consumer spending. Thus, in period 3 consumer spending is $8 billion higher as a result of tax reduction applied to the base level of GNP, $4 billion respent from period 2's $8 billion, and $2 billion respent from period 2's $4 billion. Thus the rate of GNP in period 3 will be $14 billion above the base level. In period 4, it will be $15 billion higher; in period 4 (not shown) $15½ billion; and it will level off at $16 billion higher, as shown in the last column, which gives the ultimate effect. This is the pure "consumption multiplier" effect of tax reduction. It shows what would happen if nothing changed except consumption.

But investment will be affected too. To illustrate the investment effect, we have shown a possible pattern of investment response in green on the upper part of chart I [*sic*]. The amount of this response is chosen arbitrarily. We have shown it rising over time but have not indicated how far or fast it would continue to rise or where it might taper off. This is clearly an additional impact on GNP. But it is not the end of the matter. The higher incomes earned in producing capital goods are also respent, and generate incomes earned in producing consumer goods which are in turn respent. This is indicated by new bands of red at the top of the chart representing further consumer goods production. Ultimately each added billion dollars of investment will bring along with it an addition of another billion of consumer demand.

CHART 1

EFFECT OF TAX REDUCTION ON CONSUMPTION AND GNP

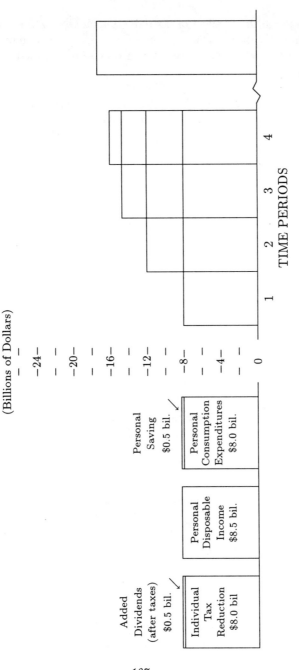

Thus the ultimate effect of tax reduction on GNP will be considerably more than the pure consumption effect. How much more it will be depends on how large an investment response is obtained.

CHART 2
DISTRIBUTION OF AN ADDITIONAL
DOLLAR OF GNP

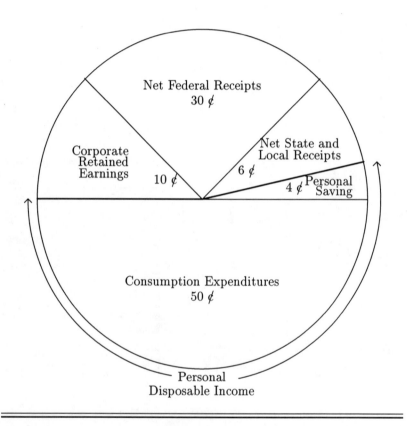

CEA STAFF MEMORANDUM ON TAX CUT

This anonymous, limited-distribution memorandum represents the "internal" position taken by the Council of Economic Advisers on the predicted effects of the tax cut. It contains more detail than Ackley's presentation at the JEC Hearings, reproduced above, and was written about a week later. It is referenced as (K28) in the Bibliography.

Copy No. 1   CEA Staff Memorandum

NOTES ON ECONOMIC ASSUMPTIONS UNDERLYING THE PRESIDENT'S TAX PROPOSALS[1]

2/6/63
[handwritten]

I. Economic prospects without tax reduction and reform

1) There are no forces now visible that would enable the economy to advance over the next several years at a faster average rate than it has since 1957. In any given year or quarter, of course, economic activity might be somewhat above or below this trend; but no long-term improvement would be expected.

2) This would imply:

a) GNP growing at 3 percent per year in real terms (the same as between 1957 and 1962) and 4-1/2 percent per year in current dollars.

b) Unemployment gradually rising from the current 5.8 percent to something slightly over 6 percent by mid-1964 and to perhaps 6-1/2 percent by mid-1965. Further, because of a lack of job opportunities, the size of the labor force would continue to fall substantially below its normal long-term trend. By mid-1965 the labor force could be some 2 million below its long-term trend size as projected by the Department of Labor.

c) Intermittent recessions would certainly interrupt this sluggish growth — we experienced two such recessions in the past five years. On the other hand, we foresee no recession in the immediate future.

II. Economic prospects with prompt (mid-year 1963) enactment
   of the President's tax proposals

1) Unemployment: When fully effective, and given time for its influence to be felt throughout the economy, tax reduction and reform can reasonably be expected to return the economy to a 4 percent unemployment rate.

2) On this basis GNP would begin climbing much more rapidly than in the "no-tax-cut" situation. The additions to GNP attributable to the tax program would be:

- - $15 to $20 billion in 1964
- - $35 to $40 billion in 1965

---

[1] Quantitative estimates are presented in a table at the end of this memorandum. All dollar amounts used in text and table are in current prices.

- - $50 to $60 billion in 1966

(These are not increases over the present level of GNP but over the level which would prevail in the relevant years under the 3% real growth assumption: i.e., without a tax cut.)

With prompt enactment of the tax program, GNP, which in the fourth quarter of 1962 amounted to $562 billion, could surpass $700 billion by early 1966, as compared with about $650 billion on the 3% real growth assumption. The average annual growth of GNP, 1962 to 1966, would be 5.8 percent in real terms, 7.4 percent in current prices.

3) Employment As compared with the slow-growth projection, employment would be higher under the tax program by about:

- - 1-1/4 million in 1964
- - 3 million in 1965
- - 4-1/2 million in 1966

(In 1966 the 4-1/2 million added employment is divided about equally between a reduction in unemployment and a return of the labor force to the level which might be expected to occur under conditions of plentiful job opportunities.)

Civilian employment in 1966 under the tax program would be about 6.7 million higher than the 1962 average of 67.8 million.

4) Tax revenue: Taking into account tax rate reduction, tax reform, and economic feedback on the revenue base, the estimated difference between administrative budget receipts under the proposed tax program and those receipts at present tax rates with 3% real economic growth are shown in the following table:

Fiscal year	Difference in revenues (billions of dollars)
1964	−2.7
1965	−2
1966	0
1967	+2

By fiscal year 1967, administrative budget revenues, under the new tax system, should be more than $20 billion higher than the $85-1/2 billion estimated for fiscal year 1963. (These revenue differences were calculated on the basis of the quarterly path of GNP with tax cut and with slow growth at existing tax rates, and of the probable distributions between corporate profits and personal incomes which would accompany these GNP's.)

III. Revenue and "other" costs of a recession

During the first two years of transition to a full employment economy, the tax program would thus "cost" some $4-1/2 billion in lost revenues.

However, one moderate recession — of a magnitude slightly larger than 1960–61, but smaller than 1957–58 — would cost about $8 billion in lost revenues, spread over several fiscal years. In one year alone such a recession would cost $6 billion in lost revenues, compared to the $2.7 billion revenue cost of the tax program in fiscal 1964. The new tax program would make the prospect of a recession in the near future much less likely. And among the important effects of a recession, which might thereby be avoided, are the loss of about 1-1/2 million man-years of employment and $20 to $25 billion of GNP.

IV. Budgetary impact of tax reduction

    1) There are three essential points:

a) Personal incomes and corporate profits will rise sharply as the economy moves toward full employment, under the stimulus of the tax program. Even with tax reductions occurring, revenues will rise rapidly in the next three to four fiscal years.

b) As the tax cut becomes fully effective and the economy climbs toward full employment, a substantial part of the revenue increases must go toward eliminating the transitional deficit.

c) If unemployment continued high, as it would under the 3% growth assumption with no tax program, there would be additional upward pressures on Federal spending; examples include unemployment compensation, extended unemployment benefits for those who exhausted their coverage, other welfare measures, aids to small business, area redevelopment, and accelerated public works. Some of these would be automatic under existing legislation; others would result from pressures for new legislation in response to high unemployment.

    2) Budget expenditures will rise over the next several years. Some increases in outlays for defense and space will occur merely to meet our existing national security and space exploration commitments. Increases in population and in private wages and salaries will also tend toward increased Federal outlays.

    3) However, especially during the years of transition to full employment and higher revenues, expenditure increases will be held to the minimum necessary to meet defense and space commitments and the domestic responsibilities of the Government. Both existing and proposed programs will be screened to see whether they meet this test of maximum essentiality, and all programs will be examined to insure that their basic objectives are being achieved at minimum cost to the Government.

V. "Multiplier" and "induced investment" effects

1) Individual tax reductions and increased dividends from corporate tax reduction (after personal taxes) constitute direct increases in disposable personal income. At current levels of income, these would amount to about $9-1/2 billion (with the program in full effect). At 1966 levels of income (projected on the basis of the slow growth assumptions) such additions to disposable income would be around $11 billion. Consumers have regularly saved between 6 and 8 percent of disposable income and spent the rest. Thus at the time the direct increase in consumption demand from the tax cut would be over $10 billion.

2) Incomes earned in producing added consumer goods are subject to taxation; some part is also added to corporate retained earnings. In total, about 55 cents of each added dollar of GNP reaches disposable income, generating about 50 cents of added consumer spending for each dollar of extra GNP. This gives rise to a "multiplier" of 2, and thus added consumption and GNP of over $20 billion from the original tax cut injection. (This includes the over $10 billion direct consumption described in the preceding paragraph.)

3) Higher utilization rates, greater profitability and increased cash flow will stimulate added investment. Added plant and equipment expenditures approaching $12–$14 billion (above the slow growth case) might easily result. In addition, residential construction, State and local spending, and inventory investment could increase by $4–6 billion above the no-tax-cut, slow-growth case. These expenditures are also subject to a multiplier effect, inducing roughly a further $18 billion of added consumption, and a total of $34–$38 billion of GNP.

4) The added purchases and GNP thus amount to $50–$60 above the "no-tax-cut," slow-growth case.

5) Business fixed investment expenditures at this level would be slightly above 10 percent of GNP. This ratio is appreciably lower than prevailed in the early post-war years, and lower than prevailed the last time unemployment approached 4 percent (10.7 percent in both 1956 and 1957). It is, of course, higher than the approximately 9 percent ratio of the past five years. This higher ratio of fixed investment to GNP is sustainable in an economy which is advancing at its full employment potential.

VI. Feasibility of projected increases in GNP

1) The $50 to $60 billion increases in GNP, which could be expected from the tax cut in 1966 can be accommodated within the manpower and capacity availability of the Nation.

a) These increases promise to bring GNP up to its "potential" without serious inflationary pressures from bottlenecks in the use of resources, because the stimulus is carefully phased over several years.

b) That potential is an estimate of the economy's ability to produce at a 4 percent unemployment level. The estimate of potential is based on an examination of past relationships between unemployment, working hours, and productivity. (For a detailed explanation, see pp. 26–28 of the 1963 Annual Report of the Council of Economic Advisers.)

c) The estimate of potential is also consistent with evidence of the utilization of industrial capacity. Production at potential does not mean production at 100 percent capacity, but rather at a level of utilization which is more or less in line with historical rates of utilization which have occurred during periods of relatively full employment.

d) The estimate of potential is a conservative one. It assumes that potential will grow at some $3\frac{1}{2}$ percent per year over the next four years. Actually, potential may grow even faster than this because the $3\frac{1}{2}$ percent growth rate may not allow sufficiently for the expected speedup in the rate of growth in the labor force. As the postwar "baby boom" begins to affect the labor force in the next several years, it will rise by some $1\frac{1}{2}$ million per year, compared to the 1.1 to 1.2 million "normal" growth of the last few years.

2) Increases in GNP which do not carry it beyond potential should not put undue pressure on our resources of manpower or industrial capacity. Hence the kinds of GNP increases expected to result from the tax cut, when fully effective, are not too large to be accommodated within the Nation's capacity. In turn, this means that the increases in GNP are not expected to strain against resource ceilings. The mobility of labor and other resources should continue to advance. And the retraining, vocational education, and other measures proposed in the 1964 budget should help speed the adaptability of the labor force to the growing and changing pattern of demand.

GNP, EMPLOYMENT, UNEMPLOYMENT
AND BUDGET REVENUES
– TAX CUT, 3% GROWTH, AND RECESSION MODELS –

| | | With no tax cut | | Differences | | |
	With tax cut	3% growth model	Recession model	Tax cut vs 3% growth	3% growth vs recession	Tax cut vs recession
GNP (billion $)						
CY						
1962	553.6	553.6	553.6	- -	- -	- -
1963	578.0	575.3	575.3	2.7	0	2.7
1964	620.5	602.5	583.3	18.0	19.2	37.2
1965	670.5	630.0	622.5	40.5	7.5	48.0
1966	715.0	657.5	657.5	57.5	0	57.5
Civilian Employment (millions of persons)						
C.Y.						
1962	67.8	67.8	67.8	- -	- -	- -
1963	68.2	68.1	68.1	.1	0	.1
1964	70.1	68.8	67.9	1.3	.9	2.2
1965	72.6	69.4	68.9	3.2	.5	3.7
1966	74.5	69.9	69.7	4.6	.2	4.8
Unemployment (percent)						
C.Y.						
1962	5.6	5.6	5.6	- -	- -	- -
1963	6.0	6.2	6.2	.2	0	.2
1964	5.3	6.3	7.3	1.0	1.0	2.0
1965	4.4	6.4	6.6	2.0	.2	2.2
1966	4.0	6.5	6.6	2.5	.1	2.6
Federal administrative budget revenues (billion $)						
F.Y.						
1963	85.5	85.5	85.5	- -	- -	- -
1964	86.9	89.6	89.3	−2.7	0	−2.7
1965	92.8	94.7	88.9	−1.9	5.8	3.9
1966	99.6	99.6	98.0	0	1.6	1.6
1967	106.5	104.5	104.4	+2.0	.1	2.1

February 6, 1963

THE REVENUE ACT OF 1964

Public Law 88-272 became *The Revenue Act of 1964* when it was passed and signed on 26 February 1964. Its purpose was "to amend the Internal Revenue Code of 1954 to reduce individual and corporate income taxes, to make certain structural changes with respect to the income tax and for other purposes." It is contained in *United States Statutes at Large*, Vol. 78, pp. 19–145. Its Section 1 is a "Declaration of Congress" that reads as follows:

> It is the sense of Congress that the tax reduction provided by this Act through stimulation of the economy, will, after a brief transitional period, raise (rather than lower) revenues and that such revenue increases should first be used to eliminate the deficits in the administrative budgets and then to reduce the public debt. To further the objective of obtaining balanced budgets in the near future, Congress by this action, recognizes the importance of taking all reasonable means to restrain Government spending and urges the President to declare his accord with this objective.

Title I deals with tax rates and related items, Part I of which pertains to individuals and heads of households. In Sec. 111, two sets of tax rates are specified for each group. Beginning 1 January 1964, marginal tax rates are between 16 and 77 per cent for both groups. Previously, tax rates ranged between 20 and 91 per cent. The lowest rate applied to taxable income of $500 for individuals and $1,000 for heads of households. The highest rate was levied on taxable incomes in excess of $200,000 for both groups. Beginning in 1965, marginal tax rates were again reduced, this time to 14 per cent as the lowest rate and 70 per cent as the highest. For individuals, the maximum rate was payable on taxable income in excess of $100,000 and for heads of households, on income exceeding $180,000.

Part II of Title I relates to the taxation of corporations. According to Sec. 121, the "normal tax" was 30 per cent for a taxable year beginning before 1 January 1964 and 22 per cent for a taxable year beginning after 31 December 1963. In addition, a "surtax" of 22 per cent was payable for taxable years beginning before 1 January 1964, 28 per cent for taxable years beginning after 31 December 1963 and before 1 January 1965, and 26 per cent for taxable years beginning after 31 December 1964. There was a surtax exemption of $25,000 for any taxable year.

Title II, the largest part of the bill, deals with structural changes to the Internal Revenue Code of 1954 that are not germane to the macroeconomic aspects of the tax cut, except to the extent that they raised or lowered tax revenue or altered private expenditure decisions significantly. A useful summary of these provisions of the tax bill was contained in *The New York Times* for 27 February 1964, p. 19.

Finally, Title III stipulates an "optional tax" if adjusted gross income is less $5,000. More importantly for the timing of the effects of the tax cut, Sec. 302 reduced the withholding rate from 18 per cent to 14 per cent, effective 7 days after the enactment of the legislation. For a person earning the average weekly wage of $91.33 in the private nonagricultural sector and with four exemptions, the amount of income tax withheld was $5.60.

ACKLEY'S FISCAL-POLICY MEMORANDUM

This memorandum to the President contains the earliest and strongest indication that the previous expansionary fiscal policy had to be reversed at the first opportunity. It also provides disturbing evidence that the Council advised suppressing damaging information.

THE CHAIRMAN OF THE
THE COUNCIL OF ECONOMIC ADVISERS
WASHINGTON

December 26, 1965

MEMORANDUM FOR THE PRESIDENT

Subject: Budget Policy for FY 1967

1. *The "Troika" has now nearly completed its estimates* of the state of the economy in 1966. The changes are sufficiently large that I feel I must revise the views you requested on December 16, and contained in my memorandum of December 17.

2. The *new estimate of 1966 GNP is $729 billion,* for an advance of $53 billion or 7.9% over the new higher figure of $675.7 billion for 1965. This would be a *distinct step-up* from the $47 billion or 7.5% rise this year.

   - A few months ago, the Quadriad agreed that any GNP above $720 billion for 1966 had worrisome implications for price stability. We could stretch beyond that to some degree, but $729 seems to stretch too far.

   - Similarly, a few months ago, we were hoping to reach the 4% unemployment target in 1966. Now, we would expect unemployment to go below $3^1/2$% and approach 3% late in the year. Only in World

War II and during and after Korea has unemployment been that
low.

3. $729 billion is the estimate for 1966 *without any tax measures to
moderate the advance.* However, we have now staffed out the effects
of an April 1 effective date for

- - graduated withholding,

- - the restoration of pending excise taxes on autos and
telephones, and

- - a further speed-up of corporate tax payments.

These measures would reduce GNP in 1966 by only $2 billion, and,
at an annual rate, by less than $4 billion in the fourth quarter of
1966.

4. *Even with these measures,* the fast advance of the economy in 1966
would carry *serious risk of a significant step-up in the rate of price
advance.* To be sure, our crystal-ball is far from perfect. We could be
surprised by a slower pace of demand, just as we have been surprised
by its strength in recent months. We also remember that, as late as
last May, we were told Defense spending was not on the rise. We
could get new surprises on that front in 1966 — in either direction.
But one forecast is easy: *once business and financial economists learn
and digest the basic information we have recently received*

- - the bigger GNP numbers for the first 3 quarters of this
year,

- - the huge GNP advance in the current quarter, and

- - the budgetary outlook,

everyone will be talking about overheating in 1966. Once attitudes
change, the task of preventing inflation can strain the guidepost approach to the breaking point.

5. Incidentally, in view of psychological risks, *I do not believe the Administration can publicly forecast a GNP anywhere close to $729 bil-
lion,* regardless of the policy measures adopted. If we point to an
acceleration over the huge gains of this year, no one will believe that
prices can be held in check. *We can make a conservative and still
sensible forecast,* although this will not completely fool many outside
experts. Unfortunately, it will also cut somewhat into our revenue
estimates.

6. The *only conclusion I can reach* is that an increase of individual
   and corporate income tax rates should be planned, *whatever the FY
   1967 budget* may be (within the limits we have heard discussed).
   Tactically, it may only be feasible to propose higher taxes later in
   the year. *From an economic standpoint, it needs to be done as soon
   as possible.*

Gardner Ackley

THE REVENUE AND EXPENDITURE CONTROL ACT OF 1968

After a long public debate *The Revenue and Expenditure Control Act
of 1968* was signed into law on 28 June 1968 as Public Law 90-364
and is contained in *United States Statutes at Large*, Vol. 82, pp. 251–
74. It was intended "to increase revenues, to limit expenditures and
new obligational authority, and for other purposes." The following is a
brief description of the most important parts, as they pertain to macroeconomic considerations.

Title I deals with the tax surcharge. Section 102 specifies: "In addition to the other taxes imposed by this chapter, there is hereby imposed
on the income of every individual (other than an estate or trust) whose
taxable year is the calendar year a tax as follows:" and then outlines the
extra tax to be paid by individuals in various categories. In calendar
year 1968, this generally amounted to 7.5 per cent of the adjusted tax
that would normally be calculated and paid. In calendar year 1969, it
was 5 per cent of the adjusted tax. The effective dates for withholding
rules applied to paychecks received after 31 March 1968 and before 1
July 1969. Hence the surcharge could be calculated as 10 per cent on
adjusted taxes during the final 9 months in 1968 and the first six months
in 1969, especially since there were provisions for persons who had irreg-
ularly spaced income during any calendar year. For estates and trusts,
the surcharge was 7.5 per cent in 1968 and 5 per cent in 1969, while for
corporations it was 10 per cent in 1968 and 5 per cent in 1969.

Section 105 allowed for the continuation of excise taxes on communi-
cation services and on automobiles. The former would be taxed at 10 per
cent until 1 January 1970 and decline to 1 per cent thereafter, while the
latter were taxed at 7 per cent until 1 January 1970 and decline to 1 per
cent. Finally, Section 110 stated, "Not later than December 31, 1968,
the President shall submit to the Congress proposals for a comprehensive
reform of the Internal Revenue Code of 1954."

In Title II, Congress attempted to limit expenditures during fiscal year 1969. Section 201 specifies the limitation on the number of civilian officers and employees in the executive branch to those existing on 30 June 1966, but with a multitude of exceptions. Section 202 (a) is quoted in its entirety:

> Sec. 202 (a) Expenditures and net lending during the fiscal year ending June 30, 1969, under the Budget of the United States Government (estimated on page 55 of House Document No. 225, Part 1, 90th Congress as totaling $186,062,000,000), shall not exceed $180,062,000,000, except by expenditures and net lending — (1) which the President may determine are necessary for special support of Vietnam operations in excess of the amounts estimated therefor in the Budget, (2) for interest in excess of the amounts estimated therefor in the Budget, (3) for veterans' benefits and services in excess of the amounts estimated therefor in the Budget, and (4) for payments from trust funds established by the Social Security Act, as amended, in excess of the amounts estimated therefor in the Budget.

In Section 203, using similar wording, the obligational and loan authority ending 30 June 1969 was reduced by $10 billion. Finally, Title III contains amendments to the Social Security Act.

OKUN: HOW POLITICAL MUST THE CEA BE?

At the December 1973 meetings of the American Economic Association, Okun made the following remarks that were not included in the May 1974 issue of the *American Economic Review*; they were found in his papers (J96) and represent an important view of the role of the CEA after his departure.

HOW POLITICAL MUST THE CEA BE?

A. M. Okun

American Economics Association Meeting
December 29, 1973

Since I promised Eileen Shanahan to stick to a five-minute opening statement, I shall rattle off some hopefully provocative thoughts with no explanation or justification.

First, the most important political task of the Council of Economic Advisers is internal politicking within the Executive Branch — the bureaucratic infighting to win the heart and mind of the President. The Council had better be effective in that invisible politicking. But it had better be nonpolitical enough to give the President the straight unadulterated truth about the economy and economic policy, even when he won't enjoy hearing it.

Second, CEA must be loyal to the President; it exists to advise the President — not the press, the public, or the profession. Its effectiveness depends entirely on its relationship with the President, and would be impaired — even destroyed — if it were to criticize Administration policy.

Third, silence in public is the great reconciler of loyalty and integrity. Although a CEA member can never say everything he believes, he should never say anything he doesn't believe. If silence is inadequate, if the disagreement is fundamental, the CEA member should fold up his tent, silently and politely steal out of the Administration, and then speak out on economic issues. The man who resigned with a blast because the President didn't take his advice would be a heel, not a hero.

To illustrate autobiographically, during 1966 economic policy veered substantially off my preferred course. Starting in December 1965, the Ackley Council urged a tax increase upon President Johnson, basing the initial judgment on the same defense estimates made public in the January 1966 budget. Subsequent repeated upward revisions of defense spending that were given us confidentially (and not released to the public) merely reaffirmed our conviction. Although I found public silence golden (cancelling a couple of speeches in the summer), I felt that professional responsibility called for staying in the political battle to get fiscal policy back on course. To be sure, in the light of years of history and perhaps in the cold light of objectivity that shines on independent scholars, the issues of Vietnam in general and suppressing budgetary information in particular look very different to me today. But I would reaffirm the basic decision to battle internally and shut up externally.

Fourth, the public role of CEA should reflect the preferences and talents of CEA members. In nearly four years of CEA chairmanship, Walter Heller must have spoken publicly about ten times as much as Arthur Burns. And yet both were great CEA Chairmen. Being telegenic, witty, and an extrovert should neither qualify nor disqualify a man for Council chairmanship.

Finally, when he does speak out publicly, the CEA member should maintain his role as an expert and an analyst. There are some treacherous pitfalls. One is cheer leading. Obviously, no CEA member will ever say that the economy is going to Hell and there's no way to stop it. But evaluations of the economy should not see only the bright side. And we ought to repeal the idiotic tradition that requires every economic statistic to be evaluated by CEA.

The second pitfall is the overselling of programs. CEA should display its professional enthusiasm about economic proposals and programs — especially about its own babies. But selling should not become overselling. I wince rereading my speeches in behalf of the tax surcharge in 1967–68 — I promised too much and hedged too little. And this problem continues undiminished. Whatever the merits of the excise tax on crude oil proposed by the Administration last week, it was not an excess profits tax and it was part of a broader unannounced decision to retreat from reliance on a two-price system to avoid windfalls.

A third pitfall is electioneering, an issue that has been widely discussed of late and that should get an airing today. Campaigning by CEA does not violate the Hatch Act, but it breaks the law of comparative advantage. Campaign speeches are a peculiar art form, combining love poetry for one's candidate and invective for his opponent. No matter how well and how temperately that art form is practiced, the product is not professional analysis, by any standard. And the only reason for such a speech to be delivered by a CEA chairman is to invoke the professional prestige of the nation's top economic expert. Such a use of that scarce resource is bound to depreciate its value in more vital objective uses. When next a CEA chairman is urged to roll up his sleeves and electioneer, he should be able to decline by insisting that the criticism will cost more votes than the speeches will gain. He can offer instead to pitch in with speech inputs for others.

In summary, if CEA can be effective in internal politicking; if it can maintain its loyalty to the President and its professional integrity, invoking silence if necessary; and if, when it speaks publicly, it can avoid cheer leading, overselling, and electioneering, then it will have solved the problem of how political to be. In that case, it will merely have to solve the problem of providing sound economic advice for the President.

Bibliography

PUBLISHED MATERIAL

Some of the publications in this list were reprinted in books that are now more easily located than the original. In such cases, the following convention is used for citations in the text: Okun (1968; 1970, p. 345) indicates that 1968 was the year of original publication and that the reference is to p. 345 in the 1970 version, both of which are listed below.

Ackley, Gardner (1961), *Macroeconomic Theory*, New York: Macmillan.

Ackley, Gardner (1966), "The Contribution of Guidelines," in *Guidelines: Informal Controls and the Market Place*, edited by George P. Schultz and Robert Z. Aliber, Chicago: University of Chicago Press, pp. 67–78.

Adams, Charles and David T. Coe (1990), "A Systems Approach to Estimating the Natural Rate of Unemployment and Potential Output for the United States," *International Monetary Fund Staff Papers*, **37**, pp. 232–93.

Almon, Shirley (1965), "The Distributed Lag between Capital Appropriations and Expenditures," *Econometrica*, **30**, pp. 178–96.

Ando, Albert and E. Cary Brown (1963), "Lags in Fiscal Policy: Summary," research study prepared for the Commission on Money and Credit, *Stabilization Policies*, Englewood Cliffs, NJ: Prentice-Hall Inc.; reprinted in Smith and Teigen (1970, pp. 358–63).

Ando, Albert and Franco Modigliani (1963), "The 'Life Cycle' Hypothesis of Saving Behavior: Aggregate Implications and Tests," *American Economic Review*, **53**, pp. 53–84.

Auerbach, Alan J. and Joel Slemrod (1997), "The Economic Effects of the Tax Reform Act of 1986," *Journal of Economic Literature*, **35**, pp. 589–632.

Birnbaum, Jeffrey H. (1992), *The Lobbyists*, New York: Times Books.

Cochrane, D. and Guy H. Orcutt (1949), "Application of Least-squares Regressions to Relationships Containing Auto-correlated Error Terms," *Journal of the American Statistical Association*, **44**, pp. 32–61.

Council of Economic Advisers (1961), *The American Economy in 1961: Problems and Policies*, reprinted in Tobin and Weidenbaum (1988, pp. 17–86).

deLeeuw, Frank *et al.* (1980), "The High-Employment Budget: New Estimates, 1955–80," *Survey of Curent Business*, **60** (11), pp. 13–43.

Dernburg, Thomas F. (1985), *Macroeconomics: Concepts, Theories and Policies*, 7th edition, New York: McGraw-Hill Book Company.

Dernburg, Thomas F. and Duncan M. McDougall (1960), *Macro-economics*,
New York: McGraw-Hill Book Company.

Diebold, Francis X. (1998), "The Past, Present, and Future of Macroeconomic
Forecasting," *Journal of Economic Perspectives*, **12**, pp. 175–92.

Dixit, Avinash and Barry Nalebuff (1991), *Thinking Strategically*, New York:
W.W. Norton & Company.

Duesenberry, James S., Gary Fromm, Lawrence R. Klein and Edwin Kuh
(1965), *The Brookings Quarterly Econometric Model of the United States*,
Chicago: Rand McNally & Co.

Eckstein, Otto (1970), "The Economics of the 1960's: A Backward Look,"
Public Interest (Spring), pp. 86–97.

Eizenstat, Stuart E. (1992), "Economists and White House Decisions," *Journal of Economic Perspectives*, **6** (Summer), pp. 65–71.

Farrell, M.J. (1959), "The New Theories of the Consumption Function," *Economic Journal*, **69**, pp. 678–96.

Feldstein, Martin (1997), "The Council of Economic Advisers: From Stabilization to Resource Allocation," *American Economic Review: Papers and
Proceedings*, **87**, pp. 99–102.

Fellner, William (1982), "The High-Employment Budget and Potential Output," *Survey of Current Business*, **62** November, pp. 26–33.

Flash, Edward S. Jr. (1965), *Economic Advice and Presidential Leadership*,
New York: Columbia University Press.

Friedman, Milton (1957), *A Theory of the Consumption Function*, Princeton
NJ: Princeton University Press.

Friedman, Milton (1968), "The Role of Monetary Policy," *American Economic
Review*, **58**, pp. 1–17.

Galbraith, John Kenneth (1958), *The Affluent Society*, Boston: Houghton
Mifflin Company.

Gordon, H. Scott (1961), *The Economists versus the Bank of Canada*, Toronto:
Ryerson Press.

Gordon, Robert J. (1982), "Inflation, Flexible Exchange Rates, and the Natural Rate of Unemployment," in Martin N. Baily, editor, *Workers, Jobs,
and Inflation*, Washington: Brookings Institution, pp. 89–152.

Gordon, Robert J. (1984), "Unemployment and Potential Output in the
1980's," *Brookings Papers on Economic Activity*, 2:1984, pp. 537–68.

Gordon, Robert J. (1993), *Macroeconomics*, 6th edition, New York: Harper-
Collins.

Gordon, Robert J. (1997), "The Time-Varying NAIRU and its Implications
for Economic Policy," *Journal of Economic Perspectives*, **11**, pp. 11–32.

Hamilton, Lee H. (1992), "Economists as Public Policy Advisers," *Journal of
Economic Perspectives*, **6** (Summer), pp. 61–4.

Hansen, Alvin H. (1953), *A Guide to Keynes*, New York: McGraw-Hill Book
Company.

Hargrove, Erwin C. and Samuel A. Morley, editors (1984), *The President and the Council of Economic Advisers: Interviews with CEA Chairmen*, Boulder, CO: Westview Press.

Harr, Jonathan (1996), "The Crash Detectives," *The New Yorker*, 5 August, pp. 34–55.

Heilbroner, Robert L. (1974), "The Clouded Crystal Ball," *American Economic Review: Papers and Proceedings*, **64**, pp. 121–4.

Heilbroner, Robert L. and Peter L. Bernstein (1963), *A Primer on Government Spending*, New York: Vintage Books.

Heller, Walter W. (1962), "Why We Must Cut Taxes," *Nation's Business*, **50**, November, pp. 40–42.

Heller, Walter W. (1967), *New Dimensions of Political Economy*, New York: W.W. Norton.

Henderson, James M. and Richard E. Quandt (1958), *Microeconomic Theory: A Mathematical Approach*, New York: McGraw-Hill Book Company.

Hendry, David and Neil Ericsson (1990), "Modelling the Demand for Narrow Money in the United Kingdom and the United States," manuscript, Washington: Board of Governors, Federal System.

Hicks, John R. (1937), "Mr. Keynes and the Classics: A Suggested Interpretation," *Econometrica*, **5**, pp. 147–59.

Johnson, Lyndon B. (1971), *The Vantage Point: Perspectives of the Presidency 1963-1969*, New York: Holt, Rinehart & Winston.

Johnston, John (1963), *Econometric Methods*, New York: McGraw-Hill Book Company.

Kearns, Doris (1976), *Lyndon Johnson and the American Dream*, New York: Harper & Row.

Keyserling, Leon H. (1956), "The Council of Economic Advisers' Tasks in the Next Decade," in *The Employment Act, Past and Future: A Tenth Anniversary Symposium*, edited by Gerhard Colm, Washington: National Planning Association, pp. 66–73.

Mankiw, N. Gregory (1986), "The Term Structure Revisited," *Brookings Papers in Economic Activity*, 1:1986, pp. 61–96.

Manley, John F. (1970), *The Politics of Finance: The House Committee on Ways and Means*, Boston: Little, Brown & Company.

McLure Charles E. Jr. (1972), *Fiscal Failure: Lessons of the Sixties*, Special Analysis No. 22, Washington: American Enterprise Institute for Public Policy Research.

McLure, Charles E. Jr. (1988), "The 1986 Act: Tax Reform's Finest Hour or Death Throes of the Income Tax?" *National Tax Journal*, **41**, pp. 303–15.

Meade, James E. (1951), *The Theory of International Economic Policy*, Volume I: *The Balance of Payments*, London: Oxford University Press.

Modigliani, Franco (1949), "Fluctuations in the Saving–Income Ratio: A Problem in Economic Forecasting," in National Bureau of Economic Research *Studies in Income and Wealth*, No. 11.

Modigliani, Franco (1986), "Life Cycle, Individual Thrift, and the Wealth of Nations," *American Economic Review*, **76**, pp. 297–313.

Modigliani, Franco and Richard Brumberg (1954), "Utility Analysis and the

Consumption Function: An Interpretation of Cross-Section Data," in Kenneth Kurihara, editor, *Post-Keynesian Economics*, New Brunswick, NJ: Rutgers University Press, pp. 388–436.

Mundell, Robert A. (1962), "The Appropriate Use of Monetary and Fiscal Policy for Internal and External Stability," *International Monetary Fund Staff Papers*, **9**, pp. 70–79.

Mundell, Robert A. (1963), "On the Selection of a Program of Economic Policy with an Application to the Current Situation in the United States," *Banca Nazionale Del Lavoro Quarterly Review*, **16**, pp. 262–84.

Norton, Hugh S. (1977), *The Employment Act and the Council of Economic Advisers, 1946–1976*, Columbia, SC: University of South Carolina Press.

Ohanian, Lee E. (1997), "The Macroeconomic Effects of War Finance in the United States: World War II and the Korean War," *American Economic Review*, **87**, pp. 23–40.

Okun, Arthur M. (1962), "Potential GNP: Its Measurement and Significance," *Proceedings of the Business and Economic Section of the American Statistical Association*, reprinted in Smith and Teigen (1970, pp. 313–22).

Okun, Arthur M., editor (1965), *The Battle Against Unemployment*, New York: W.W. Norton.

Okun, Arthur M. (1968), "Measuring the Impact of the 1964 Tax Reduction," in Walter W. Heller (ed.), *Perspectives on Economic Growth*, New York: Random House, pp. 27–49; reprinted in Smith and Teigen (1970, pp. 345–58).

Olson, Mancur (1971), *The Logic of Collective Action*, Cambridge, MA: Harvard University Press.

Organization for Economic Co-operation and Development (OECD) (1965), *Techniques of Economic Forecasting*, Paris.

Perry, George L. (1966), *Unemployment, Money Wage Rates and Inflation*, Cambridge, MA: MIT Press.

Phelps, Edmund S. (1967), "Phillips Curves, Expectations of Inflation and Optimal Unemployment over Time," *Economica*, **34**, pp. 254–81.

Pindyck, Robert S. and Daniel L. Rubenfeld (1991), *Econometric Models and Economic Forecasts*, third edition, New York: McGraw-Hill, Inc.

Prachowny, Martin F.J. (1969), *A Structural Model of the U.S. Balance of Payments*, Amsterdam: North-Holland Publishing Company.

Prachowny, Martin F.J. (1993), "Okun's Law: Theoretical Foundations and Revised Estimates," *Review of Economics and Statistics*, **75**, pp. 331–6.

Prachowny, Martin F.J. (1994), *The Goals of Macroeconomic Policy*, London and New York: Routledge.

Prachowny, Martin F.J. (1997), *Working in the Macroeconomy: A Study of the US Labor Market*, London and New York: Routledge.

Romer, Christina D. (1993), "The Nation in Depression," *Journal of Economic Perspectives*, **7**, pp. 19–39.

Romer, David (1996), *Advanced Macroeconomics*, New York: McGraw-Hill Company.

Samuelson, Paul A. (1939), "Interaction between the Multiplier Analysis and the Principle of Acceleration," *Review of Economic Statistics*, **21**, pp. 75–8.

Samuelson, Paul A. (1954), "Pure Theory of Public Expenditures," *Review of Economics and Statistics*, **36**, pp. 387–9.

Schlesinger, Arthur M. Jr. (1965), *A Thousand Days: John F. Kennedy in the White House*, Boston: Houghton Mifflin Company.

Schultze, Charles L. (1996), "The CEA: An Inside Voice for Mainstream Economics," *Journal of Economic Perspectives*, **10**, pp. 23–40.

Sherwood, Robert E. (1950), *Roosevelt and Hopkins: An Intimate History*, New York: Grosset & Dunlap.

Smith, Warren L. and Ronald L. Teigen, editors (1970), *Readings in Money, National Income and Stabilization Policy*, revised edition, Homewood, IL: Richard D. Irwin.

Solow, Robert M. (1966), "The Case Against the Case Against the Guideposts," and "Comments," in *Guidelines: Informal Controls and the Market Place*, edited by George P. Schultz and Robert Z. Aliber, Chicago: University of Chicago Press, pp. 41–54 and 62–6.

Solow, Robert M. (1997), "It Ain't the Things You Don't Know That Hurt You, It's the Things You Know That Ain't So," *American Economic Review: Papers and Proceedings*, **87**, pp. 107–8.

Solow, Robert M. and James Tobin (1988), "Introduction," in *Two Revolutions in Economic Policy*, edited by James Tobin and Murray L. Weidenbaum, Cambridge, MA: MIT Press, pp. 3–16.

Sorensen, Theodore C. (1965), *Kennedy*, New York: Harper & Row.

Stadler, George W. (1994), "Real Business Cycles," *Journal of Economic Literature*, **32**, pp. 1750–83.

Stein, Herbert (1988), *Presidential Economics: The Making of Economic Policy from Roosevelt to Reagan and Beyond*, 2nd revised edition, Washington: American Enterprise Institute.

Stein, Herbert (1996a), *The Fiscal Revolution in America: Policy in Pursuit of Reality*, 2nd revised edition, Washington: AEI Press.

Stein, Herbert (1996b), "A Successful Accident: Recollections and Speculations about the CEA," *Journal of Economic Perspectives*, **10**, pp. 3–21.

Stiglitz, Joseph (1997), "Looking Out for the National Interest: The Principles of the Council of Economic Advisers," *American Economic Review: Papers and Proceedings*, **87**, pp. 109–13.

Stiglitz, Joseph (1998), "The Private Uses of Public Interests: Incentives and Institutions," *Journal of Economic Perspectives*, **12**, pp. 3–22.

Taylor, John B. (1993), *Macroeconomic Policy in a World Economy: From Econometric Design to Practical Operation*, New York: W. W. Norton & Co.

Teigen, Ronald L. (1970), "The Effectiveness of Public Works as a Stabilization Device," in Smith and Teigen (1970, pp. 333–9).

Thurow, Lester C. (1969), "A Fiscal Policy Model of the United States," *Survey of Current Business*, **49** (6), pp. 45–64.

Tobin, James (1980), "Stabilization Policy Ten Years After," *Brookings Papers on Economic Activity*, 1:1980, pp. 19–71.

Tobin, James and Murray L. Weidenbaum, editors (1988), *Two Revolutions in Economic Policy*, Cambridge, MA: MIT Press.

US Congress, Joint Economic Committee (1963a), *Hearings Before the Joint Economic Committee*, 28–31 January, 1, 4–6 February, 1963, 88th Congress, 1st Session, Washington: Superintendent of Documents.

US Congress, Joint Economic Committee (1963b), *Report of the Joint Economic Committtee on the January 1963 Economic Report of the President*, 88th Congress, 1st Session, Washington: Superintendent of Documents.

US Congress, Joint Economic Committee (1964), *Hearings Before the Joint Economic Committee*, 23–29 January 1964, 88th Congress, 2nd Session, Washington: Superintendent of Documents.

US Congress, Joint Economic Committee, Subcommittee on Fiscal Policy (1965a), *Hearings Before the Subcommittee on Fiscal Policy*, 89th Congress, 1st Session, Washington: Superintendent of Documents.

US Congress, Joint Economic Committee, Subcommittee on Fiscal Policy (1965b), *Statements by Individual Economists and Representatives of Interested Organizations*, 89th Congress, 1st Session, Washington: Superintendent of Documents.

US Department of Commerce (1966), *The National Income and Product Accounts of the United States, 1929–65: Statistical Tables*, Washington: Superintendent of Documents.

US Department of Commerce (1977), *The National Income and Product Accounts of the United States, 1929–74: Statistical Tables*, Washington: Superintendent of Documents.

US Department of Commerce (1982), *Fixed Reproducible Tangible Wealth in the United States, 1925–79*, Washington: Superintendent of Documents.

US Department of Commerce (1993), "Fixed Reproducible Tangible Wealth in the United States: Revised Estimates for 1990–92 and Summary Estimates for 1925–92," *Survey of Current Business*, **73**, September, pp. 61–9.

US President (1953–98), *Economic Report of the President*, Washington: Superintendent of Documents.

Whealan, Ronald E., compiler and editor (1993), *Historical Materials in the John Fitzgerald Kennedy Library*, Boston: John Fitzgerald Kennedy Library.

ARCHIVAL MATERIAL

This material is listed in chronological order and citations in the text are to the number attached to each item, with a prefix K for the Kennedy Library, B for the Bentley Historical Library at the University of Michigan and J for the Johnson Library in Austin Texas. In view of the overlap of Heller, Ackley and Okun as members and chairmen of the Council, material authored by one of them was found in the files of the others. Thus Ackley papers are found in the Heller collection and vice versa.

Description: Author and Recipient (if any), "Title," Date, Name of Collection (Box Number: Folder Title). "—" is used if information is unavailable; "?" is used to denote uncertainty about information; if no title is available, quotation marks are omitted and short description of contents is provided. Only last names are given for well-known participants.

John F. Kennedy Library

Information about historical material at the Kennedy Library is provided in Whealan (1993). Only a few of the collections are mentioned below. Abbreviations: HP – Walter H. Heller Papers, POF – Presidential Office Papers, WHCF – White House Central Files.

K1   Heller to File, "Conversation with Senator Kennedy on Economic Issues," 4 October 1960, HP (4: 7/60–10/60).

K2   Heller to Tobin and Gordon, "Eventual Memo to the President on Tax Cut," 20 February 1961, HP (21: 11/60–3/61).

K3   Heller to President, "Shea Article in Wall Street Journal," 28 February 1961, POF (63a: 1961).

K4   CEA, "The Role of the Council of Economic Advisers," 6 March 1961, HP (3: 2/16/61–9/2/64).

K5   Solow to Heller, "Brief Note on 4% unemployment rate," 15 March 1961, WHCF (113 FG 011: 1/1/61–7/31/61).

K6   Heller to President, "The Economics of the Second-Stage Recovery Program," 17 March 1961, HP (5: 3/61).

K7   Heller to President, "Retroactive Income Tax Cut for 1960," 21 March 1961, HP (5: 3/61).

K8   Heller to Tobin, Gordon, and Solow, "Activities from March 17 through March 24, 1961," 27 March 1961, HP (3, 2/61–3/61).

K9   Heller to Gordon, Tobin, and Solow, "Preparation for Resumed Hearings," 3 April 1961, HP (3: 2/61–3/61).

K10 Heller to Tobin, Gordon, Solow, and Okun, "Talk with Paul Samuelson," 15 May 1961, HP (5: 5/61–6/61).

K11 Consultants to the Subcommittee, "Memorandum to the Subcommittee on Sound Wage and Price Policies," 4 August 1961, HP (24: 2/61–12/61).

K12 Heller to President, "Outline of Economic Report: Appendix A," 18 October 1961, HP (3: 9/61–10/61).

K13 Heller to President, "What it takes to get to full employment," 3 March 1962, HP (5: 3/3/62).

K14 Heller to President, "That Slevin Story, Shadow and Substance," 3 March 1962, WHCF (113 FG 011: 8/1/61–3/31/61).

K15 Heller to President, "The Slowdown in the Recovery and Its Implications for Policy," 21 March 1962, HP (5: 3/6/62–3/15/62).

K16 Kennedy to Johnson and McCormack, letter explaining bill on standby authority to reduce taxes, 8 May 1962, WHCF (476: LE000/FI11 4/6/62–7/15/62).

K17 —, "Notes on JFK's Yale Commencement Speech in June, 1962," —, HP (4: 8/60–11/61).

K18 Okun to Records and Tobin, "BOB-CEA Meeting of May 29," 1 June 1962, HP (4: 4/62–9/62).

K19 — to President, "Wednesday's Meeting on Budget and Tax Policy — Draft," 9 June 1962, HP (5: 6/62).

K20 Heller to President, memo on Gallup poll, 31 July 1962, WHCF (113: FG011, 4/1/62).

K21 Gordon to Heller and Ackley, "Miscellaneous Developments While you Were Gone," 13 October 1962, HP (4: 10/62–12/62).

K22 Okun, "A Post-Mortem on 1962 and a Pre-Natal Look at 1963," 28 November 1962, POF (75a: 11/16/62–5/31/63).

K23 Cabinet Committee on Economic Growth to President, "Programs to Promote Economic Growth in the 1963 Administration Program," 2 December 1962, POF (75a: 11/16/62–5/31/63).

K24 Heller to President, "Recap of Issues on Tax Cuts (and the Galbraithian alternative)," 16 December 1962, HP (5: 12/62).

K25 Heller to President, "Report on tax and other fronts," 21 December 1962, HP (5: 11/62–12/62).

K26 Office of Tax Analysis, "Table 3: Tax Program for Individuals," 22 January 1963, HP (22: 1/16/63–1/31/63).

K27 Ackley to Sorensen, "Economic Comparisons — With and Without Tax Program," 29 January 1963, HP (22, 1/16/63–1/31/63).

K28 CEA Staff, "Notes on Economic Assumptions Underlying the President's Tax Proposals," 6 February 1963, HP (23: 6/63).

K29 Humphrey to O'Brien, letter on support for President's tax message, 15 February 1963, WHCF (476: LE000/FI 11/1–11/3).

K30 Duesenberry to Harris, "Impact of Tax Reduction," 19 February 1963, HP (22: 2/1/63–2/28/63).

K31 Heller to President, "The improved economic outlook," 21 March 1963, HP (5: 6/63).

K32 Heller to President, "Background for meeting with Senator Paul Douglas tomorrow," 28 March 1963, POF (75a: 11/16/62–5/31/63).

K33 Heller to President, "Sustaining Recovery through 1964: Preliminary Report," 5 April 1963, HP (6: 4/63).

K34 Heller to Lippmann, "Response to your March 14 column," 9 April 1963, HP (6: 4/63).

K35 Heller to President, "How Large a Deficit Can We Stand to Get Us to Full Employment?" 4 May 1963, HP (6: 5/63).

K36 Heller to Evelyn Lincoln, draft of letter by Kennedy on tax reduction, 5 May 1963, HP (23: 5/63).

K37 Schulze, Charles L. speech, "Tax Policy and Economic Growth," 8 May 1963, HP (23: 5/63).

K38 Heller to President, draft of letter by academic economists, 18 May 1963, HP (23: 5/63).

K39 Heller speech, "Tax Reduction for an Expanding Economy," 20 May 1963, POF (75a: 11/16/62–5/31/63).

K40 Heller to President, "A Primer on Government Spending," 1 June 1963, POF (76: 6/63–11/63).

K41 Heller to President, "Structural unemployment once again," 7 June 1963, HP (6: 6/63).

K42 Heller to President, personal note on 1963 tax reform, 7 June 1963, POF (76: 6/63–11/63).

K43 Heller to President, "Tax Reform: Our Nemesis?" 7 June 1963, HP (23: 6/63).

K44 Heller to President, Samuelson articles, 8 June 1963, POF (76: 6/63–11/63).

K45 Heller to President, "Assuring Economic Expansion through 1964," 23 June 1963, HP (6: 6/63).

K46 Heller to President, "Milestones in the Kennedy Expansion," 15 June 1963, HP (6: 6/63).

K47 Heller to President, University of Michigan survey, 25 June 1963, HP (6: 6/63).

K48 Heller to President, "Proposed Discount Rate Boost," 7 July 1963, HP (6: 7/63).

K49 Chandler, Lester V. to Kennedy, letter with statement, 12 July 1963, WHCF (476: LE000/FI11 7/16/63).

K50 Heller?, draft concerning Fed testimony to Congress, 23 July 1963, HP (23: 7/63).

K51 Heller to President, "Economic Round-up Meeting with AFL-CIO Economists," 5 August 1963, HP (6: 8/63).

K52 Heller to President, "Fiscal Strategy – Or 1964 Comes First," 7 August 1963, HP (6: 8/63).

K53 Dillon statement to House Ways and Means Committee, 12 August 1963, HP (23: 8/1/63–8/13/63).

K54 Kennedy to Mills, letter of appreciation for work on tax bill, 19 August 1963, WHCF (476: LE000/FI11 2/11/63).

K55 Heller to President, "The tax cut and full employment," 4 September 1963, POF (76: 6/63–11/63).

K56 Heller to President, "Seymour Harris," 2 October 1963, POF (76: 10/1/63–10/7/63).

K57 Heller to Professional Staff, "Initial Assignments for the 1964 Annual Report," 10 October 1963, POF (76: 6/63–11/63).

K58 Anderson, W.H.L., "GNP in 1964 With and Without Tax Cut," 4 November 1963, HP (22: 11/63).

K59 Heller to President, "A Quick Economic Round-up," 23 November 1963, HP (6: 11/23/63–12/31/63).

K60 Ackley notes, "Troika Meeting with President Johnson, November 25, 1963," 26 and 30 November 1963, HP (23: 11/63).

K61 Musgrave, Richard A., statement to Senate Finance Committee, 3 December 1963, HP (23: 12/63).

K62 Heller to President, "Prices and Wages in 1964," 6 December 1963, HP (6: 11/23/63–12/31/63).

K63 Heller to Sylvia Porter, letter concerning tax-cut effects, 16 December 1963, HP (23: 12/63).

K64 —, "Derivation of the $30 to $40 billion Estimate of Additional GNP and of the 2 to 3 million Additional Jobs," —, HP (23: 10/63 undated).

K65 —, "Tax Cut Considerations," —, HP (23: undated 1963).

K66 Okun to Heller, "The Payoff on the tax cut," —, HP (23: undated 1963).

K67 Hanson, Lee and Burton Weisbrod to Heller, "Some Thoughts on Assessing the Effects of the Tax Cut," 13 February 1964, HP (24: 3/64–4/64).

K68 Heller speech, "Notes on the Economic Situation, Outlook and Policies in the United States," 21 February 1964, HP (24: 1/64–2/64).

K69 Anderson, Locke to John Lewis, "Surveying the Tax Cut," 25 February 1964, HP (24: 1/64–2/64).

K70 Lepper, Susan J. to Lewis, "Studying Reactions to the Tax Cut: Some Goals and Some Tools," 4 March 1964, HP (24: 3/64–4/64).

K71 —, "Indications of Response to the Tax Cut," 15 May 1964, HP (24: 5/64–8/64).

K72 Lusher, David to the Council, "Tax-cut Consumption II-1964," 7 August 1964, HP (24: 5/64–8/64).

K73 Heller to President, "The Goldwater tax-cut plan," 9 September 1964, HP (6: 8/64–9/64).

K74 Heller to President, "Business Week's request for a Presidential written interview," 23 September 1964, HP (6: 8/64–9/64).

K75 —, "Gibson's revised language," 4 October 1964, HP (4: 12/63–10/64).

Bentley Historical Library

The only collection relevant to this study is the Gardner Ackley Papers, for which "Finding Aids" are available from the Library. It lists the titles of all folders in each of the 28 boxes. Box numbers and folder titles are given for each entry.

B1 Okun, "What We Can't Say About the Budget," 10 November 1961 (7: Troika – 1961).

B2 Galbraith to President, "Tax Reduction," 6 June 1962 (15: Memos to White House Staff – John Kenneth Galbraith).

B3 Teeters, Nancy to Council, "Problems in the full-employment surplus concept," 10 October 1962 (6: 1963 Tax Bill).

B4 Heller to William McC. Martin, memorandum concerning easier monetary policy, 16 October 1962 (5: Monetary Policy – 1962).

B5 Ackley to Heller and Gordon, "Some Thoughts on the Economic Considerations Bearing on the Size of the 1963 Tax Reduction," 7 November 1962 (6: 1963 Tax Bill).

B6 Lusher, David to Ackley, "Some Appropriate Estimates Bearing on the Size of the 1963 Tax Reduction," 14 November 1962 (6: 1963 Tax Bill).

B7 Proxmire to Kennedy, letter concerning tax-cut effects on revenue, 28 February 1963 (17: Congressional correspondence with William Proxmire).

B8   Ackley to Paul Volcker, "Attached Draft Letter from the President to Senator Proxmire," 19 April 1963 (17: Congressional correspondence with William Proxmire).

B9   Musgrave, Richard A., "Comments on Tax Policy," 4 May 1963 (7: Troika – 1963)

B10 Heller to President, memorandum on tax reform, 10 June 1963 (6: 1963 Tax Bill).

B11 —, "Distributional Effects of the Tax Reduction – Tax Reform Plan," 10 June 1963 (6: 1963 Tax Bill).

B12 Heller to Ackley, memorandum concerning possible overstimulation by tax cut, 17 October 1963 (6: Senate Finance Committee Hearings, Nov. 12, 1963 – Staff Memos).

B13 Weisbrod, Burton A. to Heller, "Finance Committee Testimony of William McC. Martin," 10 December 1963 (6: Senate Finance Committee Hearings, Nov. 12, 1963 – Staff Memos).

B14 Heller to President, "The Goldwater tax cut plan," 9 September 1964 (14: Memos to the President [regarding Senator Goldwater's Tax plan]).

B15 Ackley to President, "A Stronger Fiscal Policy for 1965?" 13 December 1964 (13: Memos to the President – Nov.–Dec. 1964).

B16 Dillon, Gordon, and Ackley to President, "Troika Review of Economic and Fiscal Outlook," 31 March 1965 (13: Memos to the President – March–April 1965).

B17 Ackley to President, "Jawbone Price Control," 23 July 1965 (13: Memos to the President – July–Aug. 1965).

B18 Ackley to President, "Economic Aspects of Vietnam," 30 July 1965 (13: Memos to the President – July–Aug. 1965).

B19 Ackley to President, "Scare Talk on Tax Increase," 2 September 1965 (13: Memos to the President – Sept.–Oct. 1965).

B20 Ackley to Bill Moyers, "Comments on Secretary Fowler's Speech Draft," 18 November 1965 (16: Memos to White House Staff – Bill Moyers – Oct.–Dec. 1965).

B21 Mills to Ackley, letter and attached speech, 14 December 1965 (17: Congressional correspondence with Wilbur Mills).

B22 Ackley to President, "Policy Implications of the Budget," 17 December 1965 (13: Memos to the President – Nov.–Dec. 1965)

B23 Pechman, Joseph A. to Ackley, letter concerning contribution of economists to policy formation, 20 December 1965 (9: AEA–AFA luncheon).

B24 Ackley to President, "Budget Policy for FY 1967," 26 December 1965 (13: Memos to the President – Nov.–Dec. 1965).

B25 Ackley to Joseph A. Califano, "Shoe Prices," 8 February 1966 (15: Memos to White House Staff – Joseph Califano – Jan.–Feb. 1966).

B26 Ackley, Okun, and Duesenberry to President, "The Economics of a Tax Increase," 12 March 1966 (13: Memos to the President – March 1966).

B27 —, "The Fiscal/Monetary Policy Mix: Alternative Possibilities in 1966–67," 1 June 1966 (5: Economy (state of) – June 1966).

B28 Welsh, Carol, memorandum for the secretaries to the special assistants,

21 June 1966 (16: Memos to White House Staff – Bill Moyers – Jan.–June 1966).

B29 Heller to President, "Conversation with Wilbur Mills, August 19, 1966," 20 August 1966 (14: Memos to the President – Aug. 1966).

B30 Ackley to President, "Why We Need the Investment Credit Suspension *Now*," 3 October 1966 (14: Memos to the President – Oct. 1966).

B31 Ackley to President, "The State of the Economy," 1 December 1966 (14: Memos to the President – Dec. 1966).

B32 Ackley to Leon H. Keyserling, letter concerning budget policy, 3 December 1966 (14: Memos to the President – Dec. 1966).

B33 Ackley to President, "Briefing Paper on Economic Policy for 1967," 4 January 1967 (14: Memos to the President – Jan. 1967).

B34 Ackley to President, "Reactions to your Economic Policy Program," 25 February 1967 (14: Memos to the President – Feb. 1967).

B35 Fowler, Schultze, and Ackley to President, "Troika Review of Economic Situation and Fiscal Policy," 29 March 1967 (14: Memos to the President – March 1967).

B36 Okun to Ackley and Duesenberry, memorandum on defense spending, 14 April 1967 (7: Tax Issues – Feb.–Aug. 1967).

B37 Heller to Ackley, memorandum with attached report on Ditchley Foundation Conference, 13 July 1967 (5: Guideposts).

B38 Ackley to President, "Economic Outlook," 19 June 1967 (7: Tax Issues – Feb.–Aug. 1967).

B39 Ackley to President, "The Economy and the Tax Proposal," 15 July 1967 (14: Memos to the President – July 1967).

B40 Ackley to President, "Weekly Price Report," 29 July 1967 (11: Meetings – Regarding Prices – Aug. 4, 1967).

B41 Ackley to President, "Tire and Steel Price Increases," 1 August 1967 (11: Meetings – Regarding Prices – Sept. 1, 1967).

B42 Ackley to President, "Views of Economists on the Tax Bill," 4 August 1967 (14: Memos to the President – Aug. 1967).

B43 Ackley to President, "Weekly Price Report," 12 August 1967 (11: Meetings – Regarding Prices – Aug. 18, 1967).

B44 Ackley to Joseph A. Califano, "Steel Plate Price Increase," 17 August 1967 (11: Meetings – Regarding Prices – Aug. 18, 1967).

B45 Ackley to President, "Weekly Price Report," 19 August 1967 (11: Meetings – Regarding Prices – Aug. 25, 1967).

B46 Ackley to President, "Weekly Price Report," 1 September 1967 (11: Meetings – Regarding Prices – Sept. 8, 1967).

B47 Ackley to President, "Economists' Statement," 9 September 1967 (14: Memos to the President – Sept. 1967).

B48 Ackley to President, "Weekly Price Report," 9 September 1967 (11: Meetings – Regarding Prices – Sept. 15, 1967).

B49 Okun to James B. Reston, letter concerning *New York Times* editorials, 2 October 1967 (14: Memos to the President – Oct. 1967).

B50 Ackley to President, "The Cost of *Not* Increasing Taxes," 4 October 1967 (14: Memos to the President – Oct. 1967).

B51 Ackley to President, "Weekly Price Report," 14 October 1967 (11: Meetings – Regarding Prices – Oct. 20, 1967).

B52 Ackley to President, "Weekly Price Report," 28 October 1967 (11: Meetings – Regarding Prices – Nov. 3, 1967).

B53 Okun to President, "Weekly Price Report," 10 November 1967 (11: Meetings – Regarding Prices – Nov. 17, 1967).

B54 Okun to President, "Weekly Price Report," 18 November 1967 (11: Meetings – Regarding Prices – Nov. 24, 1967).

B55 Ackley to President, "Weekly Price Report," 25 November 1967 (11: Meetings – Regarding Prices – Dec. 1, 1967).

B56 Ackley to President, "View of Economists," 18 December 1967 (14: Memos to the President – Dec. 1967).

B57 Proxmire to Ackley, letter concerning surtax effects, 30 January 1968 (17: Congressional correspondence with William Proxmire).

B58 Ackley to Proxmire, letter replying to previous item, 2 February 1968 (17: Congressional correspondence with William Proxmire).

B59 Ackley, "The Role of the Economist as Policy Adviser in the United States," Essays in honour of Giuseppe Ugo Papi, 1973 (26: Speeches, Journal Articles and Letters to the Editor).

Lyndon B. Johnson Library

The most important collection here is the Arthur M. Okun Papers; almost all of the entries are from that collection, which is identified as OP. Unfortunately, less than half of the 253 boxes are currently open for research. The only other collection used in this study is the White House Central Files, which is identified by WHCF. Finding aids for both collections are available from the Library. More detailed information is contained in *Historical Materials in the Lyndon Baines Johnson Library*.

J1 table, GNP Projections, 18 September 1961, OP (163: Troika Projections 1961–62).

J2 —, "Countercyclical Tax Flexibility: A New Proposal," 4 December 1962, OP (25: Tax Cut).

J3 Tobin to Heller, "Tax Reductions and Full Employment Investment," 27 March 1963, OP (19: Plant & Equipment).

J4 P. Diamond, "Productivity," 23 August 1963, OP (22: Productivity).

J5 Locke Anderson to Council, "The 3 1/2 percent Trend Line," 29 October 1963, OP (22: Productivity).

J6 Heller to President, "Unemployment Cost of Budget Cutting," 14 December 1963, OP (22: Productivity).

J7 David Lusher to Heller, "The Latest Troika Exercise," 19 December 1963, OP (22: Productivity).

J8 Barbara Berman to Heller, letter, 30 December 1963, OP (30: Wages, Prices, Guideposts: 1963).

J9   Heller to President, "Meeting the Threat of Tighter Money," 31 December 1963, OP (156: Memos for the President, Jan.–March 1964).

J10 Heller to President, "Is the Tax Cut Inflationary?" 3 February 1964, OP (156: Memos for the President, Jan.–March 1964).

J11 Locke Anderson, "1964 As It Looked Early in The Year," 14 February 1964, OP (163: Troika (1964)).

J12 Heller to Hodges, Wirtz, and Dillon, memo about 'economic (good) news notes' for the President, 21 March 1964, OP (156: Memos for the President, Jan.–March 1964).

J13 —, "A Review of the Economic Impact of the Revenue Act 1964 to Date," 16 September 1964, OP (25: Tax Cut).

J14 Heller to President, "Goldwater's latest fiscal 'me too'," 18 September 1964, OP (157: Memos for the President, Sept. 1964).

J15 Heller to President, "The Outlook for Price Stability in 1964 – A Second Look," 8 October 1964, OP (157: Memos for the President, Oct.–Nov. 1964).

J16 Dillon, Gordon, and Ackley to President, "Troika Review of Economic and Fiscal Outlook," 7 December 1964, OP (163: Troika (Summary File)).

J17 Ackley to President, "Economic Welfare and the Pace of Expansion," 11 December 1964, OP (157: Memos for the President, Dec. 1964).

J18 Eckstein to Okun and Lusher, "Economic Projections," 17 December 1964, OP (163: Troika (Dec. 1964)).

J19 Ackley to President, "Program for Reducing the Unemployment Rate," 11 January 1965, OP (157: Memos for the President, Jan.–Feb. 1965).

J20 —, "An Explanatory Note on the Council's 1965 Annual Report," 2 April 1965, OP (82: The Growth of Potential GNP).

J21 — to President, "Consolidating Our Job Gains," 10 April 1965, OP (158: Memos to the President, Mar.–April 1965).

J22 Dave Starrett to Council, "Impact of Government Fiscal Policy," 2 July 1965, OP (163: Troika (Mar.–Sep. 1965)).

J23 Ackley to President, "Economic Aspects of Vietnam," 30 July 1965, OP (158: Memos to the President, July–Aug. 1965).

J24 Louis Paradiso to Okun, "Consumption function used in tax analysis," 17 September 1965, OP (83: Tax Cut Speech, Back-up Material).

J25 —, "Summary of CEA Consultants Meeting on Guideposts," 24 September 1965, OP (30: Wages, Prices, Guideposts: 1965).

J26 Ackley to President, "Chrysler and GM '66 Model Prices," 24 September 1965, OP (159: Memos for the President, 1965).

J27 Ackley to President, "Civil Service Paybill" and attached hand-written note, 17 October 1965, OP (159: Memos for the President, 1965).

J28 —, "Preliminary Look at Possible Tax Actions for 1966," 5 December 1965, OP (26: Taxes, Dec. 1965).

J29 William Capron to Ackley, "Tactics of a Tax Increase," 15 December 1965, OP (26: Taxes, Dec. 1965).

J30 Ackley to President, "Revision of 1965 GNP," 22 December 1965, OP (248: Memos to the President, November–December, 1965).

J31 Ackley to President, "Wage Guideposts for 1966," 28 December 1965, OP (30: Wages, Prices, Guideposts: 1965).

J32 Council, "Statement," 1 January 1966, OP (23: Steel Announcements).

J33 Ackley to President, "Weekly Price Report," and attached "Checklist on our Marching Orders from the President," 12 March 1966, OP (159: Memos for the President, Jan.–Mar. 1966).

J34 Terry Colvin to Okun, memo and attachments, 24 March 1966, OP (164: Troika (Mar.–Apr. 1966)).

J35 table, "GNP Under Alternative Tax Programs," 6 April 1966, OP (164: Troika (Mar.–Apr. 1966)).

J36 Ackley to President, "Republican Blast on Inflation," 21 April 1966, OP(160: Memos for the President, Apr.–May 1966).

J37 Saul Nelson to Ackley, "The Current Price Outlook," 4 May 1966, OP (22: Price Outlook).

J38 Ackley to President, "The Case for Higher Taxes," 10 May 1966, OP (164: Troika (1966 Summary)).

J39 — to President, "The effect of a Tax Increase," 11 May 1966, WHCF (59: FI 11–4, 4/20/66–7/6/66).

J40 Okun to Califano, draft of memo to President, 31 May 1966, WHCF (59: FI 11–4, 4/20/66–7/6/66).

J41 —, "The Case *For* a Tax Increase Now," 30 June 1966, OP (26: Taxes, Dec. 1965).

J42 Ackley to President, "Senator Jacob Javits' Tax Proposal," 18 July 1966, WHCF (60: FI 11–4, 7/7/66–10/10/66).

J43 — to Fowler, Schultze, and Ackley, "Troika Review," 19 July 1966, OP (162: Troika).

J44 Ackley to President, "Stand-by Tax Authority," 25 July 1966, WHCH (60: FI 11–4, 7/7/66–10/10/66).

J45 Fowler, Schultze, and Ackley to President, "The FY 1967 Budget Outlook," 22 August 1966, OP (164: Troika (Aug. 1966)).

J46 Ackley to President, "Why We Need the Investment Credit Suspension *Now*," 3 October 1966, OP (160: Memos to the President, October 1966).

J47 Califano to President, memo concerning need for tax increase, 14 October 1966, WHCF (60: FI 11–4, 10/11/66–12/15/66).

J48 Okun to Ackley, "Troika Notes," 20 October 1966, OP (162: Troika).

J49 Wallace, Zwick, and Okun to Fowler, Schultze, and Ackley, "Troika Review," 1 November 1966, OP (162: Troika).

J50 Ackley to President, "Further Thoughts on the State of the Economy," 8 November 1966, OP (160: Memos to the President, November 1966).

J51 Fowler, Schultze, and Ackley to President, "Economic Outlook and Policy for 1967," 11 November 1966, OP (163: Troika (Summary File)).

J52 Ackley to President, "Budget Reductions," 25 November 1966, OP (160: Memos to the President, November 1966).

J53 —, "Issues of Policy Flexibility for 1967," 7 December 1966, OP (163: Troika (Summary File)).

J54 Okun to Ackley and Duesenberry, "Nightmare Model," 9 December 1966, OP (163: Troika (Summary File)).

J55 William McC. Martin to President, memo concerning tax question, 13 December 1966, WHCF (60: FI 11–4, 10/11/66–12/15/66).

J56 Barr, Schultze, and Ackley to President, "A Second Look at the Economic Outlook and Policy for 1967," 14 December 1966, OP (159: Memos for the President, Dec. 1966).

J57 Fowler, Schultze, and Ackley to President, "Further Tax Considerations," 30 December 1966, OP (26: Tax Issues 1966).

J58 Fowler, Schultze, and Ackley to President, "Third Troika Review," 30 December 1966, OP (163: Troika (Summary File)).

J59 Fowler to President, memo on column about tax increase, 16 January 1967, WHCH (60: FI 11–4, 1/16/67–1/24/67).

J60 Ackley to President, "Economic Outlook," 6 February 1967, OP (161: Memos to the President, Jan.–June 1967).

J61 Okun to Ackley and Duesenberry, "The Party Line on Stabilization Policy," 28 March 1967, OP (164: Spring 1967 Troika Exercise).

J62 Ackley to President, "Suggested Agenda for Quadriad Meeting," 24 May 1967, OP (161: Memos to the President, Jan.–June 1967).

J63 Ackley to President, "Economic Outlook," 19 June 1967, OP (161: Memos to the President, Jan.–June 1967).

J64 Okun to Ackley and Duesenberry, "Tax Issues," 3 July 1967, OP (164: Summer 1967 Troika Exercise).

J65 Ackley to President, "The Case for a Tax Increase," 11 July 1967, OP (161: Memos to the President, July–Dec. 1967).

J66 Lerman and Schmallensee, "Draft Reply to Expenditure Cut vs. Tax Increase Question," 31 July 1967, OP (27: Tax Program 1967–68, Congressional File).

J67 Ackley to Califano, "Government Organization for Prices and Wage Stabilization Efforts," 10 August 1967, OP (162: Memos for WH Staff, July–Dec. 1967).

J68 Ackley to New York Times, letter, 11 September 1967, OP (27: Tax Program 1967–68, General).

J69 Barefoot Sanders to President, memo concerning conversation with Wilbur Mills, 13 September 1967, WHCF (61: FI 11–4, 8/15/67–9/21/67).

J70 Ackley to James Wiggins, Washington Post, letter, 5 October 1967, OP (161: Memos to the President, July–Dec. 1967).

J71 Ackley to President, "If We Don't Get a Tax Increase," 6 October 1967, OP (27: Tax Program 1967–68, General).

J72 CEA draft, "The Problem of Price and Wage Stabilization," 11 October 1967, OP (30: Wages, Prices, Guideposts: 1967).

J73 Ackley to Califano, "What Do we Do If?" 16 October 1967, OP (162: Memos for WH Staff, July–Dec. 1967).

J74 Ackley to Robert Hardesty, "Attached Draft Speeches," 19 October 1967, OP (162: Memos for WH Staff, July–Dec. 1967).

J75 Saul Hymans to Okun, "Macro Forecasting Model," 23 October 1967, OP (164: Fall 1967 Troika Exercise).

J76 Okun to Califano, "1966 Export Controls and Present Hide Prices," 26 October 1967, OP (162: Memos for WH Staff, July–Dec. 1967).

J77 CEA Troika Staff to Troika Staff, "Add-on Multiplier Tables," 8 November 1967, OP (164: Fall 1967 Troika Exercise).

J78 Ackley to Larry Levinson, memo concerning speeches, 9 November 1967, OP (162: Memos for WH Staff, July–Dec. 1967).

J79 Saul Hymans to Okun, "Credit Conditions and the Latest Forecast," 29 December 1967, OP (163: Troika (Summary File)).

J80 Okun, "Memorandum for the Files," 20 March 1968, OP (28: Tax Talking Points).

J81 Okun to President, "Economics of the Tax Bill," 13 May 1968, OP (28: Tax Talking Points).

J82 Duesenberry, Lewis, and Wallace to Fowler, Okun, and Zwick, "Troika Forecasts," 17 May 1968, OP (164: Spring 1967 Troika Exercise).

J83 Okun to President, "Quick Troika Exercise on Fiscal Alternatives," 20 May 1968, OP (178: Memos to the President, Jan.–June 1968).

J84 Okun to President, "Added Notes on the Costs of Fiscal Inaction," 20 May 1968, OP (178: Memos to the President, Jan.–June 1968).

J85 Okun to President, "Mills, Ford, and Byrnes on the Tax Bill," 20 May 1968, OP (178: Memos to the President, Jan.–June 1968).

J86 Okun, "Memorandum for the Files," 29 May 1968, OP (156: Memorandum for the Files).

J87 Okun to Califano, "The Future of Wage-Price Policy," 15 July 1968, OP (181: Memos for the WH Staff, July 1968–Jan. 1969).

J88 Okun, "Economic Issues of 1968," 14 September 1968, OP (84: Economic Issues of 1968, Sept.).

J89 table, "Estimated Effect of Calendar Year Tax Liabilities (Administrative Budget) of Tax Actions since 1962," 16 September 1968, OP (25: Tax Change Estimates).

J90 table, "Estimated Effect of Fiscal Year Receipts (Administrative Budget) of Tax Actions since 1962," 16 September 1968, OP (25: Tax Change Estimates).

J91 Okun to David Ott, "Fiscal Policy History," 4 November 1968, OP (156: Memorandum for the Files).

J92 David Ott?, "Fiscal Policy History," in two versions, one of which is dated 4 November 1968, OP (156: Memorandum for the Files).

J93 Okun to John Macey, "Federal Job Shuffling Proposal," 11 November 1968, OP (181: Memos for the WH Staff, July 1968–Jan. 1969).

J94 Okun to Califano, "CEA's History Project," 27 December 1968, OP (181: Memos for the WH Staff, July 1968–Jan. 1969).

J95 —, "The Council of Economic Advisers During the Administration of President Lyndon B. Johnson: November 1963–January 1969," —, OP (176: CEA Papers, 1963–1969).

J96 Okun, "How Political Must the CEA Be?" 29 December 1973, OP (78: AEA Meeting).

Index